THE
AUTHORIZED
GUIDE TO

2-WAY
WRIST
TV

COLLECTIBLES

THE
AUTHORIZED
GUIDE TO

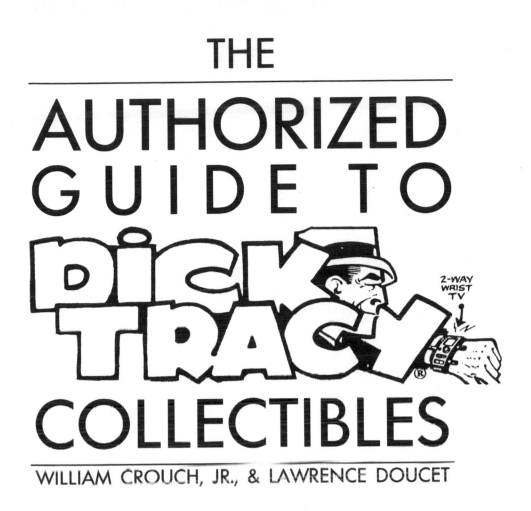

COLLECTIBLES

WILLIAM CROUCH, JR., & LAWRENCE DOUCET

Wallace-Homestead Book Company
Radnor, Pennsylvania

Published in Radnor, Pennsylvania 19089, by Wallace-Homestead,
a division of Chilton Book Company

Designed by Anthony Jacobson
Manufactured in the United States of America

Library of Congress Cataloging in Publication Data

Crouch, William.
The authorized guide to Dick Tracy collectibles / William Crouch, Jr., and Lawrence Doucet.
p. cm.
ISBN 0-87069-570-3
1. Tracy, Dick (Fictitious character)—Collectibles. I. Doucet, Lawrence. II. Title.
NK808.C77 1990
741.5'0973—dc20 90-70543
CIP

1 2 3 4 5 6 7 8 9 0 9 8 7 6 5 4 3 2 1 0

To
Patricia Doucet,
in appreciation for her full support and tolerant understanding
of my inexplicable quest for
Dick Tracy collectibles.

CONTENTS

Jean Gould O'Connell
May, 1990

FOREWORD

I was four years old when my father created his hero, Dick Tracy. During my adolescent and preteen years, I thought very little about my dad being famous. It was his job, just as my friend's father was an insurance agent.

During my childhood, my father was always bringing home Dick Tracy toys of one kind and another. I remember fingerprinting everyone in the house—even the dog—when he brought me a Dick Tracy Fingerprinting Set. Then there were handcuffs (they wouldn't fit dad's wrists—only mine and my little friends'). The rubber stamp figures were among my favorites because the figures could be colored in after stamping them, and the magic writing paper was used up right away: its invisible ink amazed me! My best friend and I had a Dick Tracy Code Book and really thought we had something BIG.

The annual newspaper convention in New York City was a special occasion: I was dismissed from school for several days to go with my family. It was always a colorful affair with celebrity guests, exciting people and many of the Tribune cartoonists. In 1947, the Ideal Toy Company was designing a new doll that was to take the country by storm. Dad, mother, and I were invited to see the operation from conception to manufacturing. This, of course, was to be Sparkle Plenty!

Today, I have very few Dick Tracy collectibles. It breaks my heart to think that I had so many and broke them, or took them to school to share with friends, but this book certainly brings back memories of the items I had as a child. The one cherished family heirloom my son has is one of the first Dick Tracy watches from the 1930s. And why shouldn't he? His name is Tracy Richard!

The World's Worst Rest in Woodstock

In a quiet plot near Woodstock, 16 white wooden markers stand solemn guard.

Beneath these simple markers, 16 scoundrels rest in peace in the tranquil countryside, some 60 miles from the Windy City where once they pursued their wicked ways.

Here under two berry bushes lie the fictional remains of the nation's most notorious felons—the 16 villains that Dick Tracy has cornered, outwitted, and undone. The cemetery is a monument to the demon detective who since 1932 has been carrying on for Tribune readers his relentless war against crime.

The man who sees to it that flowers bloom in the soil where evil ones lie buried is the same man who sees to it that justice—and Tracy—always triumph. He's Chester Gould, on whose drawing board are launched the adventures and fortunes of the world's greatest detective.

Here's How Come

Ask Chet Gould "How come?" and he'll tell you, "As a matter of fact, it was an idea of the Colonel's. He asked one day why didn't we have a graveyard to dispose of all the villains that Dick Tracy has outwitted. So as a gag, Mrs. Gould and I got together the vital statistics."

The Goulds first took boards, painted them white, and outlined them in black. With the help of Coleman Anderson and Ray Gould, Chet's brother, both cartoonists on the strip, Chet drew portraits of the characters and lettered in their names and the dates they died.

"We put the markers up for guests dropping in, and really, when we get them all down, it's quite a solemn little scene."

The meanest character he's ever created is "without a doubt old Mrs. Pruneface," Chet says. "She's the one, you know, who tried to dispose of Tracy by the fiendish scheme of resting an icebox on two cakes of ice, which, as they melted, would let down the refrigerator and

Daughter Jean and wife Edna admire Chester Gould's villains' graveyard—created at his home in Woodstock, Illinois, in 1947.

stick a steel spear into Tracy's heart. Tracy escaped, you remember, when he found out that by bumping the floor, he could move the ice cakes just enough so that the spike barely missed his body."

Crime Doesn't Pay

What character met the most horrible end? Chet thinks it's The Brow, head of a foreign espionage ring, who was impaled on a flagpole. "The Brow," Chet explains, "is the wartime spy who had the Summer sisters, May and June, to carry messages for him. Tracy hit him with an inkwell, and the impact caused him to lose his balance and go hurtling out the window where he was skewered on the flagpole in the neighborhood honor roll and

service plaque square."

An awful way to die? "Well, after all," answers Chet, who's a genius at ingenious disposal, "we deal with some mighty awful characters."

When it comes to malicious men and vicious vixen, the score boards stand 13 to three. The little white markers carry the names and faces of these creatures of crime:

Spaldoni, May 6, 1934: When Georgio Spaldoni, crook lawyer, found out that Arthur Jean Penfield's manuscript would break up the underworld's political connections, he disposed of the snooping girl writer and planted on the murder weapon the fingerprints of Tess Trueheart, Dick Tracy's sweetheart. Tracy and Junior caught

Spaldoni and his gang in their hideout in an abandoned steel mill. Spaldoni, critically wounded in an unsuccessful attempt to shoot it out with Tracy, cleared Tess in his deathbed statement.

Doc Hump, Nov. 11, 1934: Killed by a vicious dog which he planned to unleash on Tracy and Junior after he innoculated the animal with a serum producing instant rabies.

Nuremoh ("Homerun" spelled backwards), **Aug. 22, 1939:** The former baseball player, who married Tracy's sweetheart, Tess Trueheart, killed his rich aunt on the day of the wedding when she tried to change her will in favor of another nephew. Tess learned the truth, and Nuremoh was about to kill her when his sweetheart walked into the path of the bullet meant for Tess. Nuremoh's mind snapped, and he walked off the cliff with his sweetheart's body in his arms.

Stooge Viller, Jan. 7, 1940: Stooge, the only hoodlum Tracy ever sent up the river who came back, organized "Outfitters of the Underworld," to provide job pulling items like miniature acetylene torch outfits. He was shot by his little blond daughter, Binnie, as he was about to push Tracy over the fire escape. Stooge, after telling his daughter to go straight whatever happens, died in the hospital, begging Tracy to tell his daughter he'd gone up the river.

B-B Eyes, April 19, 1942: B-B Eyes bootlegged tires. When Tracy discovered the gang, he and Pat were sealed in paraffin. Tracy, not to be outdone, melted his way out and cornered the gang. On the way to headquarters, B-B Eyes threw himself out of the car, climbed down to the lower level of the bridge, lost his hold, and smashed into a bucket of slime, mud, and rubbish in a passing scow. B-B Eyes' body was found at the bottom of the bay, entwined in, of all things, an abandoned tire.

88 Keyes, July 11, 1943: The famous piano player and orchestra leader arranged the murder of millionaire A. B. Helmet and ran away with Mrs. Helmet and the 200 grand

in insurance. 88 disposed of the widow in a train accident, temporarily outwitted Tracy in the train station, and finally was shot in a shack by the railroad track where he was waiting for a freight.

Mrs. Pruneface, Sept. 26, 1943: The meanest of them all, old Mrs. Pruneface was outwitted by Tracy when she came to avenge her husband whom Tracy had trapped.

Here's Flattop's Fate

Flattop, May 21,1944: Imported by the local boys to get rid of Tracy, Flattop ran into Vitamin Flintheart, the famous actor of flea-bitten fur coat fame. Vitamin meanwhile, was innocently involved in the shooting of a bartender with Flattop's gun when Pat Patten asked him to hold it. Flattop and Vitamin escaped to a hideout in the replica of an old sailing ship used by Columbus. Cornered by Tracy, Flattop tried to escape by swimming under the pilings, but his body became wedged between the braces beneath the old ship.

The Brow, Sept. 24, 1944, speared on the flagpole.

Shakey, Jan. 21. 1945: Shakey, who sponsored a shakedown attempt on rich Nat Banks, died in a coffin of ice when he hid from Tracy under an old, filled in pier.

Itchy, Dec. 23, 1945: Itchy, Shakey's best friend, was brought into the scene by Mrs. Shakey who hoped to recover her late husband's money. Itchy and Mrs. B-B Eyes were killed by Tracy with the gun which Junior slipped in to Tracy, a prisoner at Mrs. B-B Eyes' home.

Breathless Forgives B.O.

Breathless Mahoney, Aug. 25, 1946: Breathless, Mrs. Shakey's daughter by an earlier marriage, outsmarted her mother and escaped with Shakey's shakedown money. She ran into B.O. Plenty, who outsmarted her and ran off with the money. When the cops ran into them both, B.O.'s marriage to Gravel Gertie was ended dramatically and suddenly as B.O. was taken away to jail. Breathless, the

state's only witness against B.O., died in women's prison hospital after scrawling on a pad, "Give him another chance. I forgive him."

Gargles, Nov. 10, 1946: Gargles made a racket of selling colored water as mouthwash and killed the men who got wise to him. Tracy cornered him in a glass company garage. Approaching behind a bullet proof glass, Tracy shot Gargles, who crashed thru the stair rail and was pierced by falling glass.

Mumbles, Dec. 7, 1947: The leader of a quartet and organizer of charity robberies, Mumbles apparently was cornered by Tracy after Mumbles blackmailed Singer Kis Andtel by threatening to throw acid in her face. Mumbles escaped in a stolen boat. Tracy arrived by helicopter. Mumbles took to a raft. His paddle broke, and in trying to attract the attention of a passing boat, he lost his balance, fell and speared the rubber raft with the paddle's jagged edge. He sank beneath the surface and was seen no more.

Shoulders, Feb. 22, 1948: Shoulders, the fixer who once shot little Themesong two years earlier, made his getaway in July, 1946, in a plane which, immediately after takeoff, hit a large gas tank and exploded. He was heard of no more until he cut off the top of an orange marble monument imported from India and found 2,000 precious stones. He tucked these safely away in his shoulder pads while he posed as an Emptier Brush company salesman. Later, hiding out in Miss Varnish's antique shop, he accidentally shot himself as the cops closed in.

Mrs. Volts, May 2, 1948: This electrical equipment blackmarketeer, hiding from police at her nephew Briar's home, was asphyxiated under the sink when a gas line accidentally broke. Her nephew and his young wife dumped her body on a golf course near B.O. Plenty's home where six yards of sand were to be dumped the next day.

ACKNOWLEDGMENTS

We would like to thank Robert S. Reed, President/C.E.O. and Elyce Small Goldstein, Director of Licensing, both of Tribune Media Services, for believing in this project.

We thank Dawn Honnaka and Robin Tynan of The Walt Disney Company for their assistance, and that of their staff. We also thank those licensees who were able to share information and photos on their new Dick Tracy products.

Special thanks to Jim Cavett, Customer Service Director of TMS, and, at Chilton Books, Harry Rinker, Kathryn Conover, Nancy Ellis, Tony Jacobson, and Troy Vozzella.

We appreciate our families, who didn't toss us out of our respective houses while writing this book.

Finally, thanks to Jean Gould O'Connell, Bill Gaines of MAD magazine, Jay Maeder, Larry Lowery, Steve Spencer, Bob Blair, Richard Ross Fletcher, Julio Santiago, and Don Weston.

"The American comic strip has sold more newspapers than any other feature in American journalism."

AND THERE'S NO SUBSTITUTE!

CHESTER GOULD

1 TRACY THROUGH THE DECADES

Dick Tracy is much more than a cartoon character to literally tens of millions of people. For nearly sixty years his daily activities have been an integral part of American culture. Not too long ago he appeared in more than 600 newspapers and was read every day by more than 100 million people in the United States and abroad. A poll in the late 1940s reported that Dick Tracy was the most readily recognized figure in the country, real or fictional. When ABC was planning a new TV series based upon a comic book character in 1965, a market research firm reported that Dick Tracy was the most popular of all. Batman, the third most popular, was the selected character only because rights could not be obtained for Dick Tracy (or Superman).

1931: A Hero is Born

Created by Chester Gould, *Dick Tracy* first appeared in October 1931. His appeal was immediate and his rise in popularity was meteoric. His hard-hitting, shoot-first-ask-questions-later, no-nonsense approach to dealing with crime was just what the public wanted. Within a few years, *Dick Tracy* became the Tribune Syndicate's third most popular strip, and quickly rose afterward to the number one position. Tracy was the first character to be published in the popular Big Little Book series in 1932. Tracy stories were reprinted in hardcover books as early as 1933 and in comic books as early as 1936. Mutual Radio serialized him as early as 1935, and Republic produced the first Dick Tracy movie in 1937.

Tracy's popularity accelerated through the 1940s as the villains became more and more grotesque and the artistic qualities of the strip became increasingly surreal. Increasingly intricate and enthralling storylines captured the collective imagination. There was a continual anticipation of the next day's funny papers by millions of children and adults alike to see if Tracy could manage to escape a hopeless "deathtrap" or finally capture a merciless, horrific gangster.

Tracy's supporting cast nearly rivaled him in popularity. Flattop, The Brow, The Mole, Pruneface, Breathless Mahoney, Measles and other villains became household names. Countless letters of sympathy were sent to Gould upon the death of Flattop in 1944. Gravel Gertie and B.O. Plenty were so popular that their wedding was a national event in 1946, as was the birth of their daughter, Sparkle Plenty, in 1947. Tracy's surprise marriage to Tess Trueheart

"Dick Tracy," Detective Thriller, New Trib Comic

"DICK TRACY," drawn by Chester Gould, started as a daily comic strip in the Tribune on March 22. Since January the comic has been running in the Sunday Tribune.

Last October Ches Gould joined the Chicago Tribune Newspapers Syndicate to draw "Dick Tracy," which began immediately in the *New York News* and *Detroit Mirror*.

Caricatures Teacher

The creator of "Dick Tracy" was born in Pawnee, Oklahoma—just in time

Gantter photo.
Ches Gould at his drawing board

for Thanksgiving dinner in 1900. The first time he showed signs of becoming a comic strip artist was during a chemistry exam in the local high school. Ches did a cartoon of the instructor testing a flask of Oklahoma "mule." Contrary to tradition, the teacher liked the drawing and gave him help in his progress through school.

After attending Oklahoma State College for two years Ches came to Chicago and entered Northwestern University, from which he was graduated in 1923.

His desire to draw led him to night classes in the Art Institute. For the next few years he drew comic strips for a Chicago newspaper, did commercial art work, and organized a vaudeville act.

Lives in Wilmette

Ches lives in Wilmette. When he isn't too occupied with Dick Tracy, he tries to teach his four-year-old daughter to ride a bike or to roller skate.

The popularity of Dick Tracy has been instantaneous and the Syndicate reports increasing sales to other newspapers, among them the *Kentucky World*, which has run the comic since October. Reports from this paper are that one day the Dick Tracy strips were lost in the mail. The *World* appeared minus Dick Tracy and calls from readers who missed the comic swamped the *World* office.

Fig. 1-1
Rare paper collectible from "The Trib," the in-house publication for employees of the *Chicago Tribune* (May, 1932). The photo shows Gould at about age 31.

on Christmas Eve, 1949, was applauded throughout the country, and the birth of their daughter, Bonny Braids, in 1951 was comparable in popularity to Sparkle's birth. Other regulars, such as Junior (Tracy's adopted son), Pat Patton, Sam Catchem, Lizz, Vitamin Flintheart, and Diet Smith, became widely recognized as an integral part of the "Tracy family." Each has played a prominent role in numerous storylines over the decades.

Tracy fans differ when it comes to the best periods of the strip and favorite stories and villains. Some like the 1930s best because the strips generally reflected the gangland realism to which they were accustomed. Many Tracy fans and experts consider the 1940s to be the golden age of the strip, because the most famous villains originated during this time and because artistic qualities of the strip matured to a unique style. However, many other fans consider

Fig. 1-2

Dick Tracy joined the *Honolulu Advertiser*'s comics on Sept. 24, 1945. Some collectors seek tearsheets of promo artwork and also Tracy with foreign language text (he is especially popular in Europe and South America).

the 1950s to be the golden age of the strip. It is widely believed that Gould's story writing and artwork reached their peak during this decade. Some comics experts, including the present Dick Tracy author Max Allan Collins, rate some of the Tracy stories of this era among the best ever written for the comics. By and large, particular preferences are influenced by when a reader first got hooked on a particular storyline or first started reading the strip as a youngster.

Fig. 1-3

In 1949, Gould designed a special who-done-it titled "The Black Bag Mystery" to promote subscriptions for the *Chicago Tribune*. There are 35 sequences in the story. It was also used by the *Duluth Herald* and other newspapers. In Chicago, the publisher offered to pay Gould $1 for every new subscriber: Gould won over 50,000 new subscribers, but wouldn't take the money, so the publisher gave him a new Cadillac.

The mid-1960s saw a decline in Tracy's popularity. The turbulent, free-spirited times may have had a lot to do with this. However, many Tracy fans blame Gould's "space period." Sending Tracy to the moon in 1964 was highly controversial. Moon people and anti-gravity ships were more science fiction than could be tolerated. Junior's marriage to Moon Maid and the birth of their daughter, Honey Moon, were mostly panned by the public.

Other factors abetted the strip's decline in popularity in the 1960s. First of all, although Gould's artwork continued to evolve in style and quality, his sharp storylines and interesting character development just didn't seem to be consistent any longer. Another key factor was the reduction in strip size. Gould himself claimed that the shrinking space allowed for comics in most papers restricted his artistic creativity. A movement by some editors to eliminate violence in comic strips also cramped Gould's style. Because of such censorship, he could no longer show villains being impaled on flag-poles, pierced by panels of glass, or blasted by sub-machine guns. It is not easy to forget those numerous earlier panels where bullets were shown penetrating the victim and tumbling end-over-end out of the other side when a villain was foolish enough to fight it out with Tracy. In the 1970s, after Gould decided to minimize space exploits, Tracy's popularity improved somewhat, but it never again reached that of earlier decades.

Fig. 1-4

The current *Dick Tracy* movie isn't the first tie-in between Disney and Tracy. This March 17, 1957, clipping from the *Minneapolis Star* shows a newspaper promotion for a trip to Disneyland.

Fig. 1-5

Tracy was featured in a series of Ford Autolite Spark Plug print ads that used bizarre villains such as Piston Puss and Strip Gear. These ads from the 1960s were ghosted by Gould's assistant, Rick Fletcher. A good volume of advertising artwork featuring Tracy awaits the collector.

Fig. 1-6

A 1984 ad for ITT hypes its engineers with Tracy and his wrist radio. The strong graphic design of Tracy has made him a visual attention grabber.

The Collins/Fletcher/Locher Era

Gould retired in December, 1977, and was replaced by Max Collins and Rick Fletcher. Collins, an award-winning mystery novelist, was hand-picked by the Tribune Syndicate to write the Tracy strip stories. Fletcher, Gould's assistant since 1961, became the strip's artist; many consider his artwork on Tracy and other strips to be among the best and most detailed of all time. Rick Fletcher passed away in 1983 and was replaced by Dick Locher, the current strip artist. Locher, a Pulitzer Prize-winning editorial cartoonist, worked as an assistant of Gould from 1956 through 1961.

Critical acclaim has greeted storylines and outstanding artistry during the Collins, Fletcher and Locher era. Some of the villains introduced since 1977, including Flattop's daughter Angeltop, Art Dekko, Torcher, Dye and Oxen Cixot, and Upward Lee-Mobile, compare favorably to Gould's best villains. In addition, Collins has devised ingenious ways of bringing back some of Gould's popular villains. For example, cloning was used to reintroduce Mumbles, cryonics (freeze drying) was used to reintroduce Pruneface, and the discovery of "top secret declassified documents" was used in a new flashback story featuring Flattop, Shaky, Pruneface, and others.

No dramatic surges in Tracy's popularity have occurred in recent years. To

Fig. 1-7
Products for children, such as Plymouth, Inc.'s, pads, binders, and bookcovers and Panini USA's poster and sticker book, aim to make Dick Tracy a household name for a whole new generation. © Disney.

many, the "new" Dick Tracy of Collins and Locher is merely a shell of Gould's Tracy during the strip's golden years. Actually, very few—if any—comic characters or strips of *any* era are able to compare well against Gould's Tracy at its best. For those of us who collect everything Tracy, the golden era will always hold the greatest treasures—but we have plenty of room for collectibles of later eras, too, including all the great new Tracy items coming out along with the movie this year.

2 MYTH, MAGIC, AND COMMERCE

With all the confrontations between Dick Tracy and a wide variety of villains, it is easy to forget that *Dick Tracy* is more than a detective story, more than a morality play between good and evil—it is a comic strip about a family.

Historically, the most successful comic strips have been those involving a family. Today's popularity surveys continue to place *Peanuts, Calvin and Hobbes, Blondie, Hagar the Horrible, Gasoline Alley,* and *Nancy* high in the ratings. All are family strips. All easily become part of one's routine of reading the daily newspaper.

Chester Gould with his comic strip *Dick Tracy* never faltered in his mission to entertain the public. Gould drove some newspaper editors to despair when he said in truth, "The American comic strip has sold more newspapers than any other feature in American journalism." This statement rings true today as shown in the report "Teenagers and Newspapers 1989," prepared by the Newspaper Advertising Bureau. As reported in the April 7, 1989, issue of the trade journal *Editor & Publisher*, the comics are the most popular feature read by 68% of teens weekdays and 76% on Sunday; 81% of American teenagers either read or look at at least one issue of a newspaper per week. It would seem that the fear of illiterate youth, totally absorbed by rock videos, Walkman cassette players, MTV, and grade B slasher movies is greatly exaggerated.

Without dwelling on the report, it's of special interest that newspaper advertising reaches more older teenagers from high-income households. Also it reaches the greatest number of teens who claim they will attend a four-year college. These are the prime consumers of today and tomorrow.

The ninth *Dick Tracy* movie was released June 15, 1990. Much has been made in the hype of the film that Tracy doesn't have the name recognition of *Batman*—1989's summer smash hit. Nonsense. If anything, Dick Tracy is more firmly entrenched in American popular culture. The Caped Crusader made his first major mass media splash in the mid-1960s. Dick Tracy made his in the mid-1930s. What Batman lacks, even after the super hit movie, is the childhood memories of adults who were growing up in the 1930s and 40s when Dick Tracy starred in comics, on the radio, in movie theaters, and toy stores everywhere. Even today, the average teenager knew who Dick Tracy was long before hearing about the Warren Beatty–Madonna movie. Only Mickey Mouse and Popeye the Sailor can boast of a longer career of continuous newspaper syndication and successful licensing programs.

There is no doubt that Mickey Mouse is the all-time superstar in merchandising achievement. The Walt Disney Company's

involvement with the current Tracy film draws to it licensees who know Disney's long and excellent track record in the field of product licensing.

Just as Mickey Mouse is the symbol of Disney, *Dick Tracy* has been one of the main standard bearers of *The Chicago Tribune*.

In an era when nonhumorous comic strips have declined, *Dick Tracy* has held its own. This may be due in part to older readers who have seen Tracy in the comics almost all their lives. Now the current blockbuster film opens the door for a new generation to learn about the Dick Tracy family.

The Tracy Family: Personal and Professional

Dick Tracy really has two families, his professional family in the police department and his personal family. Tracy collectibles over the years have concentrated more on Tracy's family than on the villains; however, much of the new licensing will feature the bad guys.

Tracy's personal family includes his wife Tess, adopted son Junior, daughter Bonny Braids and natural son Joseph. He and Tess are grandparents to Honey Moon Tracy, the child of Junior and Moon Maid. Junior's first wife, the sexy feminine star of Gould's space period (1964–1970), was blown up when she turned the ignition key in a car boobytrapped for Tracy. Junior has subsequently married Sparkle Plenty, the daughter of Gravel Gertie and B.O. (Bob Oscar) Plenty.

While Tracy, Junior, and Bonny Braids have been stars in the Tracy licensing program over the years, not too many products feature Tess Trueheart Tracy. The Tracys' son, Joseph Flintheart Tracy, born in the early 1980s, has to date done nothing as a merchandising character.

There has been merchandising aplenty with the B.O. Plenty clan. The tobacco-chewing hillbilly was patterned, according to Gould, after rural characters he observed as a boy in Oklahoma. Bob Oscar Plenty is a man of the earth and most likely smelled that way with the not-so-subtle pun as his name. The public took an instant liking to him. His wife, Gravel Gertie, is an equal character. Gould described how he thought her up in an article he wrote for the April, 1976, issue of *Guideposts* magazine: "One morning while driving to work from my farm in Woodstock, Illinois, I passed abandoned gravel pits that abound the area. As I looked, I noticed a little shack in the bottom of one cavernous pit. Hansel and Gretel thoughts of my childhood rose and I chuckled. What would happen, I wondered, if one climbed down and found a witchlike creature living there?"

Gould played with the idea and soon Gravel Gertie appeared as a love-starved, toothless hag who develops a crush on the fugitive, The Brow. In his first appearance in the strip, B.O. Plenty helps another fugitive, Breathless Mahoney. Breathless's mythology in the comic strip is far different from her role in the new movie.

Eventually the gangly old maid and the

Fig. 2-1

Manufacturer's advertisement for paper Hingees from the 1940s. The Tracy set shown includes Chief Brandon, Tess, Junior, Pat Patton, Tracy.

earthy old reprobate marry and have a beautiful golden-haired child, Sparkle Plenty. This Gouldian twist to the *Beauty and the Beast*-type story led to one of the most successful licensed products of all time, Ideal Toy Company's Baby Sparkle Plenty Doll; it went on sale July 28, 1947. The doll cost $5.98 and sold over 500,000 units. That's almost $3 million!

This success led to the later dolls of Tracy and Tess's daughter, Bonny Braids, and their granddaughter Honey Moon, who was born in the Space Coupe halfway between Earth and the moon.

Tracy's other peer in long-term merchandising, *Popeye the Sailor,* is also a family strip with Popeye, his sweetheart Olive Oyl, Wimpy and Sweetpea. However, there is a tremendous difference in how the two cartoon characters have been handled by their respective syndicates.

Unlike Tribune Media Services (TMS), which has continued to develop the characterization of Dick Tracy, King Features, which owns Popeye, has allowed merchandising to become the driving force behind the character. Recently, cartoonist Bobby London has been doing brilliant work in the

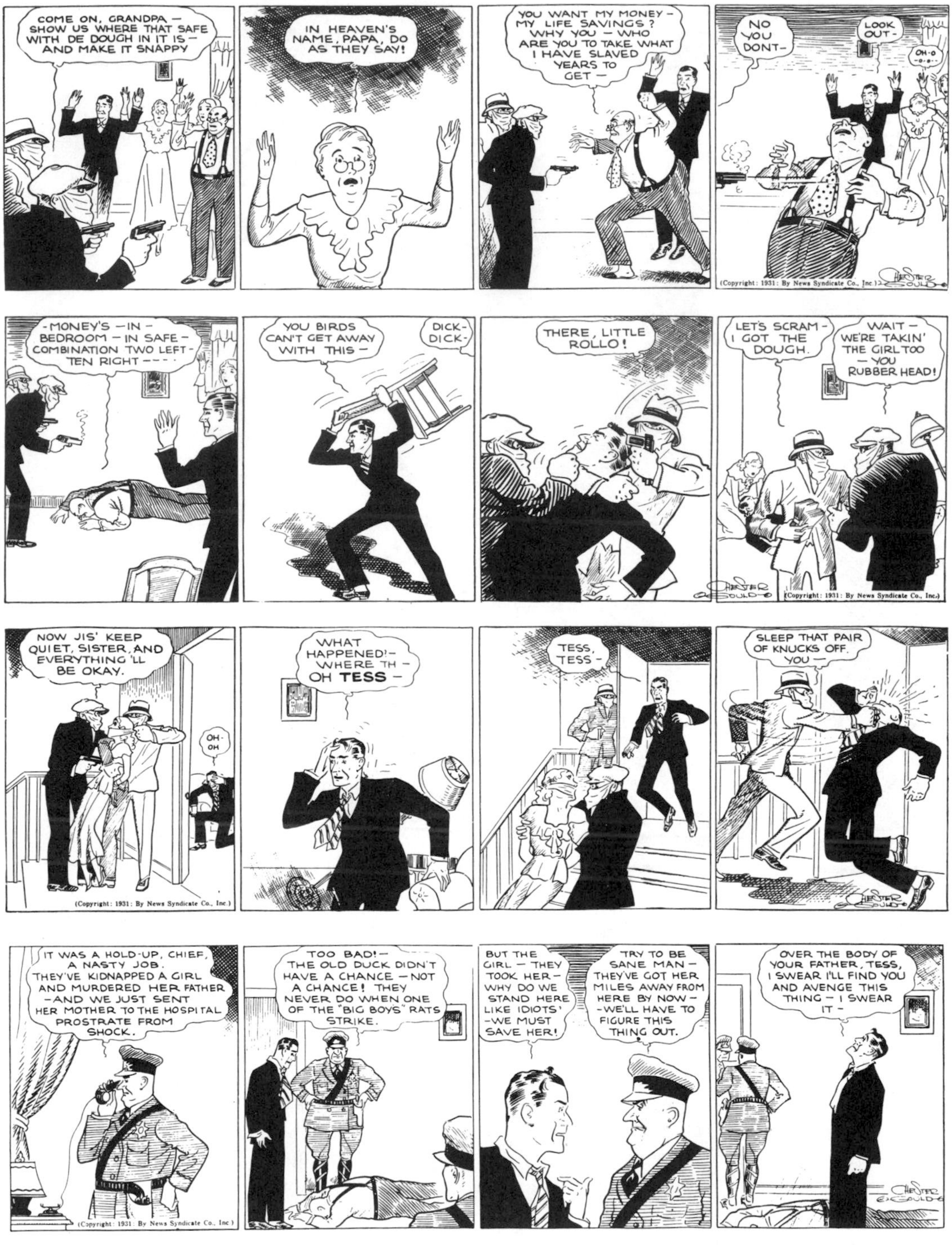
COME ON, GRANDPA — SHOW US WHERE THAT SAFE WITH DE DOUGH IN IT IS — AND MAKE IT SNAPPY
IN HEAVEN'S NAME, PAPA, DO AS THEY SAY!
YOU WANT MY MONEY — MY LIFE SAVINGS? WHY YOU — WHO ARE YOU TO TAKE WHAT I HAVE SLAVED YEARS TO GET —
NO YOU DONT—
LOOK OUT—
OH-O -O-O-
(Copyright: 1931: By News Syndicate Co., Inc.)
CHESTER GOULD
-MONEY'S —IN— BEDROOM — IN SAFE— COMBINATION TWO LEFT— TEN RIGHT - - -
YOU BIRDS CAN'T GET AWAY WITH THIS —
DICK- DICK-
THERE, LITTLE ROLLO!
LET'S SCRAM — I GOT THE DOUGH.
WAIT — WE'RE TAKIN' THE GIRL TOO — YOU RUBBER HEAD!
CHESTER GOULD
(Copyright: 1931: By News Syndicate Co., Inc.)
NOW JIS' KEEP QUIET, SISTER, AND EVERYTHING 'LL BE OKAY.
OH- OH
(Copyright: 1931: By News Syndicate Co., Inc.)
WHAT HAPPENED'— WHERE TH — OH TESS —
TESS, TESS —
SLEEP THAT PAIR OF KNUCKS OFF. YOU —
CHESTER GOULD
IT WAS A HOLD-UP, CHIEF, A NASTY JOB. THEY'VE KIDNAPPED A GIRL AND MURDERED HER FATHER —AND WE JUST SENT HER MOTHER TO THE HOSPITAL PROSTRATE FROM SHOCK.
(Copyright: 1931: By News Syndicate Co., Inc.)
TOO BAD! — THE OLD DUCK DIDN'T HAVE A CHANCE — NOT A CHANCE! THEY NEVER DO WHEN ONE OF THE "BIG BOYS" RATS STRIKE.
BUT THE GIRL — THEY TOOK HER — WHY DO WE STAND HERE LIKE IDIOTS' —WE MUST SAVE HER!
TRY TO BE SANE MAN — THEY'VE GOT HER MILES AWAY FROM HERE BY NOW —WE'LL HAVE TO FIGURE THIS THING OUT.
OVER THE BODY OF YOUR FATHER, TESS, I SWEAR I'LL FIND YOU AND AVENGE THIS THING — I SWEAR IT —
CHESTER GOULD

Fig. 2-2

The debut sequence of *Dick Tracy* is abridged here to show the death of Tess Trueheart's father. This act prompted Dick Tracy to join the plainclothes squad. Tess proves a spunky prisoner for "Big Boy," the first Gould villain. "Big Boy" was patterned after Al Capone.

Fig. 2-3

A portrait of Dick Tracy and his father, Chester Gould, drawn by Dick Locher, the Pulitzer Prize-winning editorial cartoonist of the *Chicago Tribune*. This strip was published 50 years to the day from the first Dick Tracy daily comic strip. Shown (from left) are Lizz, Junior, Sam Catchem, Chief Pat Patton, actor Vitamin Flintheart, and Tracy's wife Tess.

Fig. 2-4

Dick Tracy asked Tess Trueheart to marry him in October, 1931. However, the marriage took place "off camera," on Dec. 24, 1949. These panels from the sequence show the new husband and wife.

daily *Popeye* strip, which he both writes and draws. However, without sales support from King Features Syndicate, the strip is in only about 60 newspapers nationally. In the vast New York City market, for example, it is only read in a Spanish language newspaper. That's absurd.

Dick Tracy, on the other hand, is undergoing a revival in newspaper comics because of the new movie. Tracy consciousness has been raised. TMS is savvy enough to know this can mean new and regained client newspapers billboarding Dick Tracy every day in their newspapers.

As a result of the *Batman* movie, a syndicated comic strip is now offered by Creators Syndicate. However, launching a new strip is a far cry from nurturing and expanding the relationship with newspapers of

an entrenched part of popular culture such as Dick Tracy.

One hopes TMS will follow the advice Gould gave himself in a 1942 special drawing in Martin Sheridan's "Comics and Their Creators." In the drawing, Tracy says to Gould as he is at the drawing board, "Listen, there's got to be more action, better story, shorter balloons, and better looking girl characters."

Remarkably, one of the most impressive members of Tracy's professional family, Lizz the policewoman, has never been the subject of anything but the most peripheral presence in merchandising. She is joined as a member of Tracy's professional family by Sam Catchem, Police Chief Pat Patton, and industrialist Diet Smith. In terms of merchandising, Sam Catchem and Pat

Fig. 2-5
On Sunday, Oct. 4, 1964, Junior Tracy and Moon Maid were married. Her father, shown here with her mother, was Governor of the Moon.

Patton have, over the years, been actively depicted in products. Pat Patton was a fellow policeman with Tracy in the 1930s. Diet Smith entered the strip in 1946 as prime suspect in the death of his business partner. It was Diet's firm that developed the atom-powered 2-way wrist radio. Sam Catchem, Tracy's partner since Dec. 26, 1948, was developed as the result of a comment by Gould's friend and agent, Al Lowenthal: "You ought to have a Jewish detective in there." Gould took the suggestion to heart.

Although no collectibles of Lee Ebony currently exist, except for newspaper tear sheets of the printed syndicated strip and original art, this African-American member of Tracy's police family was developed by the creative team of Rick Fletcher and Max Allan Collins in the early 1980s. A strong, purposeful woman, Lee Ebony presents an excellent role model and certainly has great potential in the future as a character for merchandising.

This returns us to the unlikely fact that Lizz the policewoman, a very sexy character in drawings by Gould and Fletcher, has done so little in the merchandising field. She is a character often sought out by collectors of original art. Possibly she and Lee Ebony will come into their own in the future.

Fig. 2-6

Lizz and Tracy greet his daughter-in-law and granddaughter. Moon Maid makes her last appearance in the Dick Tracy comic strip on August 7, 1978, the victim of a car boobytrapped for Tracy. The artwork is by Rick Fletcher. This allowed for romance between a divorced Sparkle Plenty and widowed Junior Tracy.

Fig. 2-7
Even special family events in *Dick Tracy* cannot escape danger. Here, Junior and Sparkle marry on April 26, 1982. It's a perfect wedding, complete with time bomb.

Tracy Licensing: A Brief History

With the excitement of the *Dick Tracy* movie, prices on Tracy collectibles are currently volatile, as witnessed by doubled and tripled prices at the huge toy and collectibles show held in the early spring of 1990 in Atlantic City, N.J. This is primarily a guide to which Dick Tracy products—new and old—are available. We have included a price guide at the end of the book, to at least provide approximate ranges but remember that there's a great deal of fluctuation in the current market.

The Authorized Guide to Dick Tracy Collectibles was researched with the cooperation of The Walt Disney Company and TMS to provide a unique book. It is the only one where images of the classic TMS *Dick Tracy* and the Warren Beatty—Madonna movie *Dick Tracy* appear together.

Chester Gould was an extraordinary cartoonist. The mythology he established with Dick Tracy's two families, personal and professional, struck a nerve with the public. His appeal was to both children and adults.

The very first promotional brochure from early 1932 claims, ''Every kid wants to be a detective and wear a tin star. The same instinct for adventure and action is carried over to adult life. Evidence the unprecedented popularity of mystery stories and detective fiction. Dick Tracy is a plain-clothes man, a member of the police department. He is the prototype of the present hero ... an antidote to maudlin sympathy with society's enemies, he creates no glamour for the underworld. Children love this character, and parents and teachers approve of him.''

Right from the start, Dick Tracy would never be anything but a police detective—the force of good in a world filled with evil. If children liked the strip, they liked it even better when, early on, Junior—almost a character from a Dickins' novel—joined the

Drawn especially for Newsweek by Chester Gould

Candles for Tracy: Dick Tracy, the fearless detective of the comics, passed his 25th syndicated birthday last week. Now appearing in 500 U.S. and foreign newspapers with a total daily circulation of more than 24 million, Tracy and his assorted friends and foes have for years been bringing their originator, Chester Gould, an estimated annual income of $150,000, plus royalties on Sparkle Plenty dolls.

Fig. 2-8

cast. Now kids really had a character they could identify with!

Nothing shows the diversity of the early licensing program better than the press book for the first movie, the 15-episode Republic Pictures Saturday matinee serial *Dick Tracy,* released in 1937. Press books for all the Tracy movies are not the only great collectibles but wonderful sources of information. The press book shows a child's necktie manu-

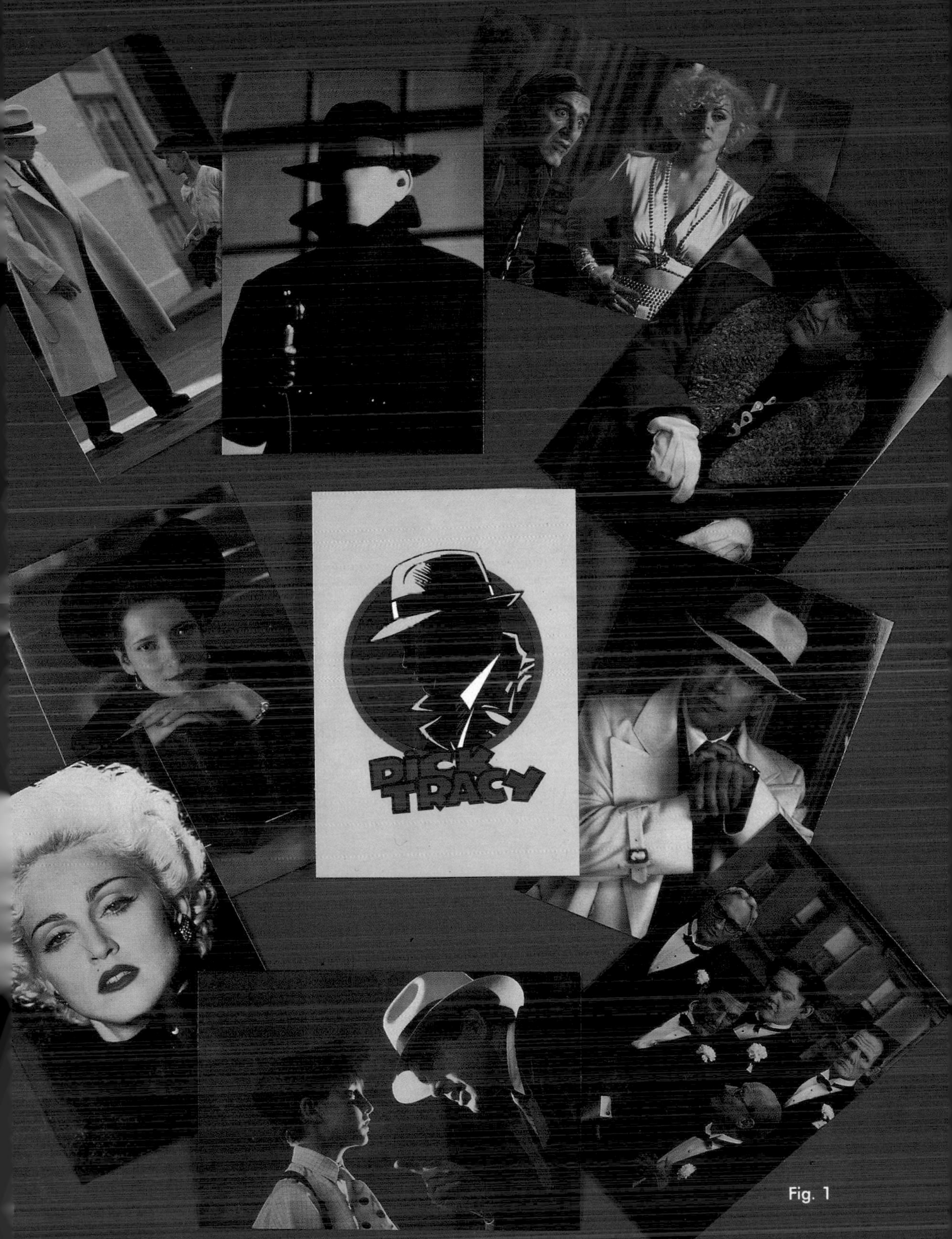
DICK
TRACY

Fig. 1

Fig. 2

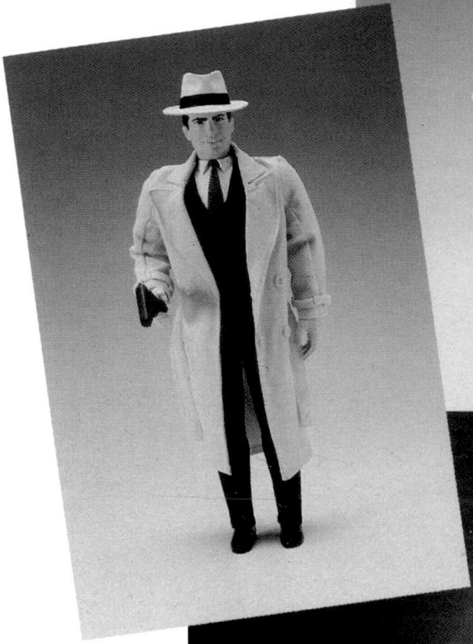

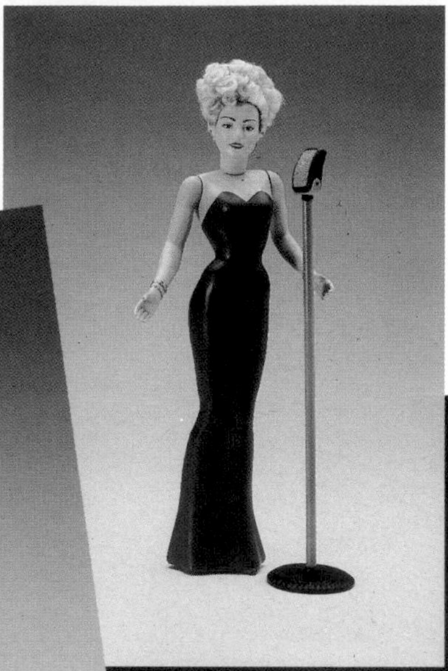

Fig. 3

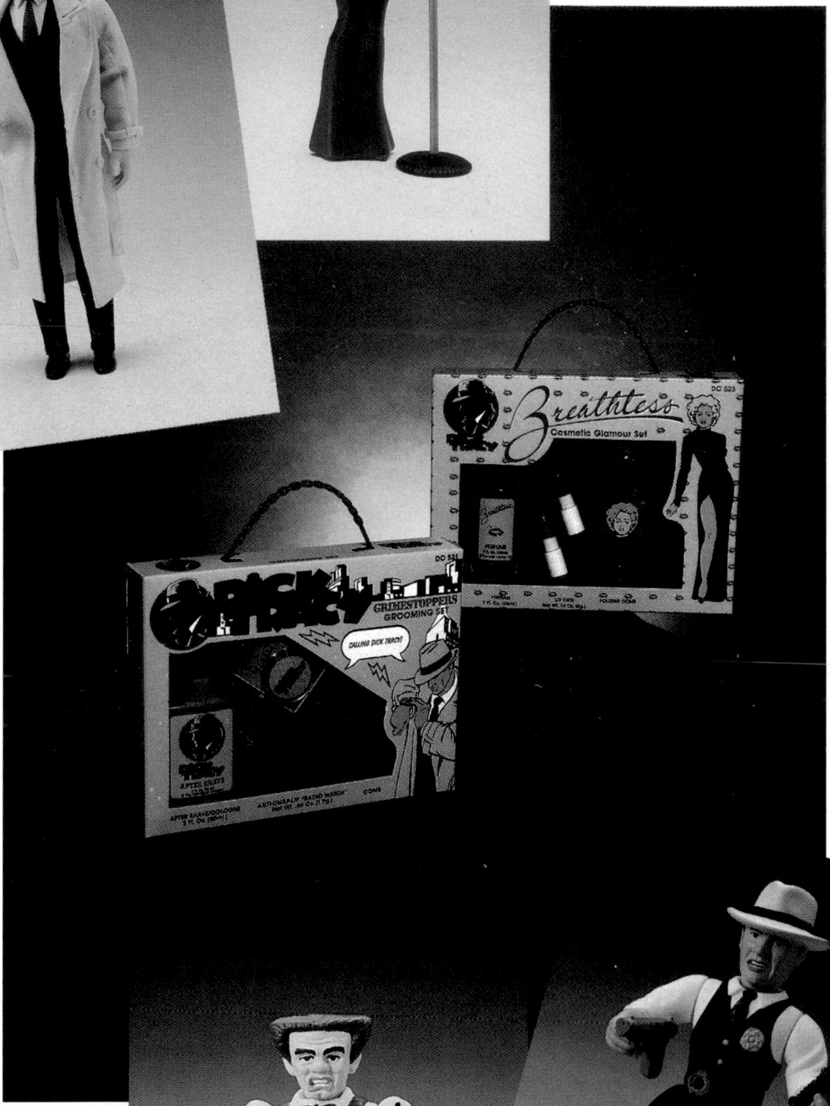
Breathless
Cosmetic Glamour Set
DC 523
GRIMESTOPPERS
GROOMING SET
CALLING DICK TRACY!

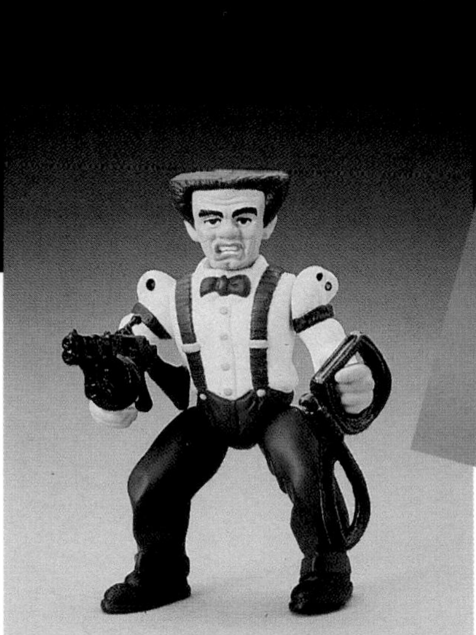

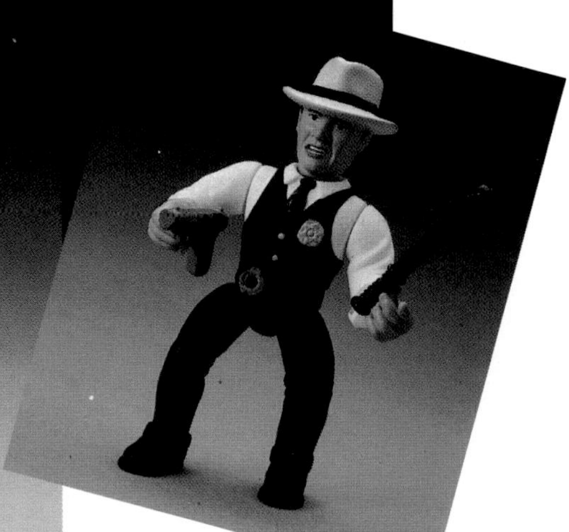

Fig. 4

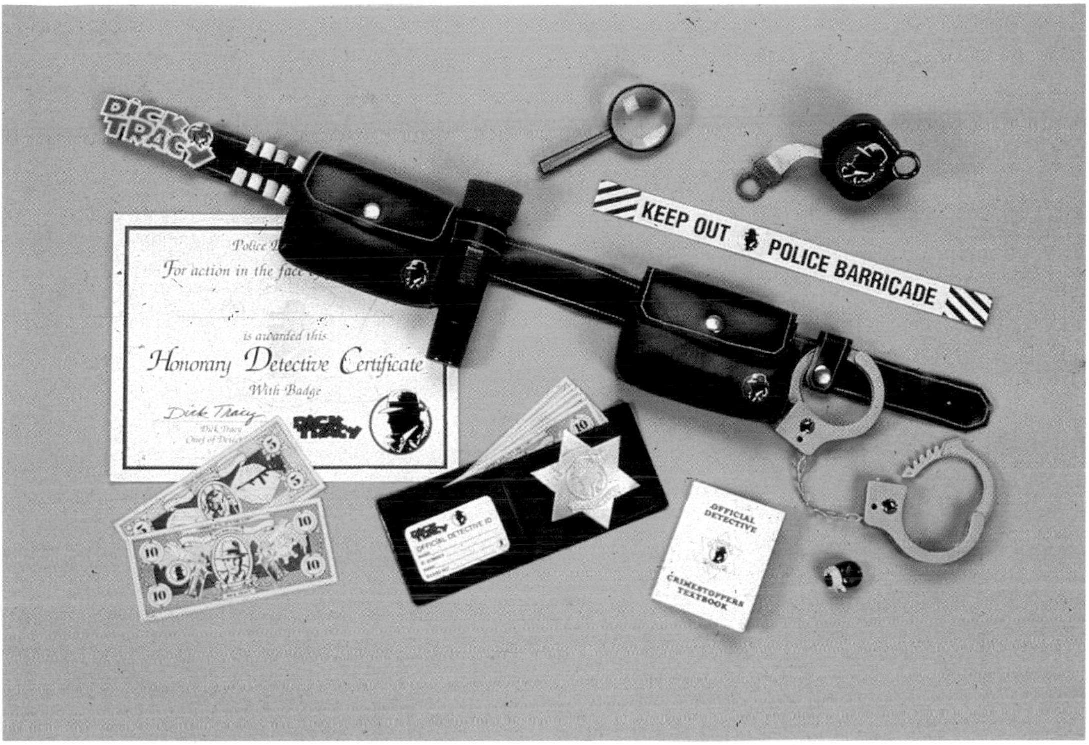
DICK TRACY
KEEP OUT POLICE BARRICADE
is awarded this
Honorary Detective Certificate
With Badge
OFFICIAL DETECTIVE
CRIMESTOPPERS TEXTBOOK

Fig. 5

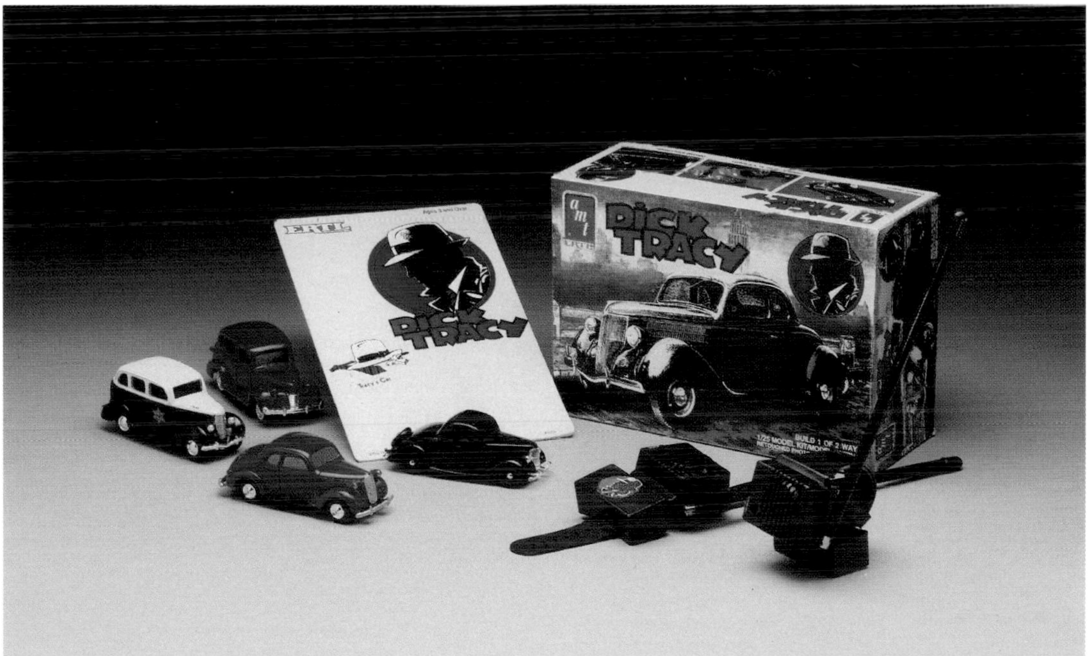
ERTL
DICK TRACY

Fig. 6

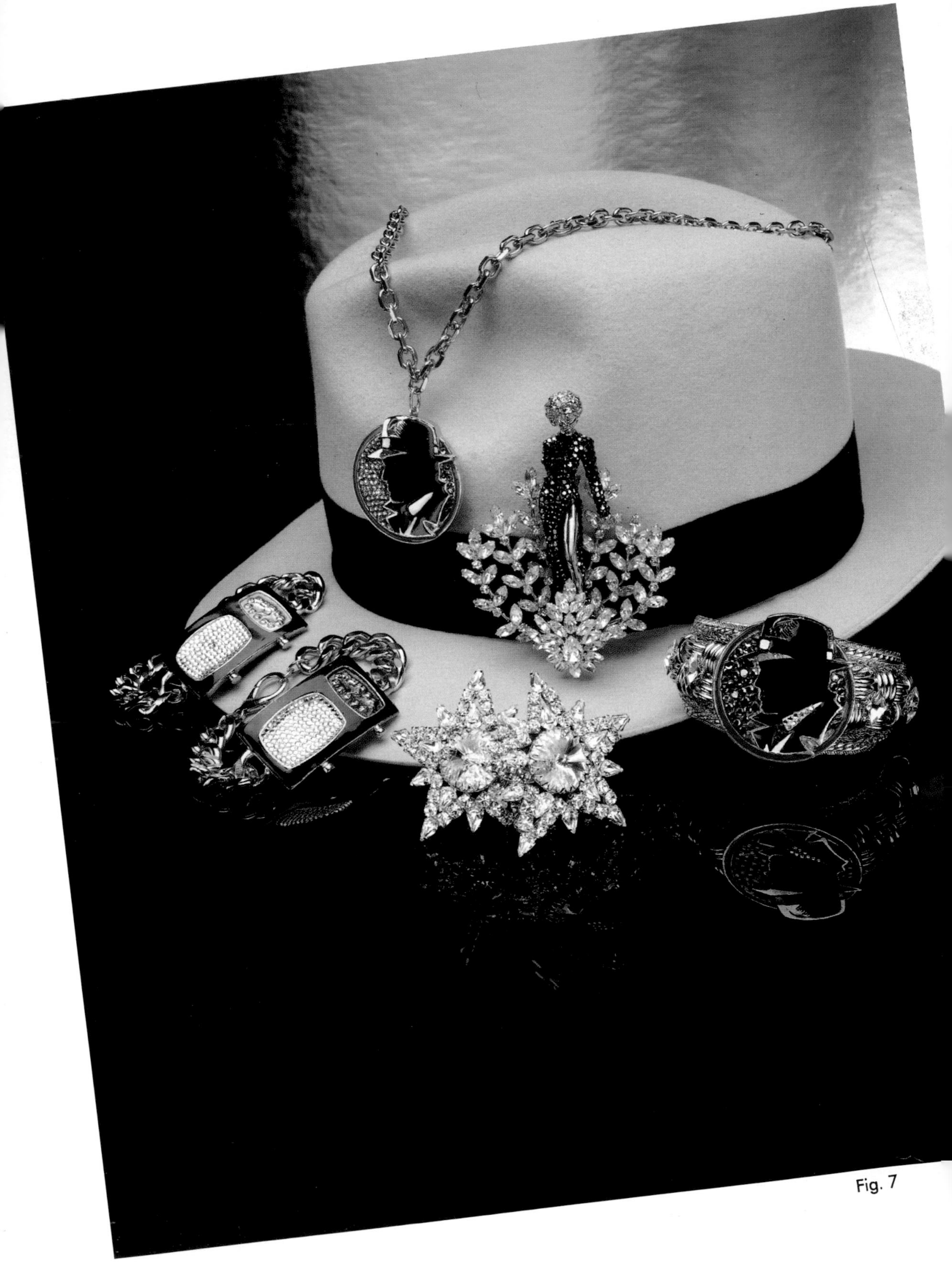

Fig. 7

LEE EBONY
POLICEWOMAN

Fig. 2-9

Lee Ebony, an African-American policewoman, was created by writer Max Allan Collins. She first appeared in the early 1980s drawn by Rick Fletcher.

factured by H. & M. Neckwear of New York City. Whitman Publishing issued "a popular priced edition of *Dick Tracy* to be retailed in five-and-ten stores, department, and book stores. This book was based on the script of the Republic serial and the illustrations are actual scene stills taken from the production."

The Dick Tracy Lite, manufactured by Micro-Lite Company of New York City, was a small pencil-like flashlight which carries a cartoon head of Tracy on the body. The Bamberger-Rheinthal Co. of Cleveland, Ohio, manufactured Dick Tracy childrens' sweaters. Some of these items are very rare.

Because the strip was born at the beginning of a decade (1931) and Chester Gould's involvement lasted almost 50 years (until Dec., 1977), it is easy to divide the history of *Dick Tracy* into decades. The same applies to Dick Tracy collectibles.

The current film depends heavily on the mythology of Gould's comic strip from the 1930s and early 1940s. Prohibition was on and gangsters and their molls were Gould's first target. Then the grotesque villains and singular names developed.

Although Gould wrote scripts where innocent citizens were sometimes drawn into criminal situations by fate, many of his villains were just plain scum who exit the strip either by what Gould called "the hot lead route" or some other appropriately bizarre method. Few readers shed a tear when The Brow, a Nazi spy, fell out of an upper story window in a 1944 fight with Tracy and was impaled on the flagpole of the local memorial to fallen American soldiers. In an interview with me (Crouch) in 1979, Gould expressed his extreme annoyance that "the lily-livered editors" left out his ending to the story when it was reprinted in the 1970 book, *The Celebrated Cases of Dick Tracy*.

The two basic books a dealer or collector needs are: *Dick Tracy: America's Most Famous Detective,* the official history of the comic strip and all the creative people involved with it, published by Citadel Press; and *Dick Tracy: The Official Biography,* published as a Plume paperback original by New American Library.

By the 1950s, following an incredible surge in popularity of the whole Dick Tracy

Fig. 2-10

Like most American families, the Goulds always sent Christmas cards. They are highly collectible and featured special art by Chester Gould. This one is from the early 1930s.

Fig. 2-11
Dick Tracy is featured in this 1946 Christmas card drawn by Chester Gould. The practice was continued by Gould until his death.

family with the birth of Sparkle Plenty, Gould repeated that success with the birth of Tracy and Tess's daughter, Bonny Braids. The infant Bonny was kidnapped by Crewy Lou, a not-so-nice woman with a crewcut in front and a long ponytail in back. While our late-20th-century sensibilities shrug this off as just a punk hairstyle, it caused a stir in 1951. Bonny Braids followed Sparkle as merchandising magic.

Fig. 2-12

In Lizz the policewoman, Gould created one of the most forceful women in comics. These two consecutive dailies from April, 1974, show why she is a favorite of collectors of Gould original art.

Gould was in his stride in the 1950s and in perfect harmony with the mood of the country. This is a favorite period for collectors of original art, as there is more post-1950 original work to be had. The Rhodent, a villain in the new movie which is set in the 1930s, actually first appeared in the comic strip in 1959. He is no doubt a cousin of the murderous Mole from 1941.

While The Mole reappeared in the strip in the Fletcher/Collins period, a totally reformed farmer in the Midwest, his granddaughter Molene was a classic villainess from the 1970s. Not just Tracy and the forces of good, but also the forces of corruption and evil fit into family groups in Dick Tracy's mythology.

Because Chester Gould created such a wonderfully bizarre gallery of evildoers, they will continue to be recycled in licensed products. Classic criminals from the 1950s are Odds Zonn, Rughead, Oodles, Joe Period, Flattop, Jr., and Miss Egghead.

The space era for Dick Tracy covered almost a decade and basically ended when man landed on the moon and it proved to be very different from Gould's fictional moon. While some fans moan and groan about this period, Gould was far too talented a writer and artist not to produce some first class material in the 1960s. Sometimes he did seem to go his own way. However, to totally dismiss this decade of his work is shortsighted and uninformed. A number of interesting collectibles appeared. The Aurora plastic model of Diet Smith's Space Coupe and the metal lunch box and thermal container decorated with Tracy space era designs are examples. The doll of Honey Moon, Dick Tracy's granddaughter, wasn't the smash hit of the earlier dolls but wasn't a flop either.

Because some of Gould's excellent evil characters from the 1960s haven't been reprinted at all, they remain fresh. Mr. Bribery, with his cigar-smoking cat, was a murderous fellow. Even his lanky, buxom sister Ugly Christine literally wore his brand on her forehead. Haf & Haf, with one side of his face handsome and the other hideously scarred, has more lives than a cat. Introduced by Gould in 1966, he reappeared in an excellent story by Max Allan Collins in spring 1978. Now he's back in 1990 as a pseudo Phantom of Hollywood.

Gould developed characters in the oddest ways. He enjoyed peanut butter on toast with bacon at breakfast. So in 1972, he introduced a 10-year-old brat named Peanutbutter. Getting Peanutbutter out of trouble provided several adventures for Tracy.

Gould mostly left the space hardware behind in the 1970s. Pouch, a former sideshow fat man whose lengthy dieting left him so many folds in his neck that he had a snap installed and hid stolen goods there, appeared in 1970. The Button, a regular member of organized crime, and The Brain, who wore a hat that looked like a human brain, appeared in 1973 and 1974, respectively.

In 1975, Z.Z. Welz, a general slimeball, is shot by his pregnant wife when she finds out that he's the one who has been terrorizing the community with obscene phone calls. Gould, who was 75 at the time, hadn't lost his punch. He ended his years on the strip as he had begun, with the basics—the crime, the chase, victory for Dick Tracy, and often death for the criminal.

While licensed products in the 1960s were fueled by the animated Tracy TV show, 1970s products were mainly inexpensive bubble-packed toys made by firms such as Larami and Ja-Ru.

With Gould's retirement in late 1977, Fletcher, as much of a technology buff as Gould, made contact with a fellow who helped place Tracy on the cutting edge of police technology. Former Deputy Sheriff Julio Santiago of Rosemount, Minnesota, became technical adviser on the strip while Fletcher handled the art. Santiago's accomplishments are impressive. The Nite-Site, a real gun sight that he co-invented, allowed Tracy to fire accurately in low-level light. Armed with a Colt .357 Magnum with a Nite-Site, Dick Tracy made short work of crooked art dealer Art Dekko in a pitch black situation in 1980.

Other Santiago innovations used by Fletcher include nylon restraining devices as emergency handcuffs, soft body armor, and 3-D police targets for life-like firearms training, to mention a few. Just for fun, Santiago agreed to help caption the toy Dick Tracy guns, and he identified some as models of specific firearms. He and Fletcher even made sure that when Art Dekko emptied a Thompson submachine gun in an attempt to kill Tracy, the correct number of spent shell casings were depicted.

What the Warren Beatty–Madonna version of Dick Tracy has done is put new excitement in the air. The time is again ripe for appreciation of Tracy and his code of honor: good always triumphs over evil. From narco-terrorists and street gangs dealing crack cocaine to the smirking, unrepentant Wall Street felons, the American public is fed up. Timing is everything. Dick Tracy's popularity is surging for a new generation. This book will let you not only see his long history in popular culture and licensed products, but serve as a valuable reference tool as well.

An Open-and-Shut Case: The Button

The most elementary level of collecting is saving the actual comic strips as printed in your local newspaper. This brief abridgement from Sunday pages gives you the flavor of Gould's work and his penchant for the unusual. This is the first time any of the Button story has been reprinted.

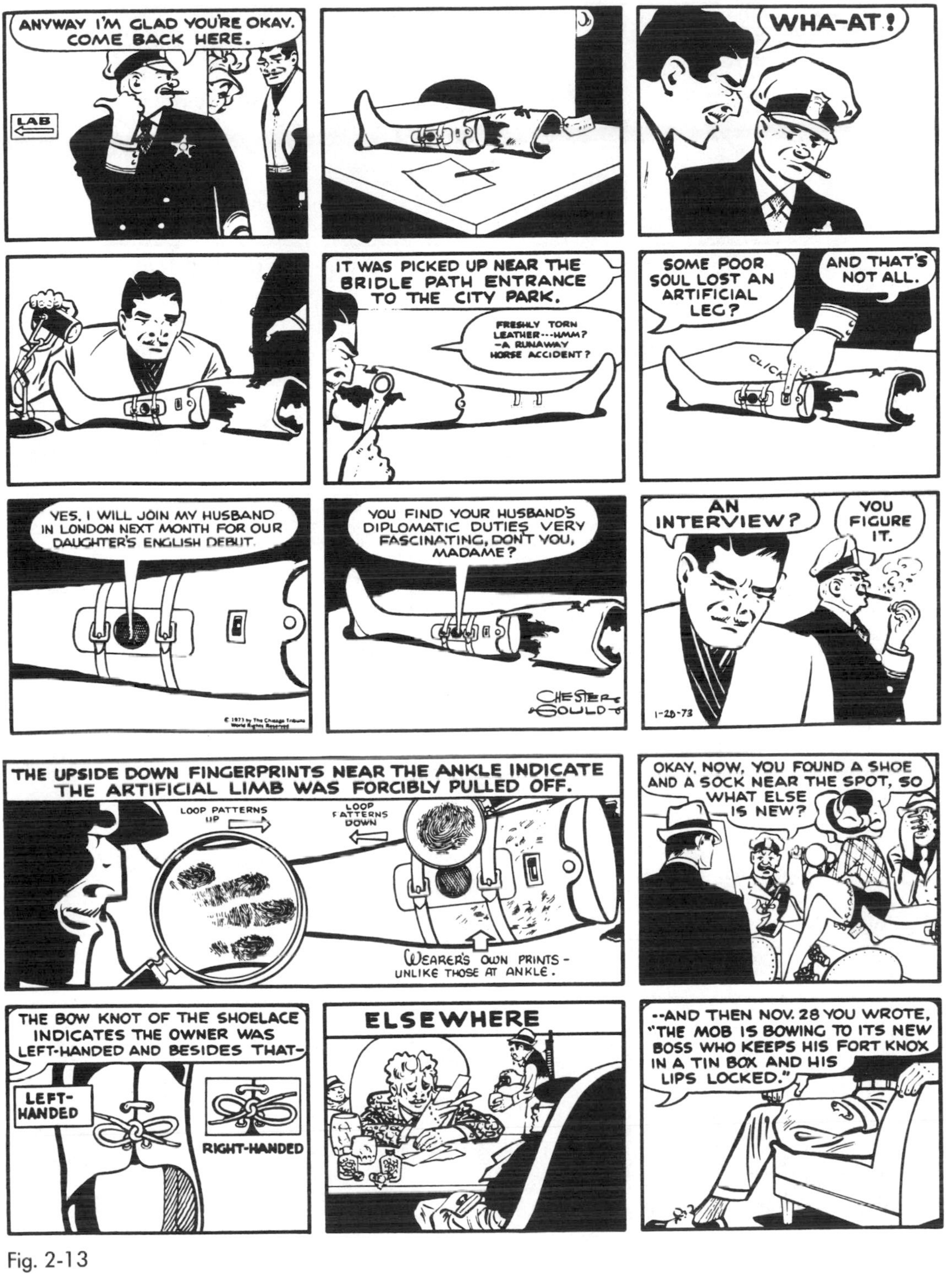
ANYWAY I'M GLAD YOU'RE OKAY. COME BACK HERE.
LAB
WHA-AT!
IT WAS PICKED UP NEAR THE BRIDLE PATH ENTRANCE TO THE CITY PARK.
FRESHLY TORN LEATHER---HMM? --A RUNAWAY HORSE ACCIDENT?
SOME POOR SOUL LOST AN ARTIFICIAL LEG?
AND THAT'S NOT ALL.
CLICK
YES, I WILL JOIN MY HUSBAND IN LONDON NEXT MONTH FOR OUR DAUGHTER'S ENGLISH DEBUT.
YOU FIND YOUR HUSBAND'S DIPLOMATIC DUTIES VERY FASCINATING, DON'T YOU, MADAME?
CHESTER GOULD
AN INTERVIEW?
YOU FIGURE IT.
1-28-73
THE UPSIDE DOWN FINGERPRINTS NEAR THE ANKLE INDICATE THE ARTIFICIAL LIMB WAS FORCIBLY PULLED OFF.
LOOP PATTERNS UP
LOOP PATTERNS DOWN
WEARER'S OWN PRINTS - UNLIKE THOSE AT ANKLE.
OKAY, NOW, YOU FOUND A SHOE AND A SOCK NEAR THE SPOT, SO WHAT ELSE IS NEW?
THE BOW KNOT OF THE SHOELACE INDICATES THE OWNER WAS LEFT-HANDED AND BESIDES THAT-
LEFT-HANDED
RIGHT-HANDED
ELSEWHERE
--AND THEN NOV. 28 YOU WROTE, "THE MOB IS BOWING TO ITS NEW BOSS WHO KEEPS HIS FORT KNOX IN A TIN BOX AND HIS LIPS LOCKED."

Fig. 2-13

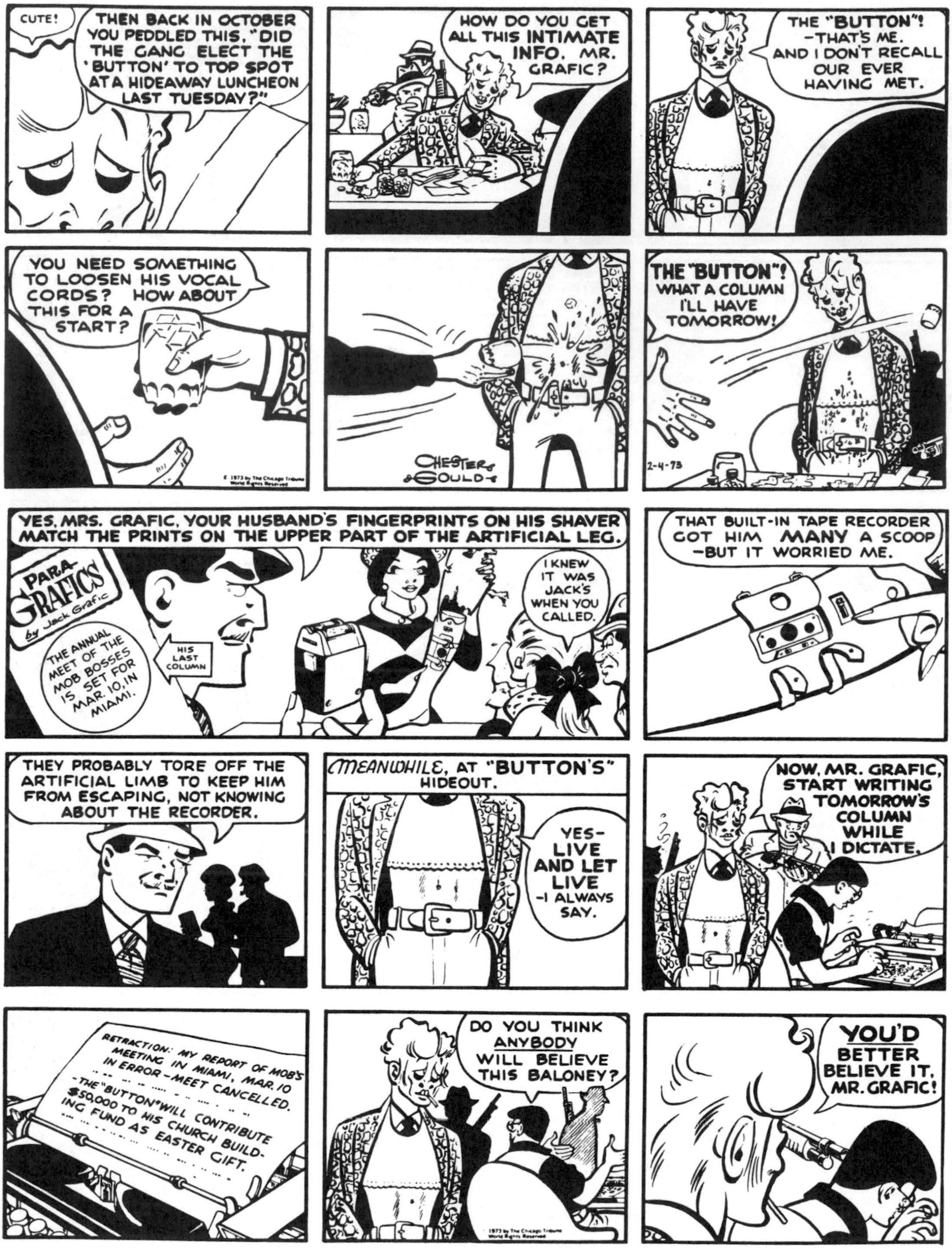
CUTE!
THEN BACK IN OCTOBER YOU PEDDLED THIS, "DID THE GANG ELECT THE 'BUTTON' TO TOP SPOT AT A HIDEAWAY LUNCHEON LAST TUESDAY?"
HOW DO YOU GET ALL THIS INTIMATE INFO, MR. GRAFIC?
THE "BUTTON"! —THAT'S ME. AND I DON'T RECALL OUR EVER HAVING MET.
YOU NEED SOMETHING TO LOOSEN HIS VOCAL CORDS? HOW ABOUT THIS FOR A START?
CHESTER GOULD
THE "BUTTON"! WHAT A COLUMN I'LL HAVE TOMORROW!
2-4-73
YES, MRS. GRAFIC, YOUR HUSBAND'S FINGERPRINTS ON HIS SHAVER MATCH THE PRINTS ON THE UPPER PART OF THE ARTIFICIAL LEG.
PARA GRAFICS by Jack Grafic
THE ANNUAL MEET OF THE MOB BOSSES IS SET FOR MAR. 10, IN MIAMI.
HIS LAST COLUMN
I KNEW IT WAS JACK'S WHEN YOU CALLED.
THAT BUILT-IN TAPE RECORDER GOT HIM MANY A SCOOP —BUT IT WORRIED ME.
THEY PROBABLY TORE OFF THE ARTIFICIAL LIMB TO KEEP HIM FROM ESCAPING, NOT KNOWING ABOUT THE RECORDER.
MEANWHILE, AT "BUTTON'S" HIDEOUT.
YES— LIVE AND LET LIVE —I ALWAYS SAY.
NOW, MR. GRAFIC, START WRITING TOMORROW'S COLUMN WHILE I DICTATE.
RETRACTION: MY REPORT OF MOB'S MEETING IN MIAMI, MAR. 10 IN ERROR—MEET CANCELLED.
-THE "BUTTON" WILL CONTRIBUTE $50,000 TO HIS CHURCH BUILDING FUND AS EASTER GIFT.
DO YOU THINK ANYBODY WILL BELIEVE THIS BALONEY?
YOU'D BETTER BELIEVE IT, MR. GRAFIC!

Fig. 2-14

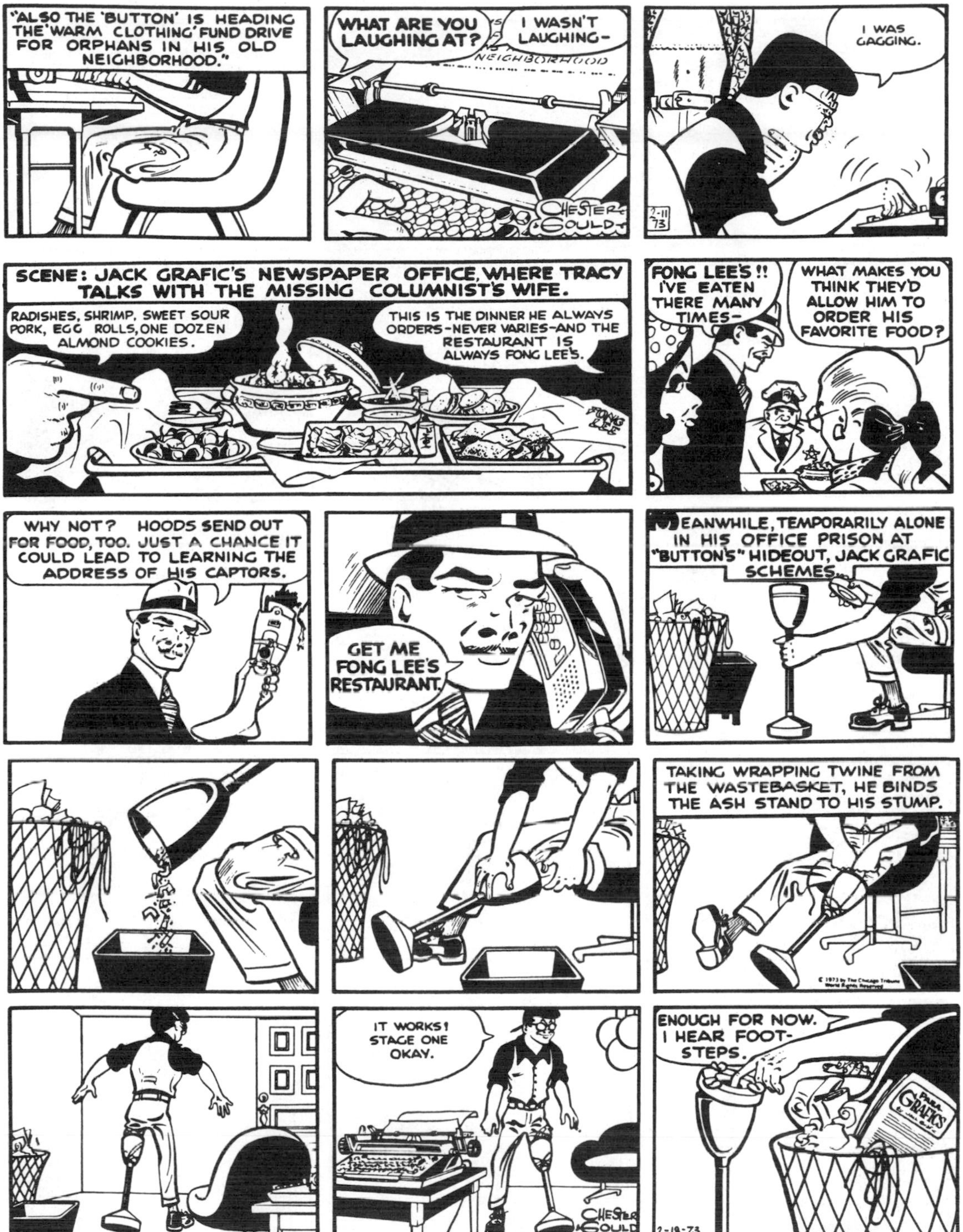
"ALSO THE 'BUTTON' IS HEADING THE 'WARM CLOTHING' FUND DRIVE FOR ORPHANS IN HIS OLD NEIGHBORHOOD."
WHAT ARE YOU LAUGHING AT?
I WASN'T LAUGHING–
NEIGHBORHOOD
CHESTER GOULD
I WAS GAGGING.
2-11-73
SCENE: JACK GRAFIC'S NEWSPAPER OFFICE, WHERE TRACY TALKS WITH THE MISSING COLUMNIST'S WIFE.
RADISHES, SHRIMP, SWEET SOUR PORK, EGG ROLLS, ONE DOZEN ALMOND COOKIES.
THIS IS THE DINNER HE ALWAYS ORDERS–NEVER VARIES–AND THE RESTAURANT IS ALWAYS FONG LEE'S.
FONG LEE
FONG LEE'S!! I'VE EATEN THERE MANY TIMES–
WHAT MAKES YOU THINK THEY'D ALLOW HIM TO ORDER HIS FAVORITE FOOD?
WHY NOT? HOODS SEND OUT FOR FOOD, TOO. JUST A CHANCE IT COULD LEAD TO LEARNING THE ADDRESS OF HIS CAPTORS.
GET ME FONG LEE'S RESTAURANT.
MEANWHILE, TEMPORARILY ALONE IN HIS OFFICE PRISON AT "BUTTON'S" HIDEOUT, JACK GRAFIC SCHEMES.
TAKING WRAPPING TWINE FROM THE WASTEBASKET, HE BINDS THE ASH STAND TO HIS STUMP.
IT WORKS! STAGE ONE OKAY.
CHESTER GOULD
ENOUGH FOR NOW. I HEAR FOOT-STEPS.
PARA GRAFICS
2-18-73

Fig. 2-15

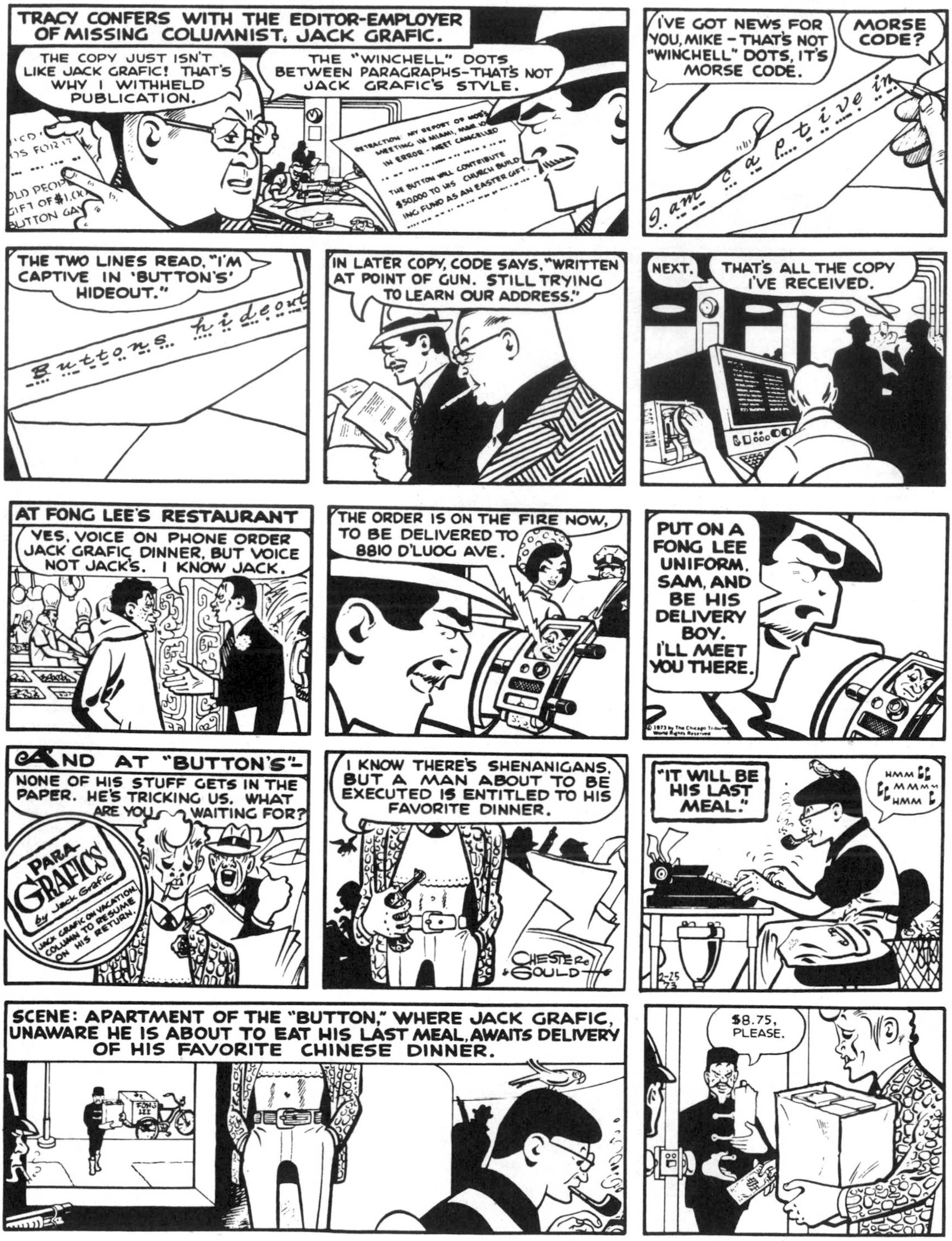
TRACY CONFERS WITH THE EDITOR-EMPLOYER OF MISSING COLUMNIST, JACK GRAFIC.
THE COPY JUST ISN'T LIKE JACK GRAFIC! THAT'S WHY I WITHHELD PUBLICATION.
THE "WINCHELL" DOTS BETWEEN PARAGRAPHS–THAT'S NOT JACK GRAFIC'S STYLE.
I'VE GOT NEWS FOR YOU, MIKE – THAT'S NOT "WINCHELL" DOTS, IT'S MORSE CODE.
MORSE CODE?
I am captive in
THE TWO LINES READ, "I'M CAPTIVE IN 'BUTTON'S' HIDEOUT."
Buttons hideout
IN LATER COPY, CODE SAYS, "WRITTEN AT POINT OF GUN. STILL TRYING TO LEARN OUR ADDRESS."
NEXT.
THAT'S ALL THE COPY I'VE RECEIVED.
AT FONG LEE'S RESTAURANT
YES, VOICE ON PHONE ORDER JACK GRAFIC DINNER, BUT VOICE NOT JACK'S. I KNOW JACK.
THE ORDER IS ON THE FIRE NOW, TO BE DELIVERED TO 8810 D'LUOG AVE.
PUT ON A FONG LEE UNIFORM, SAM, AND BE HIS DELIVERY BOY. I'LL MEET YOU THERE.
AND AT "BUTTON'S"–
NONE OF HIS STUFF GETS IN THE PAPER. HE'S TRICKING US. WHAT ARE YOU WAITING FOR?
PARA GRAFICS by Jack Grafic
JACK GRAFIC ON VACATION. COLUMN TO RESUME ON HIS RETURN.
I KNOW THERE'S SHENANIGANS. BUT A MAN ABOUT TO BE EXECUTED IS ENTITLED TO HIS FAVORITE DINNER.
CHESTER GOULD
"IT WILL BE HIS LAST MEAL."
HMM HMMM HMM
2-25 73
SCENE: APARTMENT OF THE "BUTTON," WHERE JACK GRAFIC, UNAWARE HE IS ABOUT TO EAT HIS LAST MEAL, AWAITS DELIVERY OF HIS FAVORITE CHINESE DINNER.
FONG LEE
$8.75, PLEASE.

Fig. 2-16

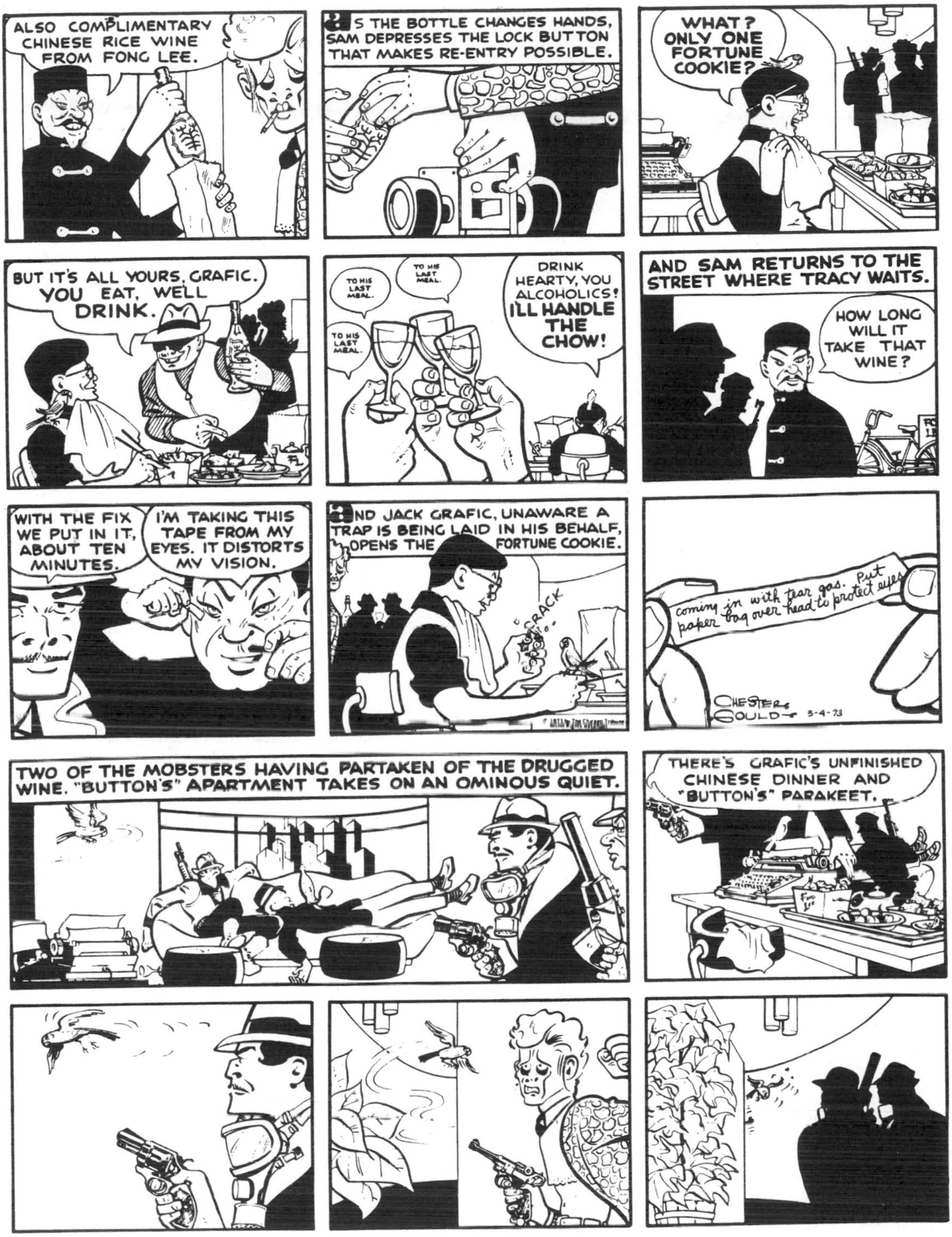

ALSO COMPLIMENTARY CHINESE RICE WINE FROM FONG LEE.
AS THE BOTTLE CHANGES HANDS, SAM DEPRESSES THE LOCK BUTTON THAT MAKES RE-ENTRY POSSIBLE.
WHAT? ONLY ONE FORTUNE COOKIE?
BUT IT'S ALL YOURS, GRAFIC. YOU EAT, WE'LL DRINK.
TO HIS LAST MEAL.
TO HIS LAST MEAL.
TO HIS LAST MEAL.
DRINK HEARTY, YOU ALCOHOLICS! I'LL HANDLE THE CHOW!
AND SAM RETURNS TO THE STREET WHERE TRACY WAITS.
HOW LONG WILL IT TAKE THAT WINE?
WITH THE FIX WE PUT IN IT, ABOUT TEN MINUTES.
I'M TAKING THIS TAPE FROM MY EYES. IT DISTORTS MY VISION.
AND JACK GRAFIC, UNAWARE A TRAP IS BEING LAID IN HIS BEHALF, OPENS THE FORTUNE COOKIE.
CRACK
coming in with tear gas. Put paper bag over head to protect eyes
CHESTER GOULD 3-4-73
TWO OF THE MOBSTERS HAVING PARTAKEN OF THE DRUGGED WINE, "BUTTON'S" APARTMENT TAKES ON AN OMINOUS QUIET.
THERE'S GRAFIC'S UNFINISHED CHINESE DINNER AND "BUTTON'S" PARAKEET. . . .

Fig. 2-17

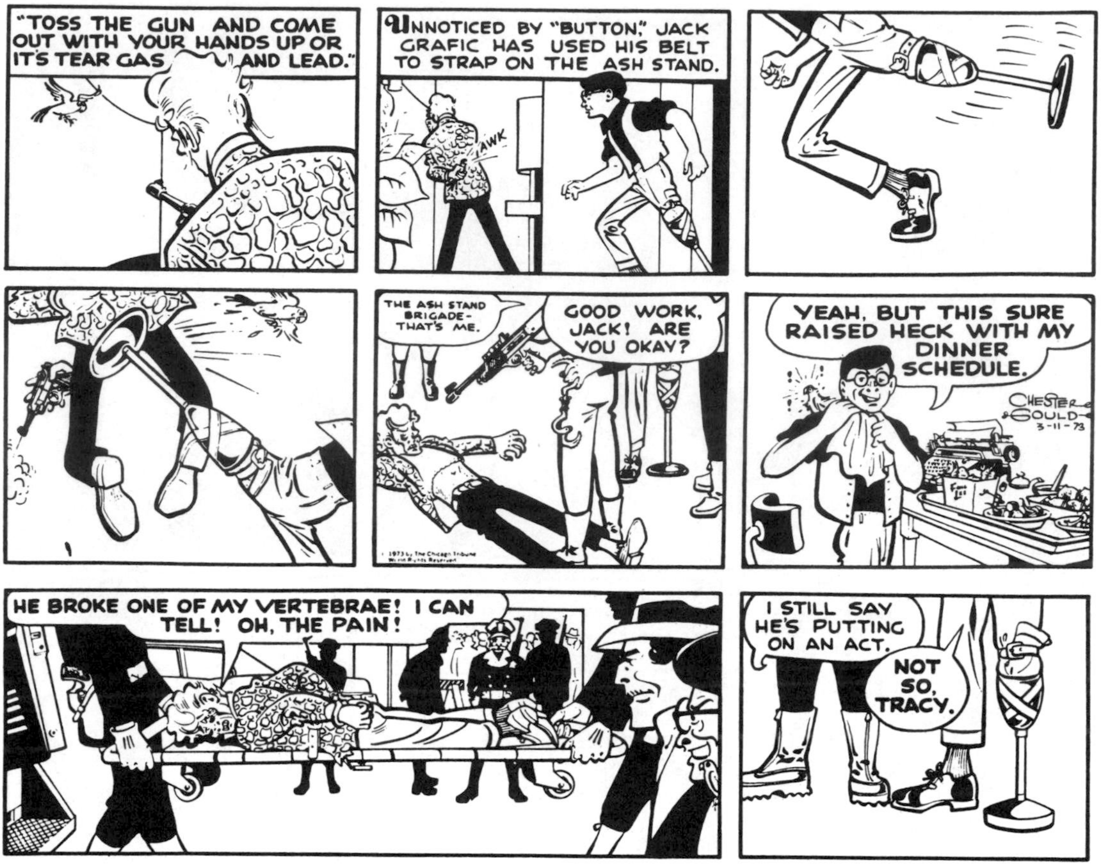
"TOSS THE GUN AND COME OUT WITH YOUR HANDS UP OR IT'S TEAR GAS AND LEAD."
UNNOTICED BY "BUTTON," JACK GRAFIC HAS USED HIS BELT TO STRAP ON THE ASH STAND.
AWK
THE ASH STAND BRIGADE- THAT'S ME.
GOOD WORK, JACK! ARE YOU OKAY?
YEAH, BUT THIS SURE RAISED HECK WITH MY DINNER SCHEDULE.
CHESTER GOULD 3-11-73
HE BROKE ONE OF MY VERTEBRAE! I CAN TELL! OH, THE PAIN!
I STILL SAY HE'S PUTTING ON AN ACT.
NOT SO, TRACY.

Fig. 2-18

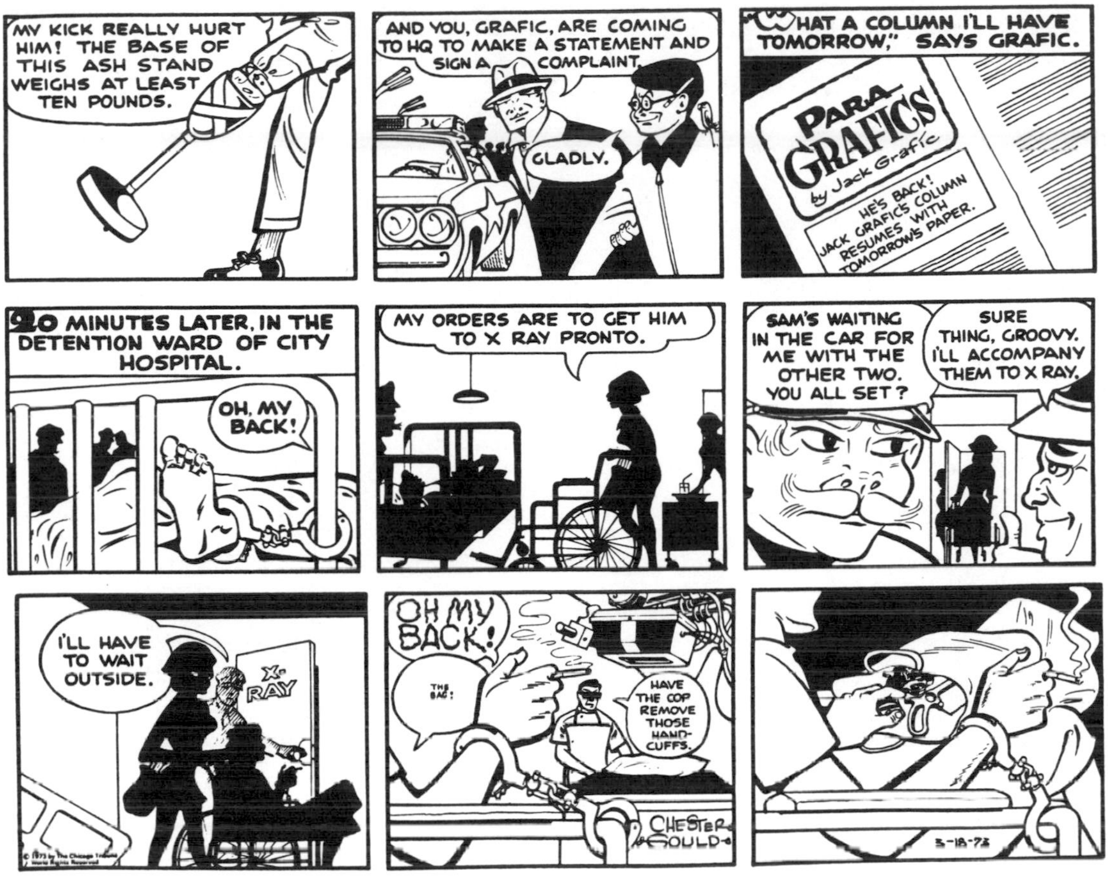
MY KICK REALLY HURT HIM! THE BASE OF THIS ASH STAND WEIGHS AT LEAST TEN POUNDS.
AND YOU, GRAFIC, ARE COMING TO HQ TO MAKE A STATEMENT AND SIGN A COMPLAINT.
GLADLY.
"WHAT A COLUMN I'LL HAVE TOMORROW," SAYS GRAFIC.
PARA GRAFICS
by Jack Grafic
HE'S BACK! JACK GRAFIC'S COLUMN RESUMES WITH TOMORROW'S PAPER.
20 MINUTES LATER, IN THE DETENTION WARD OF CITY HOSPITAL.
OH, MY BACK!
MY ORDERS ARE TO GET HIM TO X RAY PRONTO.
SAM'S WAITING IN THE CAR FOR ME WITH THE OTHER TWO. YOU ALL SET?
SURE THING, GROOVY. I'LL ACCOMPANY THEM TO X RAY.
I'LL HAVE TO WAIT OUTSIDE.
X-RAY
OH MY BACK!
HAVE THE COP REMOVE THOSE HAND-CUFFS.
CHESTER GOULD
3-18-73

Fig. 2-19

3 DICK TRACY COLLECTIBLES

Ellery Queen's introduction to *The Celebrated Cases of Dick Tracy*, a 1970 Chelsea House publication, noted that there are "more than 60 different by-products of Dick Tracy." However, any serious Dick Tracy collector would be quick to point out that this is a very low estimate. Although a comprehensive listing has never been compiled, the number of different Tracy items is well into the hundreds.

The categories in this chapter provide a representative selection of Tracy collectibles, with photos and descriptions. This is by no means intended to be a comprehensive listing.

Comic Books

Since Dick Tracy's appeal starts with the artistry and storytelling of his creator, Chester Gould, it is likely that comic books are the most widely collected Tracy items. Except for six monthly comics (Dell Nos. 19 through 24) and a few premium comics, all Dick Tracy comics contained reprints of strips from the newspapers. Dick Tracy strips were first reprinted in a pair of hardcover books published in 1933 by Cupples & Leon Co. titled *Dick Tracy & Dick Tracy, Jr. and How They Captured Stooge Viller* and *How Dick Tracy & Dick Tracy, Jr. Caught the Racketeers*. Both included strips from 1932 through 1933.

The first comic book to show Dick Tracy was Popular Comics No. 1, published by Dell in 1937. Tracy shared stories with other characters in Popular Comics between 1936 and 1948, and in Super Comics from 1938 through 1947.

The first comic book devoted *entirely* to Dick Tracy was a non-numbered Feature Book published by David McKay in 1937. There are only three known copies of this comic in existence, and it has been valued at about $3,000 in mint condition. Between 1937 and 1938, David McKay reprinted the non-numbered Feature Book as Feature Book No. 4, but with a different cover, and also published Feature Books Nos. 6 and 9.

Dell devoted six "Large Feature Book" comics and one "Large Feature Comic" to Dick Tracy stories between about 1938 and 1941. Dell's first 4-Color Comic in 1939 featured Dick Tracy, as did nine additional 4-Color Comics through 1948. Dell published Dick Tracy monthly comics Nos. 1 through 24 between January 1948 and December 1949. Harvey took over the monthly series from Dell and published it from No. 25 to No. 145 through April 1961.

Fig. 3-1

This unnumbered Feature Book, published by David McKay in 1937, was the first devoted entirely to Dick Tracy. This is one of only three known copies.

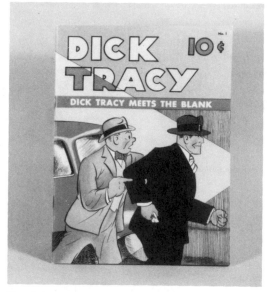

Fig. 3-2

The Blank, a villain featured in the 1990 movie, is mentioned on the cover of Dell's "Large Feature Comic" No. 1, an oversized comic book from 1938.

Several runs, or series, of Dick Tracy comics were published by Blackthorne between 1986 and 1989. These included Monthly/Weekly Series Nos. 1 through 99, Reuben Award Winner Series Nos. 1 through 24, "Dick Tracy: The Early Years" Nos. 1 through 4, and "The Unprinted Stories" Nos. 1 through 4. In 1986 Blackthorne published a 3-D comic titled "Ocean Death Trap."

The post-Gould strips done by Collins, Fletcher and Locher were published in six Dragon Lady Press comics between 1985 and 1987 and in one Ken Pierce Comic in 1986 titled "Dick Tracy's Wartime Memories."

There have been numerous miscellaneous Dick Tracy comics and reprint books published since 1933, including both hardcover and paperback books. There have also been more than a dozen premium comics published since 1939, advertising such things as shoes and hats, bread and cereal, flashlights and television sets, gas stations and department stores. The *Comic Book Price*

Fig. 3-3

Dell published Dick Tracy monthly comics Nos. 1 through 24 between January, 1948, and December, 1949. "Dick Tracy Monthly" comic book No. 1; Harvey's first "Dick Tracy Comics Monthly," which began in March, 1950, with issue No. 25 and continued as a series to issue No. 145 in April, 1961.

Guide by Robert Overstreet is the prime source of information for Dick Tracy comic collectors.

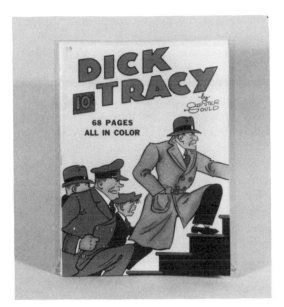

Fig. 3-4
Dell's first "4-Color Comic" in 1939 featured Dick Tracy.

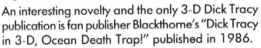

Fig. 3-5
An interesting novelty and the only 3-D Dick Tracy publication is fan publisher Blackthorne's "Dick Tracy in 3-D, Ocean Death Trap!" published in 1986.

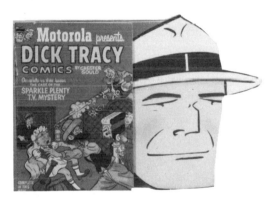

Fig. 3-6
In 1953, Motorola issued this premium comic book that came packaged with a full-color cardboard mask and vest. The mask and comic book are shown.

Premoiums

Premiums include giveaways and promotional items that were either distributed free or in exchange for boxtops, labels and the like. Some of the rarest, most expensive, and least cataloged Dick Tracy collectibles are premiums. This is probably because they were, in their time, considered common, valued lightly, and readily tossed out during housecleaning.

Among the scarce Dick Tracy comics are those freebies given away to promote such products as Buster Brown shoes, Ray-O-Vac flashlights, Sears toys, Motorola TVs, Tastee-Freeze, Esso service stations, Gilmore gas stations, Omar Bread, Popped Wheat cereal, Tip-Top bread, and Miller Brothers hats. The 1953 Motorola comic premium came packaged in a large envelope which also contained a cardboard Dick Tracy mask and vest; that mask is now far more scarce than the comic.

In the mid-1940s, Kellogg's Pep cereal included cartoon character pins in each package. These were known as Pep pins. Dick Tracy characters were featured on 9 of the 86 pins. These are prized by Tracy collectors, with the Dick Tracy and Gravel Gertie pins among the most difficult to find. Other cereal premiums sought by Tracy collectors include a Dick Tracy litho tin ring and "Decoder Cards." The ring was a premium packaged in Post Raisin Bran and Post Toasties Corn Flakes in 1948 and 1949, and the cards were packaged in Post Sugar Crisp boxes in the early 1950s.

At least three Dick Tracy premium "kits," each containing several items, are highly sought by Tracy collectors. A "Junior Dick Tracy Crime Detection Folio" and a "Dick Tracy Junior Detective Kit" were issued in 1942 and 1944, respectively, to promote the Dick Tracy radio show on the "Blue Network Station." The items in these kits were mostly colorful paper articles, such as manuals, membership certificates, mystery quizzes, puzzles, file cards, decoders, "Suspect" charts, notebooks and paper badges. These items are occasionally found individually, but they are much more prized as a packaged set.

Another premium kit of more recent vintage is a Chicago Tribune promotional package of the early 1960s. This contained such items as a red billfold, wooden decoder, metal crimestopper badge, "Crimestopper Club Fingerprint" pad, "Crimestopper Club Summons" pad, pad of "Crimestopper Textbook" features, magnifying glass, whistle, and ink pad. These all came in an unmarked box.

Several brass badges have been issued as premiums with such engravings as "Dick Tracy Detective Club," "Dick Tracy Crime Stoppers," "Dick Tracy Junior Secret Service," and "Dick Tracy, a Republic Picture." A comprehensive listing of such badges and their origins has yet to be compiled.

By far the most varied, and probably the most desirable, Dick Tracy premiums were items available for box tops of Quaker Puffed Wheat and Quaker Puffed Rice cereals through the Dick Tracy radio show between 1938 and 1939. The theme of these premiums was membership in the Dick Tracy Secret Service Patrol. More and more boxes of cereal entitled members to be promoted through the ranks and obtain increasingly important metal badges. The badges ran from blue- and gold-colored Member badges to brass badges of the rank Member, 2nd Year Member, Sergeant, Lieutenant, Captain, and Inspector General. There was also a Girls' Division Badge. The Inspector General badge is very rare, probably because only a few members could consume enough cereal between 1938 and 1939 to qualify for such a high promotion.

Besides badges, there were many other premiums available through the 1938 and 1939 Quaker-sponsored radio broadcasts. These included metal objects such as a secret compartment ring (originally called the Secret Ring of Osiris in a February, 1938, storyline), lucky dangle and wing bracelets, patrol leader bar pins, air detective wings, and a leather-pouched belt badge. Paper items included Secret Code Books of 1938 and 1939, Membership Certificates and Promotional Record Certificates. Miscellaneous items included pocket flashlights, an "Official Dick Tracy Signal Code Pencil," a balsawood "Dick Tracy's Flagship" airplane, a "Secret Detecto Kit," and a pair of "Secret Service Phones." Quaker also issued a paperback book titled "Dick Tracy's Secret Detective Methods and Magic Tricks" and two softcover booklets of Radio Play Adventure Scripts titled "Dick Tracy and the Invisible Man" and "Dick Tracy's Ghostship."

The *Illustrated Radio Premium Catalog and Price Guide* by Tom Tumbusch includes the best compilation of Dick Tracy premiums.

Fig. 3-7
For five boxtops from either Quaker Puffed Wheat or Quaker Puffed Rice in 1938 and 1939, a girl's "Dick Tracy Wing Bracelet" was offered. It shows an airplane and, in raised letters, "Dick Tracy Air Detective."

Fig. 3-8
These full-color images on 1¾" white plastic disks were issued as bread premiums in the early 1950s.

Fig. 3-10
An unusually handsome badge, this brass "Dick Tracy Detective Club" belt badge with a leather pouch back was issued in 1938 and 1939 by Quaker cereals.

Fig. 3-9
This giveaway badge promoted the early 1950s Dick Tracy television show in the Chicago area.

Fig. 3-11
Exterior packaging, such as this Post Sugar Crisp box from the 1950s, is usually rarer than the contents, in this case a free Magic Decoder. Normally the wrapper or package would be thrown away. The decoder came in both green and red.

Fig. 3-12
A rare and frameable paper premium from the mid-1940s is this full-color 7″ × 12″ portrait of Dick Tracy and Junior mounted on a 9″ × 12″ mat. Issued by Pillsbury Farina Cereal, it cost 10 cents and a boxtop.

Fig. 3-13
Dick Tracy, Breathless Mahoney, Flattop, Pruneface, and The Brow are featured in an advertising
premium by Boise-Cascade from 1971. The 11″ ×
14″ envelope showed Tracy; the full-color prints
of the criminals were inside, along with letterhead
showing pink combinations on different colored
papers.

Fig. 3-14
In 1944, a "Dick Tracy Junior Detective Kit" was issued for the radio show. Because of World War II rationing, most items were paper. Finding complete sets intact is the challenge.

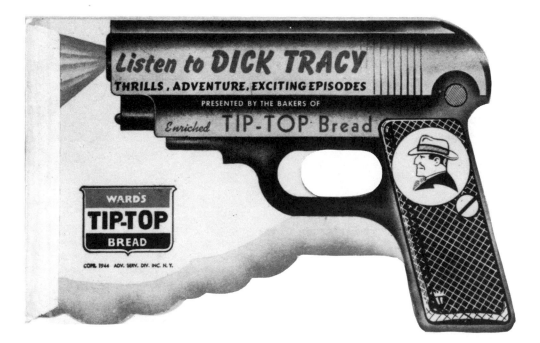

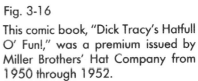

Fig. 3-16
This comic book, "Dick Tracy's Hatfull O' Fun!," was a premium issued by Miller Brothers' Hat Company from 1950 through 1952.

Fig. 3-15
Tip-Top Bread premium from 1944; a paper "pop gun" used to promote the radio show. It measures $7\frac{1}{2}'' \times 4\frac{1}{2}''$.

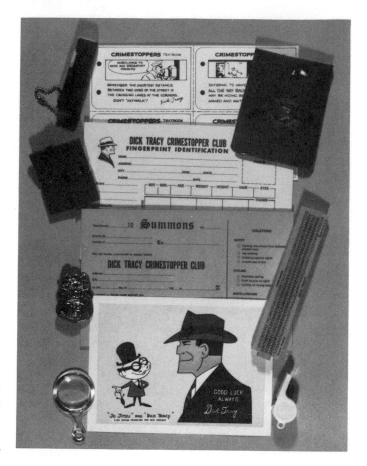

Fig. 3-17
The *Chicago Tribune* issued this promotional "Crimestopper Club" kit circa 1961 in conjunction with the animated TV show. It came in an unmarked, small corrugated kraft mailer.

Books, Coloring Books, and Paper Dolls

In 1932 the Whitman Publishing Company published the first Dick Tracy in a true book format. This was the first Big Little Book titled *The Adventures of Dick Tracy*. Over the years, a total of 27 different Dick Tracy titles were published by Whitman, second only to Mickey Mouse with 29. Other Tracy books published by Whitman included two Big Big Books, two Penny Books, and several different, softcover premium books. Whitman published two hardcover Dick Tracy books titled *Dick Tracy Ace Detective* in 1943 and *Dick Tracy Meets the Night Crawler* in 1947. In addition, several of the Whitman books have known variations in format or style, which make them highly collectible. See Appendix for list.

Among today's most prized Dick Tracy books because of its scarcity is the "Pop-Up" book published in 1935 by Pleasure Books, Inc., titled *Dick Tracy—Capture of Boris Arson*. This book features three full-color picture panels that were folded to literally pop up into three-dimensional displays when opened.

In the 1940s Dell published five Fast Action books featuring Dick Tracy. The format was similar to the Whitman books, except they had softcovers. For the most part, these books are more scarce and valuable than the Big Little Books. Dell also published an unillustrated paperback in 1947 titled *Dick Tracy and the Woo Woo Sisters*. Gould was listed as the author of the original storyline, which never appeared in the newspaper strips. Tempo published an unillustrated paperback novel in 1970 titled *Dick Tracy*. The story was written by William

Johnston, and it also never appeared in the strips.

A Little Golden Book titled *Dick Tracy* was published in 1962. This book mostly featured the early 1960s Dick Tracy television cartoon show characters, Joe Jitsu, Hemlock Holmes, and Go Go Gomez. The book and show were not drawn by Gould, Fletcher or Locher. Several different games, toys and puzzles spun off from the show, and original animation cells have surfaced as collectibles. However, the shows' cartoons and stories were considered poor and extremely childish productions. Dick Tracy appeared only briefly, and most Tracy fans were amazed that Gould and the Tribune Syndicate allowed the character to be used this way.

Several Dick Tracy books that were reprint compilations of newspaper strip stories have been published over the years. The first, and most valuable, are the two Cupples and Leon Co. hardcover books publilshed in 1933. In 1946 Rosdan Books published a hardcover reprint book titled *The Exploits of Dick Tracy* which featured the "Case of the Brow." Fawcett published three paperback reprint books in the mid-1970s titled *Dick Tracy—His Greatest Cases.* Each featured a different character. The *Celebrated Cases of Dick Tracy*, which was published by Chelsea House in 1970, reprinted strips from the first Dick Tracy episode through 1949. Chelsea House also published *Dick Tracy, the Thirties, Tommy Guns and Hard Times* in 1978. This book included reprints of the first two years of the strips from "Plainclothes Tracy" (Gould's introductory strip in 1931) through October 1933.

In 1979 and 1980, Tempo published two paperback reprint books of strips by Fletcher and Collins. The first was titled *Dick Tracy Meets Angeltop*, and the second was titled *Dick Tracy Meets the Punks*. These books are hard to find.

Included under collectible Tracy books are paint and coloring books. The Saalfield Publishing Company published a 96-page, large "Dick Tracy Paint Book" in the 1930s.

Saalfield also published two "Dick Tracy Coloring Books" in 1946, a "Baby Sparkle Plenty Book to Color" in 1948, and a "Bonny Braids Coloring Book" in 1956. Of course, Dick Tracy collectors love to find these in uncolored and unpainted condition.

In 1948 Saalfield published a "Baby Sparkle Plenty" paper doll book, and in 1951 it published a "Dick Tracy's New Daughter, Bonny Braids, and Tess" paper doll book. The Sparkle Plenty paper dolls were also published by Saalfield in a 1948 boxed set.

Dick Tracy book collectors would likely find *The Collector's Guide to Big Little and Similar Books* by Larry Lowery most valuable. In addition, a few strip compilation books are listed in Overstreet's *Comic Book Price Guide.*

Fig. 3-18
Dick Tracy's Secret Detective Methods and Magic Tricks is a 64-page softcover Quaker premium from 1939. It measures 5″ × 7½″ × ½″.

Fig. 3-19

The Adventures of Dick Tracy Detective was the first Tracy book published and also the first of Whitman Publishing Company's Big Little Books. A total of 27 different Tracy titles was included in the series, $3\frac{7}{8}'' \times 4\frac{3}{8}'' \times 1\frac{1}{4}''$.

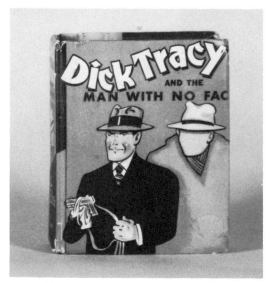

Fig. 3-20

This 1938 Big Little Book, *Dick Tracy and the Man With No Face*, retells the story of The Blank, a prominent villain in the 1990 Disney movie.

Fig. 3-21

Big Little Books also featured titles related to the Dick Tracy Republic Motion Picture serial. Shown are *Dick Tracy and His G-Men* from 1941, and *Dick Tracy Returns* from 1939.

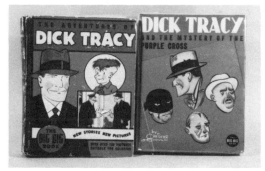

Fig. 3-22

Whitman published two Big Big Books of Dick Tracy that measure $7\frac{1}{4}'' \times 9\frac{1}{2}'' \times 1\frac{1}{4}''$. They are *The Adventures of Dick Tracy*, 1934, and the scarce *Dick Tracy and the Mystery of the Purple Cross*, 1938. The concept was that the owner would color the pictures.

Fig. 3-23

Both radio scripts are Quaker premiums from 1939. Each has 64 pages, soft covers, and measures $3\frac{3}{4} \times 3\frac{7}{8} \times \frac{3}{8}$ inches: Volume 1, *Dick Tracy and the Invisible Man*; Volume 2, *Dick Tracy's Ghost Ship*.

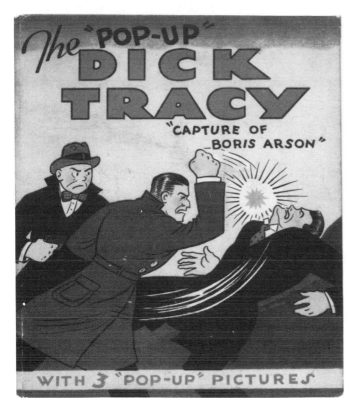

Fig. 3-24
The "pop-up" book *Dick Tracy—Capture of Boris Arson* published by Pleasure Books, Inc., in 1935 is one of the most difficult to find. It measures 8″ × 9¼″ × ¼″. Three pop-up pictures inside.

Fig. 3-25
Two of five Dell Fast Action Books: *Dick Tracy and the Frozen Bullet Murders*, 1941; *Detective Dick Tracy and the Chain of Evidence*, 1938. Each has 192 pages, soft covers, and measures 4″ × 5½″ × ⅝″.

Fig. 3-26
Whitman published two hardcover mystery novels for young adults titled *Dick Tracy Ace Detective*, 1943; and *Dick Tracy Meets the Night Crawler*, 1947. Neither from the comic strips.

Fig. 3-27
Dick Tracy, the Little Golden Book published in 1962, measures $6\frac{3}{4}'' \times 8''$ and features characters such as Joe Jitsu and Hemlock Holmes from the animated Dick Tracy television show.

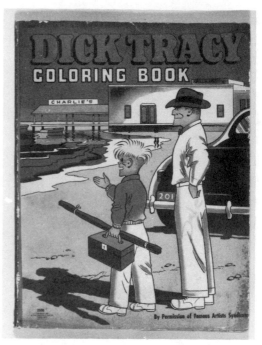

Fig. 3-29
Saalfield, 1946; "Dick Tracy Coloring Book"; #2536. $8\frac{1}{4}'' \times 11''$.

Fig. 3-28
Special cover artwork by Rick Fletcher makes these Tempo mass market paperback reprints especially attractive: *Dick Tracy Meets Angeltop,* 1979, and *Dick Tracy Meets the Punks,* 1980.

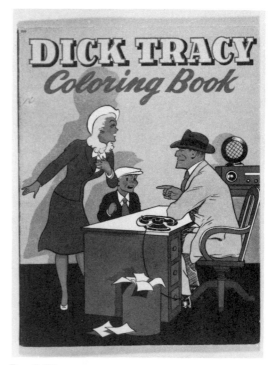

Fig. 3-30
"Dick Tracy Coloring Book"; Saalfield #399, 1946; $8\frac{1}{4}'' \times 11''$.

Fig. 3-31
Saalfield published a 96-page "Dick Tracy Paint Book" in the early 1930s. This handsome collectible measures $10\frac{3}{4}" \times 13\frac{3}{4}" \times \frac{3}{8}"$. Scarce.

Fig. 3-32
"Bonnie Braids" coloring book, Saalfield #1174; $11" \times 14"$.

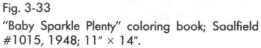

Fig. 3-33
"Baby Sparkle Plenty" coloring book; Saalfield #1015, 1948; $11" \times 14"$.

Fig. 3-34
"Baby Sparkle Plenty" paper dolls.
Saalfield Pub. Co., #1510, 1948;
11" × 14".

Fig. 3-35
"Bonny Braids," Dick Tracy's New Daughter and
Tess paper dolls. Saalfield Pub. Co., #1559, 1951;
11" × 14".

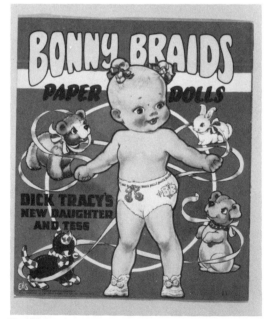

Fig. 3-36
"Bonny Braids" paper dolls. Ideal Novelty Co.,
1951.

Dick Tracy was featured on several sets of cards, similar to baseball cards, that are highly sought by collectors. The most well-known set is the series of 144 cards issued by the Walter H. Johnson Candy Company of Chicago in the early 1930s. These were commonly known as "caramel cards" because they came individually wrapped with a caramel candy. One side of each card contained a full-color rendition of a panel from the newspaper strips, and the other side contained a text of the storyline. Caramel cards are difficult to find, with card Nos. 97 to 120 being the rarest. Large quantities of card Nos. 121 to 144 have recently turned up, making them very common. A Canadian version was also issued by Willards Chocolates Limited. Although almost identical to the Johnson set, they are not valued as highly.

Big Thrill Chewing Gum Booklets, issued in 1934, are among the most interesting Dick Tracy items. Tracy was featured in six of the set of 24 different booklets. The cards were numbered one to six, and each had 8 pages. Each front contained a full-color Dick Tracy panel, along with a Big Thrill advertisement. The insides contained an illustrated story.

Different series of Penny Cards were made in the late 1930s and largely distributed as promotional items for various service stations. These cards pictured scenes from the Big Little Books and had the names of the stations on their backs.

A series of "Cartoon Comics" cards were issued in 1935 by the Chicago Tribune. Dick Tracy was featured in the first eight (Nos. 101 through 109) of the 48 cards. Each card contained a full-color strip panel, and the backs were blank.

Whitman issued a series of cards as premiums to promote their Big Little Books in 1937. Dick Tracy was featured in one of seven different sets, and the Tracy cards were numbered 33 to 64. The Dick Tracy set was taken from the Big Little Book titled *Dick Tracy in Chains of Crime*. One side of each card contained a full-color reproduc-

tion of a Big Little Book page, and the other side contained a story synopsis. These cards are scarce.

In the 1950s, Novel Corporation sold candy in two different boxes featuring Dick Tracy cards on their backs. The "Dick Tracy Candy and Toy" boxes included cards with a 4-panel, colored comic strip sequence. It is believed that as many as 20 different boxes were issued. Novel's "Dick Tracy Detective" candy boxes each had a single, colored Dick Tracy panel with a brief caption. A total of 48 different cards were issued. This set is scarce.

Tip-Top Bread and Amm-i-dent Toothpaste issued at least seven different Dick Tracy cards in 1952. Colored character pictures were on the fronts, and the backs either advertised the "Dick Tracy" TV show starring Ralph Byrd or showed a "Fingerprint File" identification puzzle.

The best source of information on Dick Tracy cards is the *Price Guide to the Non-Sports Cards* by Christopher Benjamin and Dennis Eckes.

In addition to the paper premiums noted above, the variety of Dick Tracy paper and ephemera collectibles seems endless. Almost anything depicting Dick Tracy or containing the words "Dick Tracy" or "Chester Gould" is valued by collectors. For example, advertisements for Dick Tracy toys or premiums cut from old newspapers and magazines sell for as much as $10 each. Some of the older ads sell for more than $20.

In 1941, Coca-Cola issued a set of four colorful postcards complimentary to GIs during World War II. A Dick Tracy birthday card and Christmas card were issued in the early 1950s. At least two Valentine cards were issued in the late 1940s or early 1950s. Norcross issued a set of bright, neon-colored greeting and get-well cards in the mid-1960s.

The wax-coated wrappers from Post Sugar Crisp cereal boxes advertising the "Dick Tracy Magic Decoder" is a particularly scarce item. Another collectible

Fig. 3-37
Walter H. Johnson Candy Company issued a 144-card set of Dick Tracy "caramel cards," packaged with candy in the early 1930s. Card No. 90 is shown, along with a rare card wrapper which has never been opened.

wrapper is that from the "Dick Tracy Candy Bar" sold in the early 1950s by Schutter Candy Co. However, the scarcest and most valuable wrapper is that from Caramel cards of the early 1930s.

At least three sets of Dick Tracy paper punch-out items were made. In 1937 Pillsbury manufactured "Comicooky Baking Sets" containing cookie mix, a cookie cutter and six paper cards of press-out Dick Tracy characters for decorating the cookies. In 1944 and 1945, Reed & Associates sold "Hingees" which were basically sheets of punch-out and fold-over paper dolls of Dick Tracy characters. In 1962, Golden Press published a book titled "Dick Tracy Junior Detective Kit" which comprised five pages of punch-out items.

Lobby cards and posters for the Dick Tracy movies and serials are collected by both Tracy fans and movie buffs. Republic produced four 15-chapter serials from 1937 to 1941, the RKO produced 4 feature-length Tracy films from 1945 through 1947. Lobby cards and posters were made to promote each of the movies and each of the chapters in each serial. In fact, four different lobby cards were made for each chapter of each serial.

Dick Tracy jigsaw puzzles could also be categorized as collectible paper items. The scarcest and earliest puzzle was "Famous Comics Jigsaw Puzzle No. 3—Dick Tracy" issued by Stephen Kindred & Company in the 1930s. However, Jaymar made most of the Tracy jigsaw puzzles. In 1958 Jaymar made a "2 in 1 Mystery Puzzle." The most attractive and popular puzzle was titled "Crime Does Not Pay Club." This 1940s puzzle pictured Tracy along with The Mole, The Brow, Pruneface, Mrs. Pruneface, Little Face, Flattop, Lizz, Junior, Pat Patton, Chief Brandon, Vitamin Flintheart and Gravel Gertie. Jaymar made at least two full-color jigsaw puzzles of Sunday comics from the early 1940s. In the mid-1960s, Jaymar made three puzzles featuring characters from the Dick Tracy Cartoon Show. These were titled "Bank Holdup," "Lineup," and "The Big Robbery." Saalfield also made two different tray puzzles of Bonny Braids in 1951, and Jaymar did one of Dick Tracy alone in 1952. The Dick Tracy tray puzzle is a scarce item.

In 1962 Colorforms made "Dick Tracy Cartoon Kits," and in 1963 Kenner Products made "Sparkle Paint" sets. Both of these mostly featured the characters from the Dick Tracy Cartoon Show.

Fig. 3-38

During World War II (1942–1943), Coca-Cola issued this set of four full-color postcards complimentary to GIs. (1943 cards are extremely rare.)

In 1967 Hasbro made a "Numbered Pencil Coloring Set." This was a boxed set with six pre-sketched pictures to be completed with colored pencils.

There are several Dick Tracy posters which are not only collectible but also make colorful display items. Studio One made a large poster on Mylar in 1975 for a San Diego Comic Convention. A special poster was made for a Gould art exhibit at the Museum of Cartoon Art in Port Chester, New York, between October 4 and November 30, 1978. The U.S. Government Printing Office issued a poster in 1970 with Dick Tracy saying "Protect Your Mail—Use Zip Codes." A government poster in 1976 had Dick Tracy saying "Register! Now You Can Give the Orders! Vote!" However, the most valuable poster was a limited edition, stonewash lithograph of Dick Tracy distributed in the late 1970s by Abrahms Galleries on behalf of the Newspaper Comic Council. Each numbered edition in a run of only 100 was signed by Gould.

Original art is the most valuable of numerous paper items of interest to Tracy collectors (see Chapter 4). Gould alone drew more than 16,000 daily and Sunday strips

between October, 1931, and his retirement in December, 1977. However, only a tiny fraction of these have ever been available to more than a handful of Tracy collectors. Almost no Sunday artwork is available from the 1940s or earlier, and nothing at all exists from the 1930s. As a rule, the value of original Tracy art basically hinges upon five things: age, historical significance, the presence of Tracy, the degree of violence, and the villain portrayed. Shootouts and graphic death scenes are at a premium. Favorite characters, such as Flattop and The Brow, are more desirable than others. Also, artwork depicting special events, such as the birth of Sparkle Plenty and the introduction of the 2-way wrist radio, are highly prized.

Gould monograms and autographs are highly valued paper items, including small sketches and personal notes which he sent to fans upon request. Starting in the mid-1970s, Gould sent such notes in envelopes preprinted with a Tracy profile and the return address: "Dick Tracy, Woodstock, Ill." Gould also drew personalized greeting and Christmas cards over the years, and he also designed the family Christmas cards. In addition, Gould made numerous drawings and promotional art pieces for various commercial, personal and good-will causes.

Original art done by Fletcher and Locher is also collectible. Although not considered as valuable as Gould's art, it does feature events of historical significance to the strip and introduce prime characters and villains.

As a substitute for owning original art, many Tracy collectors seek comic strip tearsheets from the newspapers. In addition to their collectible value, since comic books never reprinted all the stories from the newspapers, tearsheet collecting is the only way that most Tracy fans have been able to read or reread some of the older stories.

Other miscellaneous Tracy paper collectibles include such items as wallpaper sections from the 1950s, original art for the comic and Big Little Book covers, a Bonny Braids Punch Card, promotional materials for various toys and games, and movie theater cards.

Fig. 3-39

"I've got your HEART—Did you SUSPECT it? Say Valentine. You may DETECT it." This is Tracy's message on a greeting card from the late 1940s or early 1950s. It measures 6" × 6".

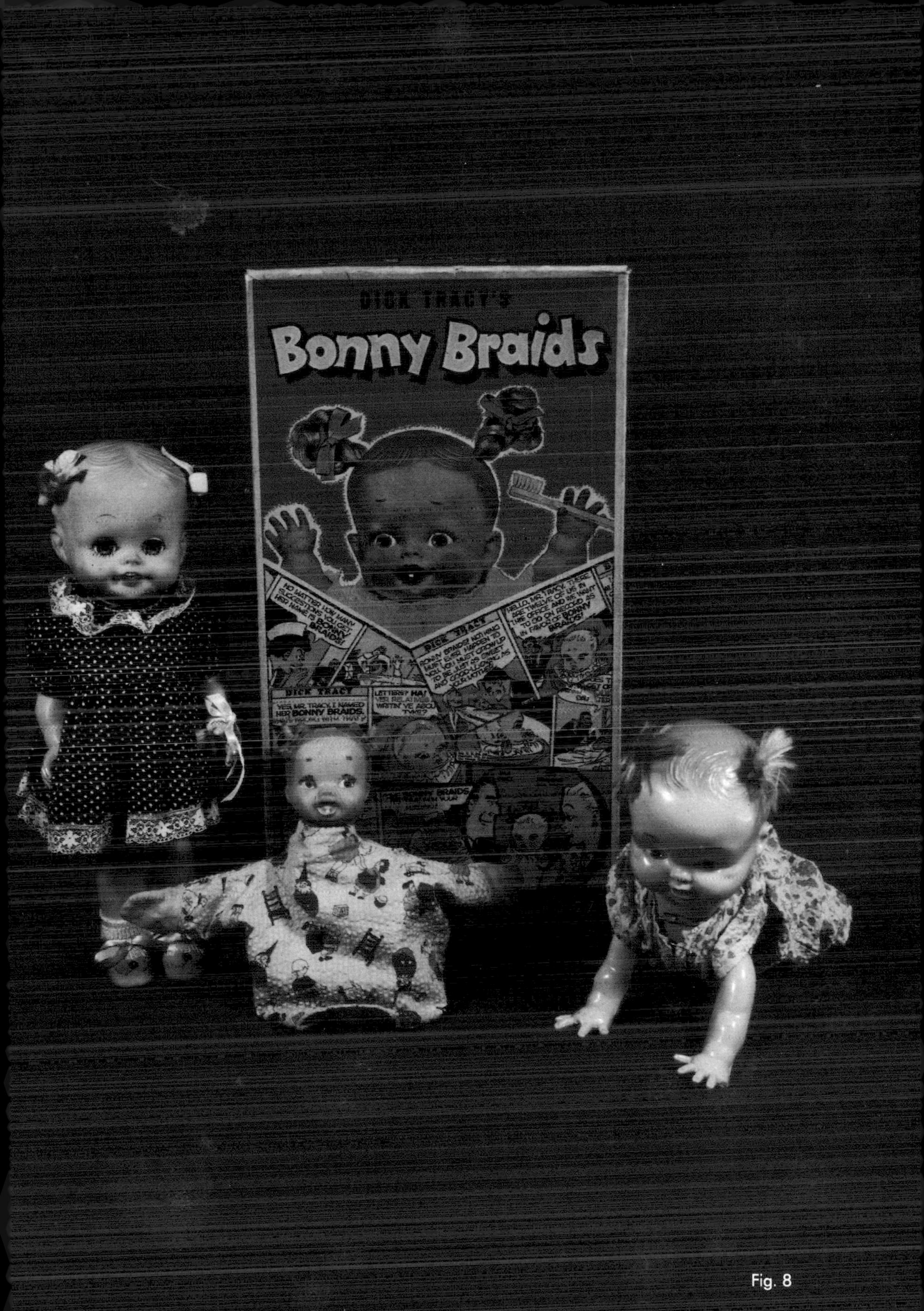
DICK TRACY'S
Bonny Braids
NO MATTER HOW MANY SUGGESTIONS YOU GOT, HER NAME IS BONNY BRAIDS!
HELLO, MR. TRACY. THERE ARE TWELVE OF US IN THE OFFICE AND WE WANT TO GO ON RECORD AS IN FAVOR OF BONNY BRAIDS!
DICK TRACY
DICK TRACY
YES, MR. TRACY, I NAMED HER BONNY BRAIDS.

Fig. 8

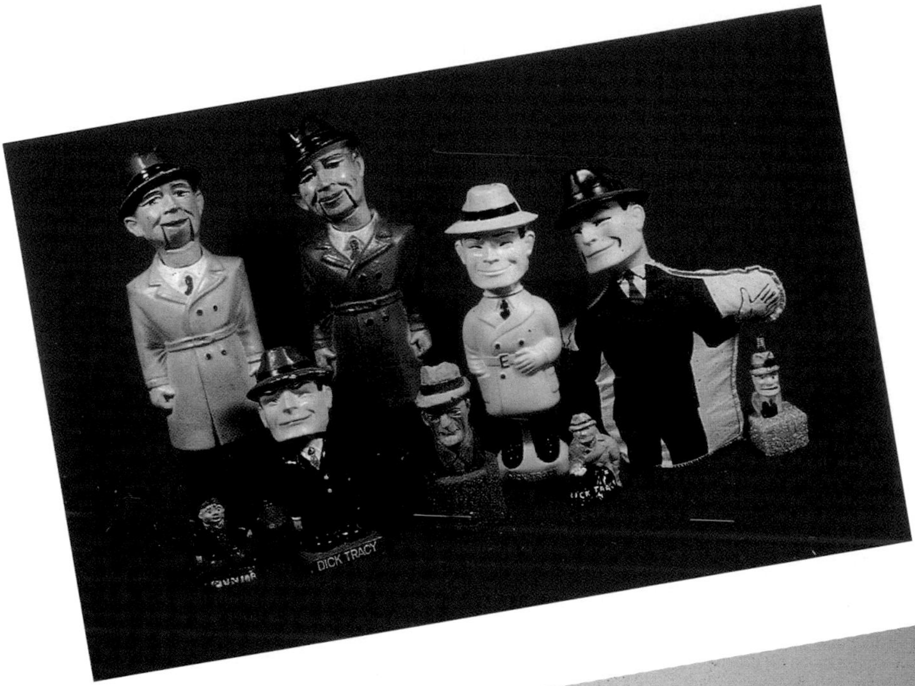
DICK TRACY

Fig. 9

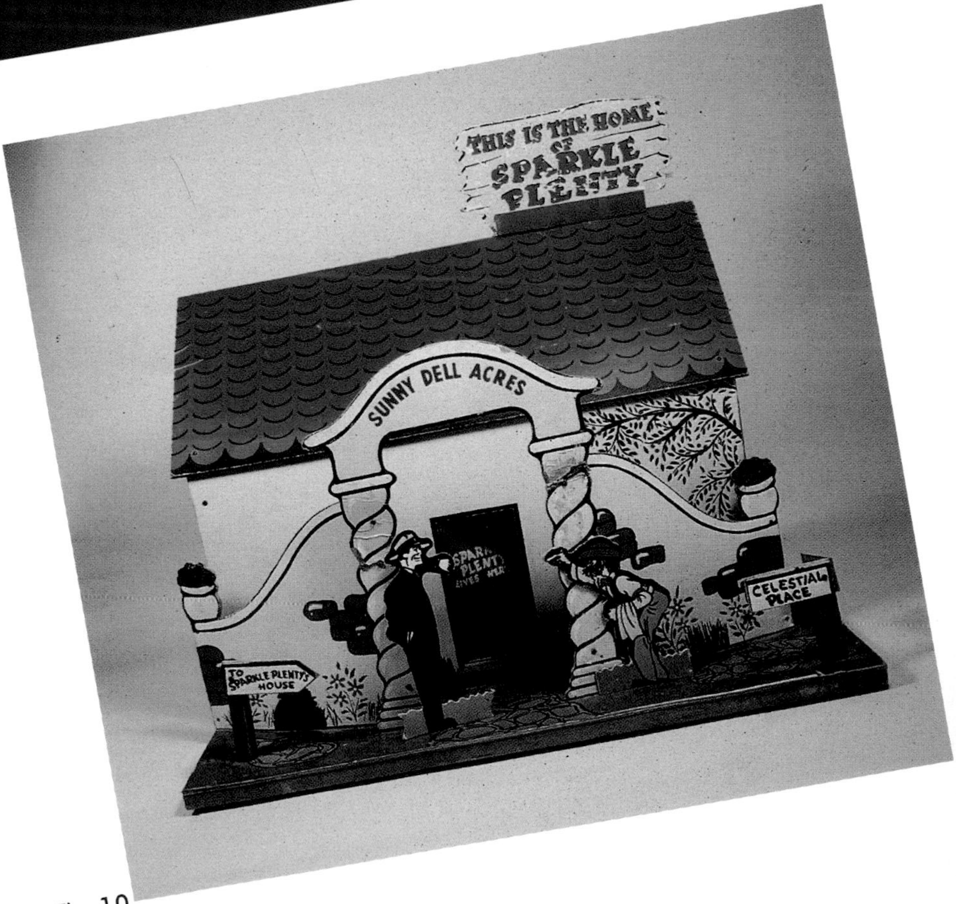
THIS IS THE HOME OF SPARKLE PLENTY
SUNNY DELL ACRES
TO SPARKLE PLENTY'S HOUSE
CELESTIAL PLACE

Fig. 10

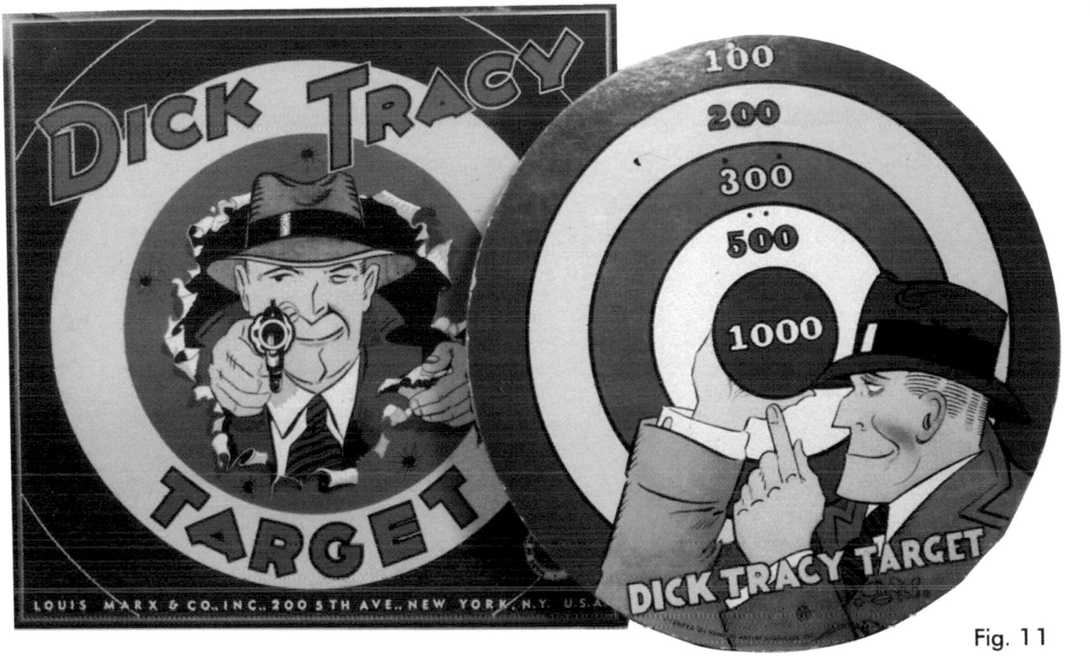
DICK TRACY
TARGET
LOUIS MARX & CO., INC., 200 5TH AVE., NEW YORK, N.Y. U.S.A.
100
200
300
500
1000
DICK TRACY TARGET

Fig. 11

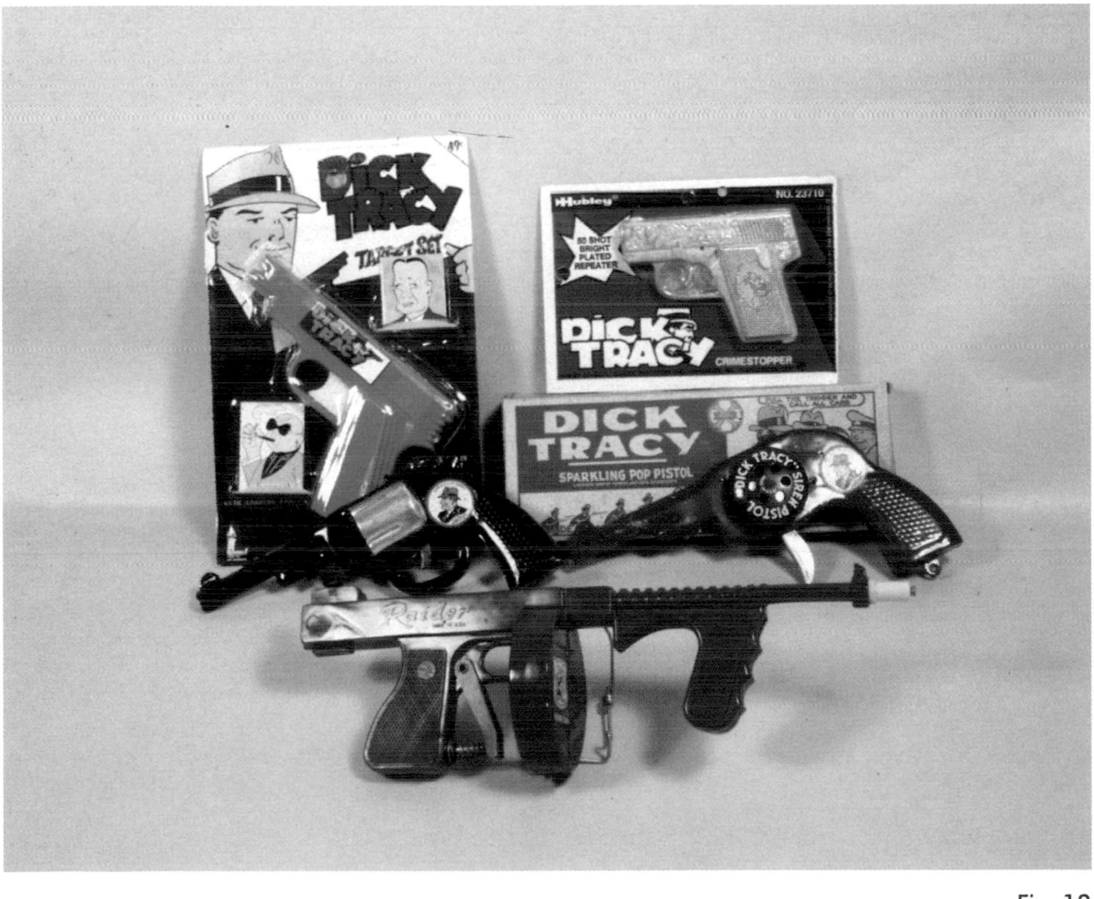
DICK TRACY
TARGET SET
Hubley
NO. 23710
50 SHOT BRIGHT PLATED REPEATER
DICK TRACY
CRIMESTOPPER
DICK TRACY
SPARKLING POP PISTOL
DICK TRACY SIREN PISTOL
Raider

Fig. 12

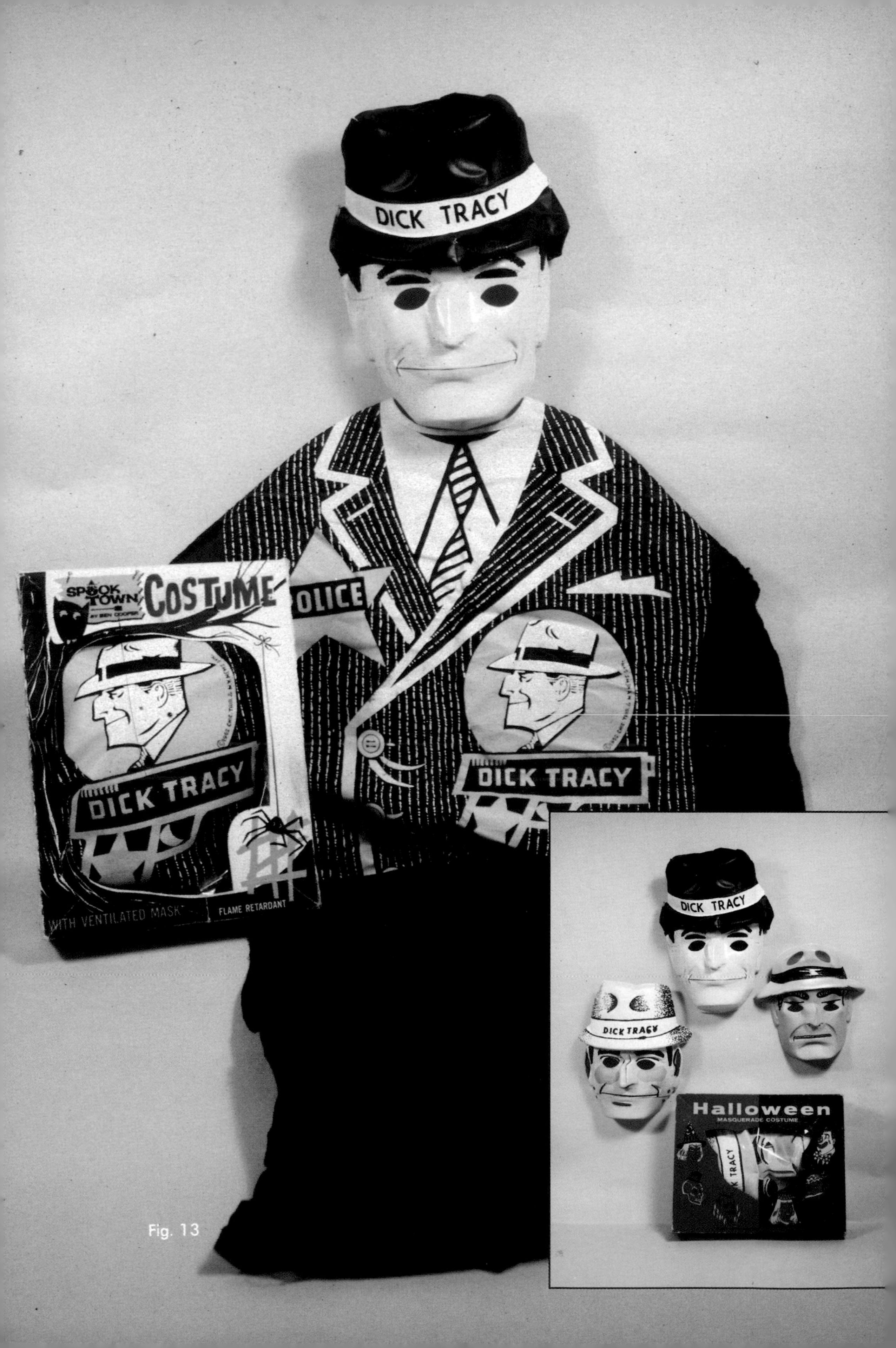
DICK TRACY
SPOOK TOWN
BY BEN COOPER
COSTUME
DICK TRACY
WITH VENTILATED MASK
FLAME RETARDANT
OLICE
DICK TRACY
DICK TRACY
DICK TRACY
Halloween
MASQUERADE COSTUME

Fig. 13

Fig. 3-40
The Pillsbury "Comicooky Baking Set" from 1937 contains mix, a cookie cutter, and six character press-out decorations (each 4½" × 6¾"). The box measures 5" × 7¼" × 1".

Fig. 3-41
Bright fluorescent backgrounds make these mid-1960s greeting and get well cards by Norcross very distinctive. Each measures 5" × 7".

Fig. 3-42
A Penny Card insert for a dispensing machine, along with several Penny Cards. They date from the late 1930s and were usually distributed by machine at gasoline stations.

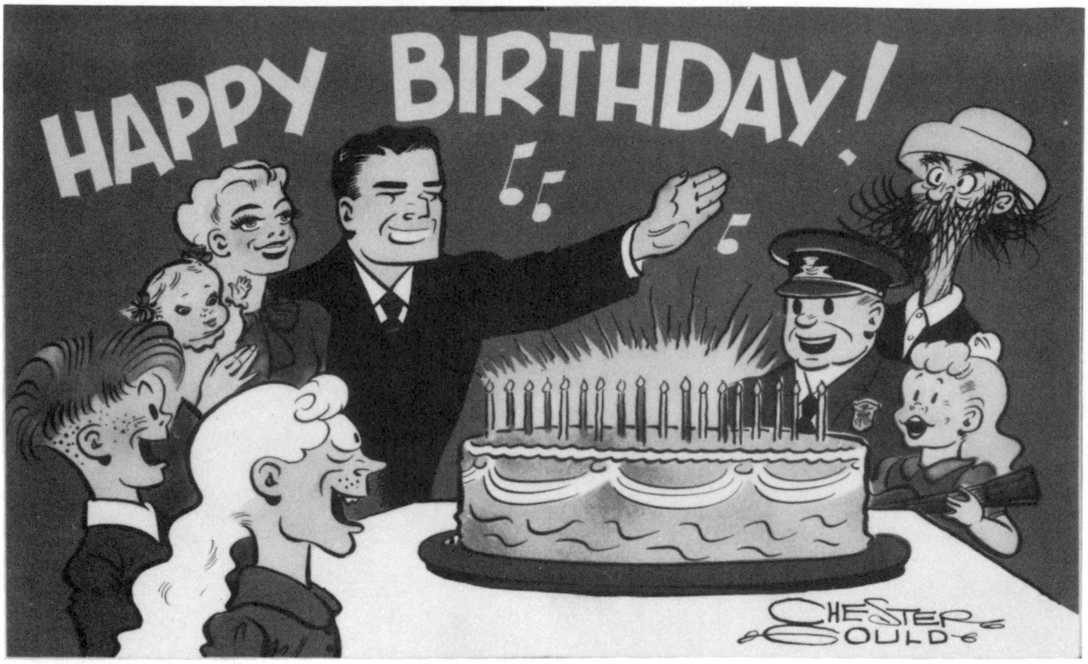
HAPPY BIRTHDAY!
CHESTER GOULD

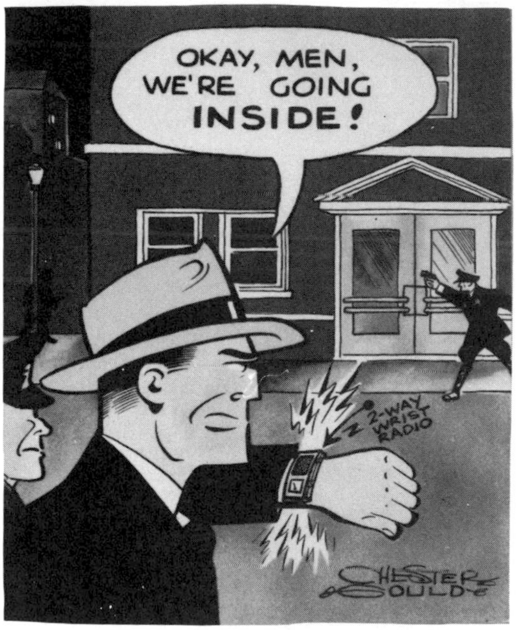
OKAY, MEN, WE'RE GOING INSIDE!
2-WAY WRIST RADIO
CHESTER GOULD

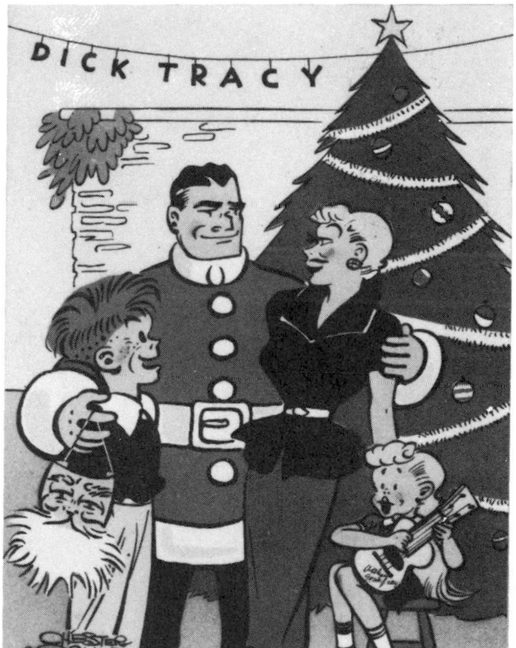
DICK TRACY
CHESTER GOULD
© CT

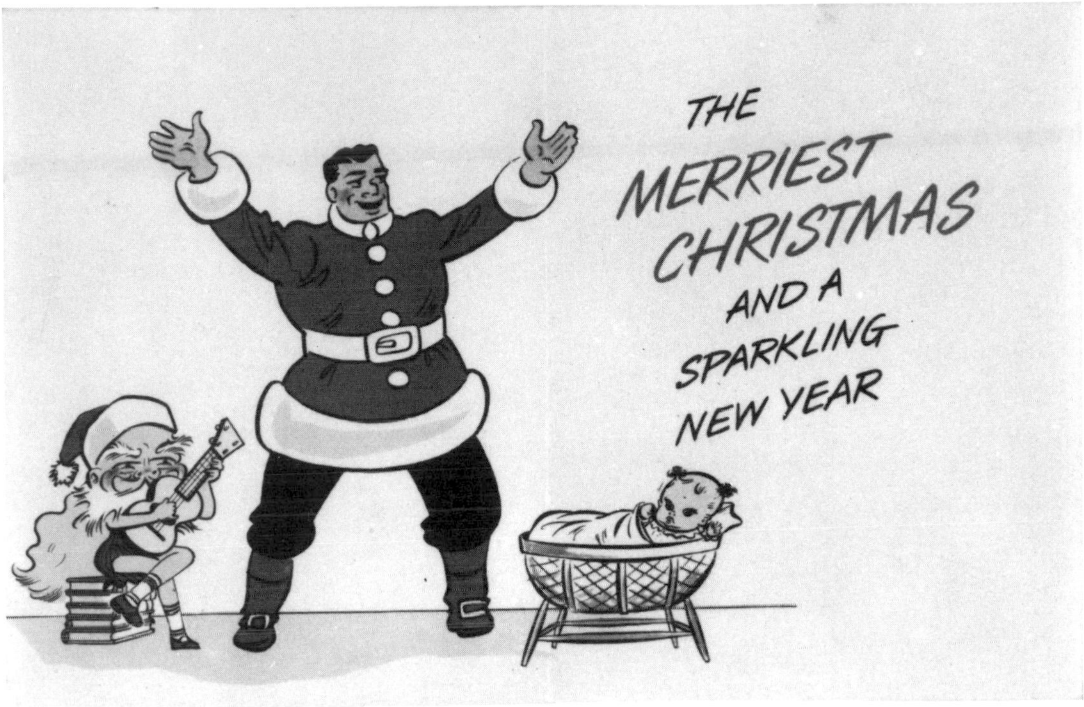
THE
MERRIEST
CHRISTMAS
AND A
SPARKLING
NEW YEAR

Fig. 3-43

These greeting cards were part of a boxed set of comic character cards from the early 1950s. The birthday card is 5″ × 6″. The Christmas card is $4\frac{1}{4}$″ × $4\frac{1}{2}$″.

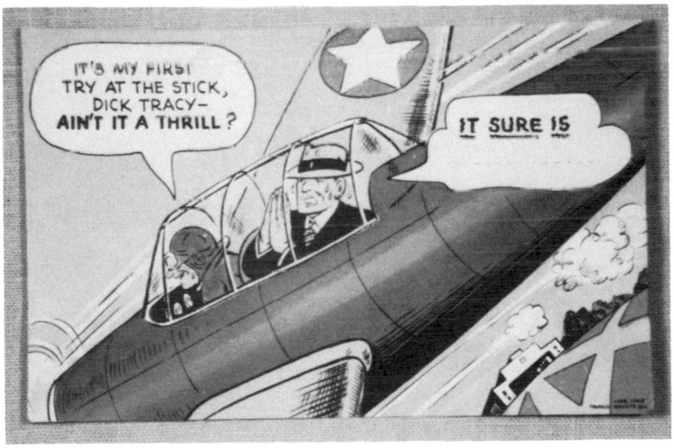
IT'S MY FIRST TRY AT THE STICK, DICK TRACY– AIN'T IT A THRILL?
IT SURE IS

Fig. 3-43a

A 1943 humorous postcard, not one of the Coca-Cola set, is quite rare.

Fig. 3-44
"Hingees," delightful punch-out, fold-over paper dolls were made in 1944 and 1945 by Reed & Associates. The set includes Tess Trueheart, Chief Brandon, Junior, Pat Patton, and Tracy. Two different packages offered the same $6\frac{1}{2}$"-tall figures. The package size is $7\frac{1}{2}$" × $11\frac{1}{2}$". Assembled figures are shown with the 1945 set.

Fig. 3-45
An 11" × 14" lobby card for Chapter 6 of the Republic Pictures Serial.

Fig. 3-46
In 1962, Golden Press published the "Dick Tracy Junior Detective Kit," shown here and in color on the front cover. It measures 7⅜" × 13" and contains five pages of punch-out items.

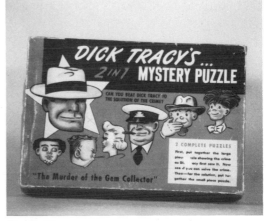

Fig. 3-47
Jaymar's "Dick Tracy's 2 in 1 Mystery Puzzle" of 1958 came in a decorative box with two complete 11" × 14" puzzles. One of the puzzles showed the crime, and the other puzzle pictured Tracy's solution.

Fig. 3-48
This 5½″ × 8″ puzzle is from the 1942 "Junior Dick Tracy Crime Detection Folio" radio show premium.

Fig. 3-49
This is one of two tray puzzles by Saalfield that celebrated the birth of Bonny Braids to Dick and Tess Tracy in 1951. It measures 10¼″ × 11½″.

Fig. 3-50
Scarce 1952 Jaymar "Dick Tracy" tray puzzle, 11" × 14"

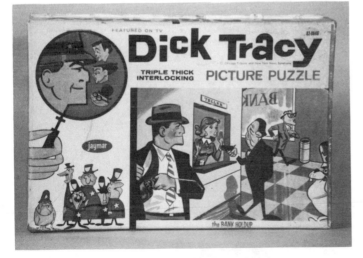

Fig. 3-50a
"The Bank Holdup" is one of three different jigsaw puzzles made by Jaymar in the 1960s featuring the characters from the animated TV cartoon show.

Fig. 3-51
This U.S. Government Printing Office ZIP Code poster is dated 1970, 11" × 14".

Fig. 3-52
The 1967 "Dick Tracy Numbered Pencil Coloring Set" by Hasbro includes six pre-sketched pictures to color. The set measures $9\frac{1}{4}$" × $10\frac{3}{4}$" × 1".

Fig. 3-53
Believed to be a promotion for caramel cards, this 6" × 8" portrait of Dick Tracy is very frameable. It dates from the early 1930s.

Louis Marx & Co. manufactured roughly a dozen different litho tin Dick Tracy cars during the late 1940s and 1950s. These included 6½″-long and 11″-long cars with variations of colors and drives. For example, the shorter cars were friction driven and had either blue or green bodies. The longer cars had either a key-wind drive or a friction drive, and their bodies were either dark green, light green or a light blue/dark blue combination. The larger cars also had battery-operated, plastic search lights. The lithos on all these cars included "Squad Car No. 1," "Police Dept.," a police shield with Tracy's profile on each side, and "Dick Tracy" on the front hood. Various characters were pictured in the windows. Tracy was always shown as the driver, and combinations of Junior, Pat Patton, Chief Brandon and Sam Catchem occupied the other seats. In several versions, a machine gun extended through the front window on the passenger side. The boxes that came with these cars had such labels as "Dick Tracy Riot Car," "Dick Tracy Siren Squad Car," and "Dick Tracy Squad Car."

Louis Marx also made a 20″-long, litho tin, convertible "squad car" in the early 1950s. This was green with friction drive, and had a battery-operated flashing signal light attached to the driver side. It came with removable plastic figures of Tracy and Sam Catchem sitting in the front seat. One of the most interesting and most valuable cars, particularly in its original box, was the Louis Marx "Police Station with Squad Car." A 7″-long, green litho tin, friction drive "Police Car" raced out of the Police Station when a wind-up siren on the side of the station was turned rapidly. The Police Station was colorful litho tin which pictured Tracy and other characters.

Louis Marx made a 9″-long, green plastic friction drive car in the 1950s. A siren sounded when the car was pushed. It had no markings other than a label on each side picturing a shield with Tracy's profile and "Dick Tracy, Police Dept." The car also had a non-removable plastic figure of Dick Tracy sitting behind the wheel.

Ideal made a 24″-long, white-and-blue plastic "Copmobile" in the early 1960s. Its only markings were a label of Tracy's profile and the words "Dick Tracy Copmobile" on the driver side. The car was battery operated and included a microphone with amplifier speaker on its top.

Fig. 3-54
Note the red light and "sparkling machine gun" on this variation of the 11″-long Dick Tracy squad car, early 1950s by Louis Marx.

Fig. 3-55

A highly sought and valuable Dick Tracy toy is the "Police Station with Squad Car" by Marx, early 1950s. It's shown with its original box. A 7"-long, green, litho tin police car races out of the police station when a wind-up siren on the side of the station is activated. Litho tin station measures $8\frac{1}{2}'' \times 5\frac{3}{4}'' \times 4''$. Box measures $9'' \times 6\frac{1}{2}'' \times 4\frac{1}{8}''$.

Fig. 3-56

Lithograph tin, early 1950s by Louis Marx. Yellow plastic top, friction drive, 7" long, dark green body. Dashboard visible inside the car.

Fig. 3-57
Litho tin, early 1950s by Louis Marx. Friction drive, 7" long. Flashing light.

Fig. 3-58
The truly awesome "Copmobile" by Ideal, 24" long, early 1960s vintage. The battery-powered car includes a siren and amplified speaker on its top. The car is all plastic.

Fig. 3-59
This 6½" Dick Tracy car is light blue and has a machine gun pointing out the front window, early 1950s by Louis Marx.

Wrist Radios and TVs

There have been several versions and adaptations of the famous 2-way wrist radio and wrist TV over the years. Probably the earliest and scarcest was a "Two Way Toy Wrist Radio" manufactured by Gaylord & Son in the late 1940s. This came packaged on an illustrated card with a detective badge. The "radio" itself was a small metal piece stamped with Tracy's profile and the words "Two Way Detective Radio"; it was mounted on a wrist strap.

Da-Myco Products made the first operable "Dick Tracy Wrist Radio" about 1947. It was a crystal set with a plastic earphone receiver on a leather wristband, embossed with "Dick Tracy" in silver. The receiver was affixed with 30″-long wires with connections for aerial and ground.

In the late 1950s, Remco made boxed sets of "Official Dick Tracy 2-Way Electronic Wrist Radios." These were plastic battery-operated transmitter–receiver units with wrist straps. A plug-in wire extension was needed to enable talking between the units, but a buzzer-like signal could be transmitted without the wire connection.

In the early 1960s, American Doll and Toy Corp. made a "Dick Tracy in 2-Way Wrist Radio" which enabled talking communication without a wire connection. This was basically a walkie-talkie set with a power-pack and wrist receiver.

Larami Corp. produced a bubble-pack "Wrist-TV" in the 1970s and, in the early 1980s, Ja-Ru reissued it as a "TV Watch." These were no more than plastic viewers (in the shape of Tracy's wrist TV) through which paper rolls of cartoon strips were threaded.

American Doll and Toy Corp. made a "Dick Tracy Transistor Radio Receiver" in 1961, complete with shoulder holster carrier and ear plug. Creative Creations made a "Dick Tracy Personal AM Wrist Radio" in 1975. It was worn with a wrist strap and listened to with an ear plug.

Fig. 3-60

This 1946 artwork shows the very first time Dick Tracy saw a wrist radio. The atom-powered 2-way wrist radio was actually invented by industrialist Diet Smith's son, Brilliant. The wrist radio, TV and computer serve as Tracy's trademark.

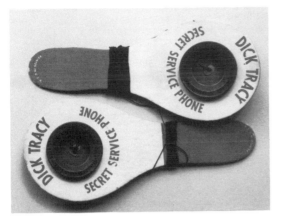

Fig. 3-61
This 1939 Quaker premium predates the actual wrist radio but is fun for its "technology." The 8" × 3½" "Dick Tracy Secret Service Phones" were made of stiff cardboard with 2" metal vibrator cups connected by string.

Fig. 3-62
Da-Myco Products' "Dick Tracy Wrist Radio," a working crystal set from about 1947, is shown next to Playmates' "Dick Tracy 2-Way Wristwatch" marketed in 1990. The wristwatch is a replica of the 2-Way Wrist Radio worn by Warren Beatty in the movie *Dick Tracy*. A button activates a red light on it, but it is not a working radio. It is a watch only. © Disney

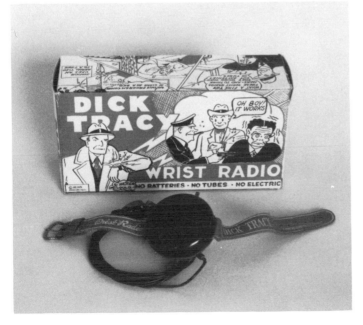

Fig. 3-63
Da-Myco Products was the first to make a "working Dick Tracy Wrist Radio" about 1947. The crystal set has a receiver on a leather band, with 30"-long wires and connections for aerial and ground. It's shown with its original box. The box is 4" × 6" × 2½". Originally sold for $3.98.

Fig. 3-64

Fig. 3-65

In 1961, American Doll and Toy Corp. released this "Dick Tracy 2 Transistor Radio Receiver." The radio measures $2\frac{1}{2}'' \times 4\frac{1}{4}'' \times 1\frac{1}{4}''$.

Fig. 3-66
Remco's boxed "Official Dick Tracy 2-Way Electronic Wrist Radios" are from the late 1950s. They are battery operated. The box measures 13" × 10" × 3".

Fig. 3-67
Different packaging—but the same Remco unit—came boxed as shown here in a carrying case 8" × 8" × 2½".

Fig. 3-68

This strip from June 23, 1956, shows the final technical improvements to the classic 2-Way wrist radio. The original art for this strip is extremely valuable due to the historical significance of the strip. It also pictures Tracy, Sam Catchem, and Diet Smith, three main characters.

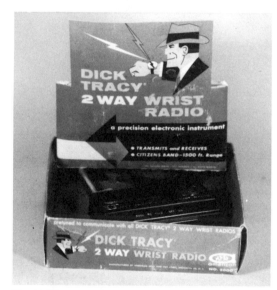

Fig. 3-69

A walkie-talkie with power-pack and receiver, the "Dick Tracy 2-Way Wrist Radio" set is by American Doll and Toy Corp. from the early 1960s. The box is 8″ × 8″ × 2″.

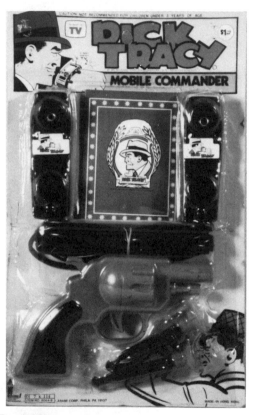

Fig. 3-70

This 1973 Larami Corp. rack toy, "Dick Tracy Mobile Commander," includes a non-working toy phone with plastic connecting tube, along with toy gun and badge.

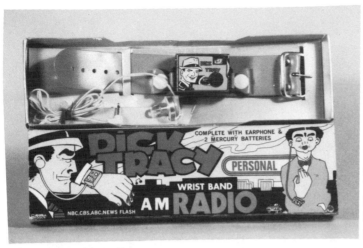

Fig. 3-71
Creative Creations made this "Dick Tracy Wrist Band AM Radio" in 1975. Its box measures $9\frac{3}{4}'' \times 2\frac{3}{4}'' \times 1\frac{1}{4}''$. It is one of the last known wrist radios prior to the new 1990 merchandise.

Fig. 3-72
The first appearance of the 2-way wrist TV in the Dick Tracy comic strip, April, 1964. It became Tracy's standard until June, 1986, and the debut of the 2-way wrist computer.

Fig. 3-73
All toy wrist TVs have been a rack-toy style, as shown in two versions here: Larami's 1973 model and Ja-Ru's model from the 1980s. Paper rolls of cartoon strips are threaded through the TV viewer.

Fig. 3-74
Larami's "Dick Tracy Mini Color Tele-Viewer" with two "movies" from 1973 is a bubblepacked rack toy. The opportunity to do a working Dick Tracy wrist TV awaits some adventurous manufacturer.

Figurines are of particular interest to Tracy collectors because they give a more "realistic" quality to the characters. These have been manufactured in various forms over the years.

The earliest, rarest, and most valuable of all Dick Tracy collectibles are 13"-tall composition Tracy dolls made in the early 1930s. Two varieties of this doll were made. One had a movable head and yellow trench coat. The other had a movable head, a mouth which opened and closed via a back pull-string, and a grey trench coat.

Allied Manufacturing made a "Dick Tracy Casting Outfit" in the 1930s; it included molds for making lead figures of Tracy, Junior and Chief Brandon. The lead figures are of interest, but the casting set itself is a prime collectible and very hard to find. Allied also made a "Playstone Funnies Kasting Kit" in the mid-1930s. This was used to make 3" to 4"-tall plaster of Paris figures of cartoon characters in molds. Dick Tracy was one of the figures.

Ceramic salt and pepper shakers of Tracy, Junior and Tess Trueheart were made in the 1940s. Sets of these came painted in different colors. A $2\frac{1}{2}$"-tall Christmas tree light bulb shaped as Dick Tracy was also made in the mid-1940s as part of a set of comic character bulbs.

In the late 1950s, Louis Marx made a set of five plastic Playset figures—ranging from about $2\frac{1}{2}$" to $3\frac{1}{2}$" tall—of Tracy, Junior, Gravel Gertie, B. O. Plenty and Sparkle Plenty. These were sold in painted and unpainted versions.

In the early 1960s, a $7\frac{1}{2}$"-tall, ceramic bobbing-head Tracy doll figure was made. This is a particularly scarce and valuable collectible.

Ideal sold boxed sets of hand puppets of Dick Tracy, Hemlock Holmes and Joe Jitsu in 1961. The puppets had rubber heads and cloth bodies. Each set also contained a small record of one of the Cartoon Shows.

In 1965 Colgate-Palmolive sold bubble bath in a 10" tall, plastic, Tracy shaped bot-

Fig. 3-75

The earliest and rarest Dick Tracy figure is this 13" composition doll with moveable head, green hats and yellow trenchcoat.

tle called a "Soaky." The empty bottle became a toy. Today these are sought-after collectibles.

Fig. 3-76

In the 1930s, the "Dick Tracy Casting Outfit" was marketed by Allied Manufacturing. The box measures $6\frac{1}{4}'' \times 3\frac{1}{4}'' \times 1''$. The casting set with original box is scarce. Shown are painted and unpainted cast figures of Tracy and Junior and unpainted figure of Chief Brandon.

Multiple Toymaker made bubble-pack sets of Dick Tracy, Junior and Flattop "Rubb'r Nik" figures in 1968. Each figure was about 6″ tall and was flexible for posing into almost any position. The Tracy set came with a tiny gun, wrist radio, and holster; the Junior set came with a magnetic air car; and the Flattop set came with a Joe Jitsu figure.

In 1968, Aurora Plastics Corp. made a plastic model assembly kit of a Dick Tracy figure descending a fire escape ladder. That same year Aurora also made a Dick Tracy Space Coupe model kit. In this kit, tiny figures of Tracy, Junior, Moon Maid and Diet Smith were mounted adjacent to the space coupe.

The Hingees set, also discussed under paper collectibles, had only figures of Tracy, Pat Patton, Chief Brandon and Tess Trueheart. However, in 1973, Ideal made a "Dick Play Set" which included 18 different, full-color, stand-up cardboard figures of Tracy characters and villains. This set also included cardboard police and getaway cars and a fold-out plastic-coated street scene for playing with the figures.

In the late 1940s, Louis Marx made a wind-up, walking litho tin B. O. Plenty. He was pictured carrying Sparkle Plenty in his right arm and a gift-wrapped package in the other. When the figure walked, its hat tipped up and down.

Sparkle Plenty was one of the most popular Tracy characters, and several of the most valuable Tracy collectibles are Sparkle items. In 1947, Ideal sold tens of thousands of the "Baby Sparkle Plenty Doll." This doll is now scarce and very valuable, particularly with its colorful box.

Two ceramic Sparkle Plenty banks were made in the late 1940s by Jayess. One had Sparkle sitting in a high chair and the other had her sitting in a large scale. Around the base of both banks were reliefs of B. O. Plenty, Gravel Gertie and Dick Tracy. These are also scarce and very valuable. Another Sparkle Plenty figure is a 4″-tall soap bar produced by Lightfoot in the late 1940s. The soap figure is colored. The box says "This is Sparkle Plenty in Her Own Little Bed."

Bonny Braids, Dick Tracy's daughter, was also a popular character. In 1951, Ideal made a Bonny Braids doll that sold as well as the Sparkle Plenty doll and is as difficult to find. In 1952, Ideal made a crawling Bonny Braids doll which was not as popular as the 1951 original, but is even more scarce today.

In 1951, the Charmore Co. made a $1\frac{1}{2}$-tall plastic Bonny Braids figure on a card. Charmore also made an interesting toy in the same year called "Watch the Nursemaid Take Dick Tracy's Bonny Braids for a Stroll." With this toy, a nursemaid would literally "walk" a tiny Bonny Braids in a baby stroller down a litho tin ramp.

Ideal made a "Little Honey Moon" doll in 1965. Honey Moon was the daughter of Junior and Moon Maid. This doll wasn't nearly as popular as the Sparkle or Bonny dolls, but it is highly collectible and hard to find. The doll came boxed with a clear plastic helmet, but few dolls found today still have the helmet.

Fig. 3-78

This 2½"-tall Christmas tree light of Tracy is part of an assorted set of cartoon characters from the 1940s.

Fig. 3-77

The semi-flat figures are about 2¼" tall. Shown are Junior and Dick Tracy.

Fig. 3-79

The 7"-tall Tracy with wrist radio and the 5" B.O. Plenty hanging the wash, came as part of the Sparkle Plenty dollhouse set of the late 1940s.

Fig. 3-80

The "Playstone Funnies Kasting Kit" by Allied Manufacturing was sold during the 1930s. The trench-coated Dick Tracy figure stands 3½" tall. Shown are the Tracy figure, an original box, size 4" × 2" × 1", and a tin of Playstone Powder, size 3" × 8½" × 1".

Fig. 3-81
Ideal Toy Company's 1961 hand puppet is shown with its original packaging. There are puppets of Dick Tracy, Hemlock Holmes and Joe Jitsu from the animated TV show.

Fig. 3-82
The 1973 Ideal Toy Company "Dick Tracy Play Set" is a self-contained carrying case that measures 17" × 7½" × 6". The case opened up into a backdrop for the 18 different cardboard figures that measure 3½" to 5" tall.

Fig. 3-83
Dick Tracy ceramic bobbing-head doll from the early 1960s is very rare.

Fig. 3-84
This 10"-tall Dick Tracy "Soaky" came with Colgate-Palmolive bubble bath in 1965. The empty bottle then became a toy.

Fig. 3-85
Tracy, Junior, Sparkle Plenty, B.O. Plenty and Gravel Gertie make up this set of Marx Toy Company plastic figures from the 1950s. Sold either painted or unpainted, the figures range in size from $2\frac{1}{2}''$ to $3\frac{1}{2}''$.

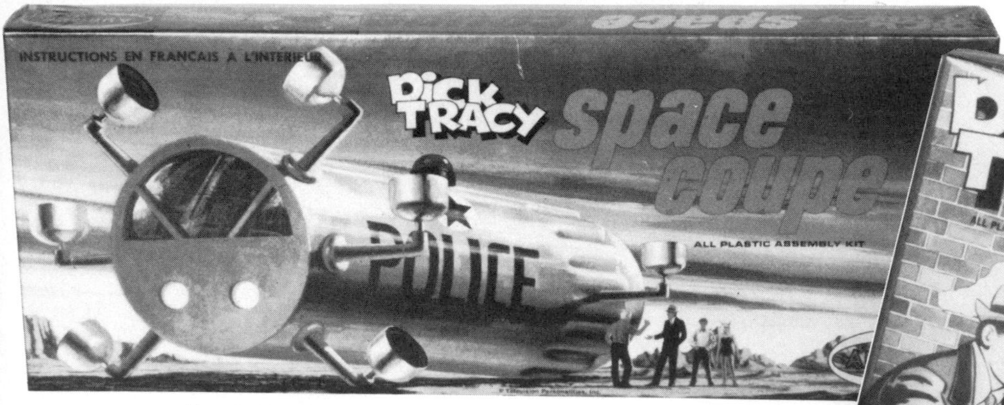
INSTRUCTIONS EN FRANCAIS A L'INTERIEUR
DICK TRACY
space coupe
ALL PLASTIC ASSEMBLY KIT
POLICE

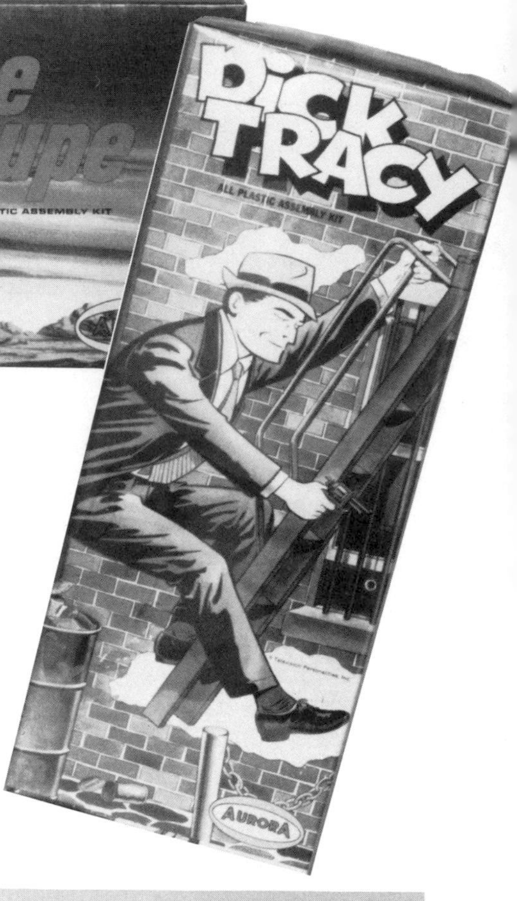
DICK TRACY
ALL PLASTIC ASSEMBLY KIT
AURORA

Fig. 3-86
Aurora Plastics Corp. issued these two kits in 1968: Dick Tracy in action, and the Space Coupe.

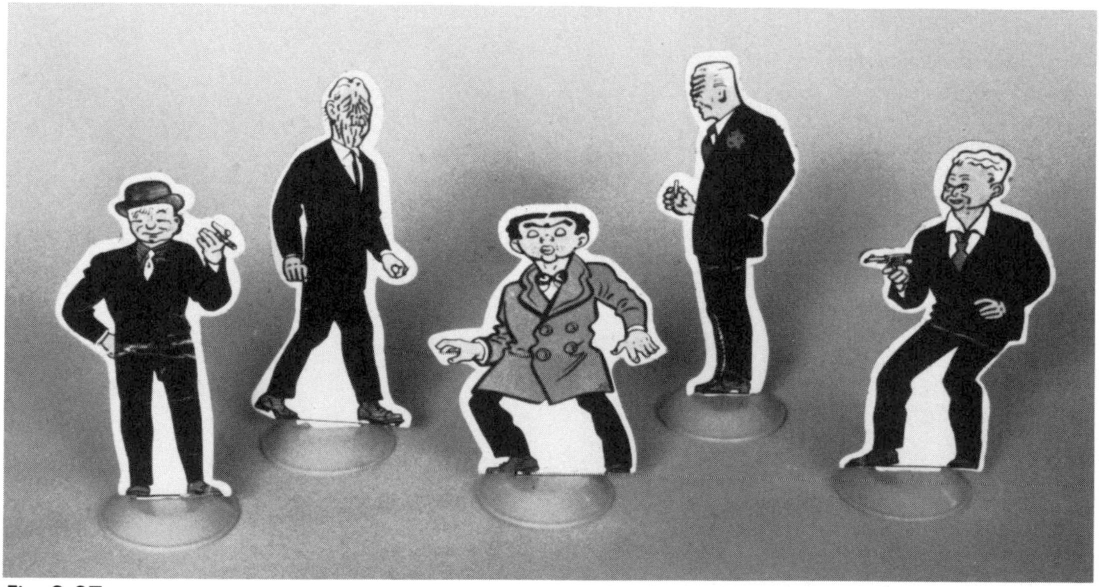

Fig. 3-87
The villains in the Ideal set include seven figures.

Fig. 3-88
Some of these panels from the Sunday announcing Sparkle Plenty's birth are used on the box design for Ideal's "Baby Sparkle Plenty Doll." The doctor visiting Gertie discovers she has pneumonia. Thus Chester Gould kept America head over heels in love with Sparkle.

Fig. 3-89
Ideal Toy Company's 12"-tall "Baby Sparkle Plenty Doll" is shown here with original packaging; it went on sale July 28, 1947, at $5.98. Even though 10,000 sold in the first five days, this doll is difficult to find today. It was the Cabbage Patch doll of its day.

Fig. 3-90

This ceramic "Sparkle Plenty Savings Bank" by Jayess is from the late 1940s. It is 12" tall and the base is $4\frac{1}{2}$" × 9". A raised medallion shows Dick Tracy as "Godfather," and medallions at either end show B.O. Plenty and Gravel Gertie. Jayess also did a 13" tall bank of Sparkle in a highchair.

Fig. 3-91

This litho tin B.O. Plenty made by Louis Marx walks, and his hat tips up and down when he's wound up with a key. The late 1940s toy shows B.O. holding baby Sparkle. It is $8\frac{1}{2}$" tall.

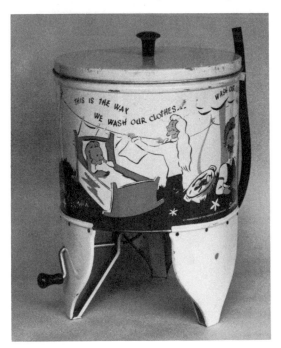

Fig. 3-92

The "Sparkle Plenty Washing Machine" made by Kalon Radio Corporation in the late 1940s is litho tin and stands 12" tall. Inside are all the components of a real washing machine. Gravel Gertie is shown doing the wash while B.O. Plenty holds baby Sparkle.

Fig. 3-93
Mounted on a base 23" × 15½", the rooftop sign proclaims, "This is the house of Sparkle Plenty." Made of heavy cardboard, the Sunny Dell Acres house is 16½" tall to its peak, not counting the sign on top. It came with cardboard figures of Sparkle, B.O. Plenty, Gravel Gertie, and Tracy. It is late 1940s vintage.

Fig. 3-94
Bonny Braids' birth was announced to Dick Tracy in the comic strip: by 2-way wrist radio, of course. She was born in the back of a police car as Tess rushed to the hospital. Elsewhere, at the same time, Tracy was duking it out with a villain named Empty Williams.

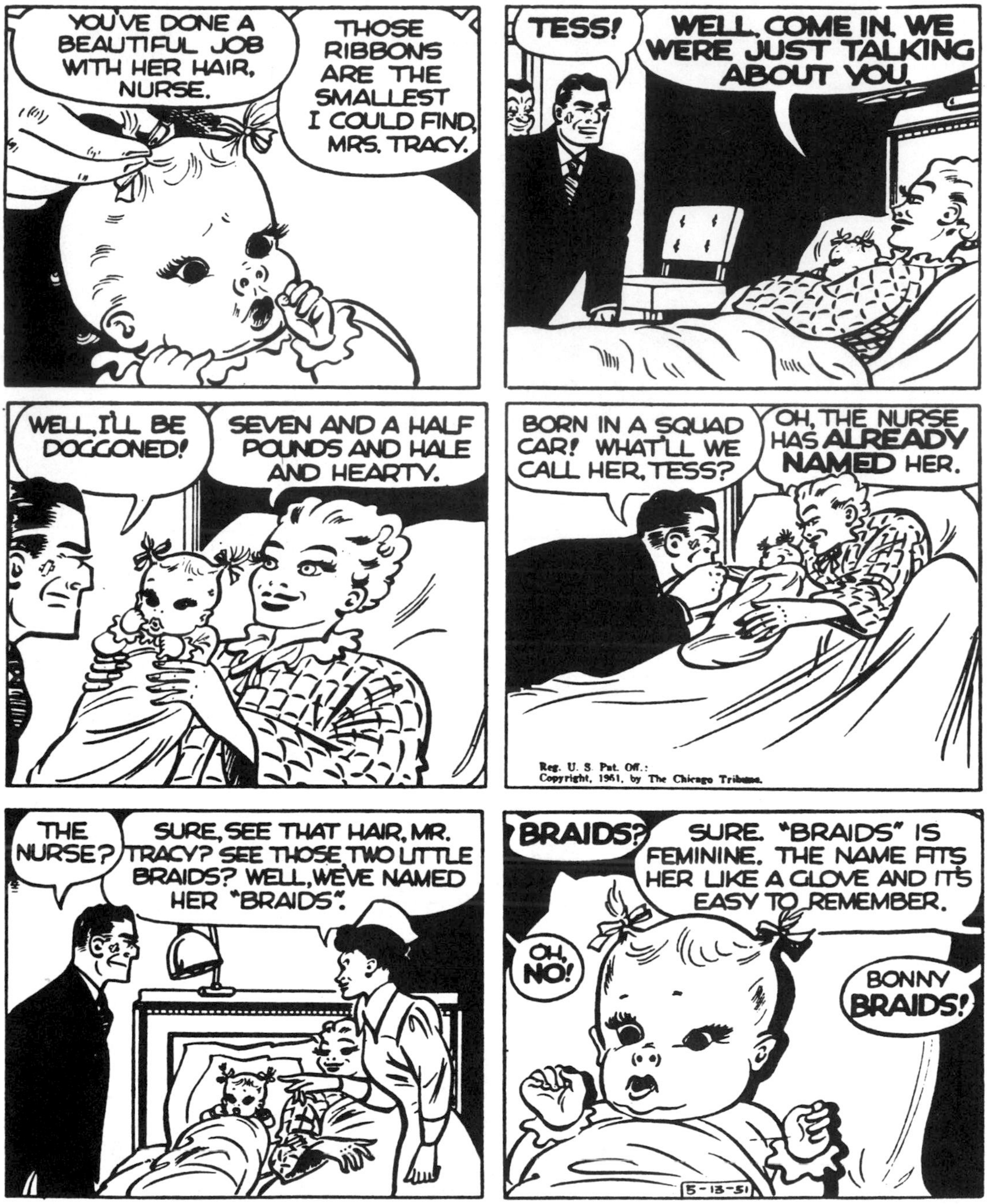

YOU'VE DONE A BEAUTIFUL JOB WITH HER HAIR, NURSE.
THOSE RIBBONS ARE THE SMALLEST I COULD FIND, MRS. TRACY.
TESS!
WELL, COME IN. WE WERE JUST TALKING ABOUT YOU.
WELL, I'LL BE DOGGONED!
SEVEN AND A HALF POUNDS AND HALE AND HEARTY.
BORN IN A SQUAD CAR! WHAT'LL WE CALL HER, TESS?
OH, THE NURSE HAS ALREADY NAMED HER.
Reg. U. S. Pat. Off.: Copyright, 1951, by The Chicago Tribune.
THE NURSE?
SURE, SEE THAT HAIR, MR. TRACY? SEE THOSE TWO LITTLE BRAIDS? WELL, WE'VE NAMED HER "BRAIDS".
BRAIDS?
SURE. "BRAIDS" IS FEMININE. THE NAME FITS HER LIKE A GLOVE AND IT'S EASY TO REMEMBER.
OH, NO!
BONNY BRAIDS!
5-13-51

Fig. 3-95

On the left is a 6″ plastic walking wobble doll of Bonny Braids (manufacturer unknown) from the early 1950s. At right is the 1952 crawling Bonny Braids doll by Ideal Toy Company. It winds up with a key and crawls. The crawling Bonny is 8″ tall and 11″ long.

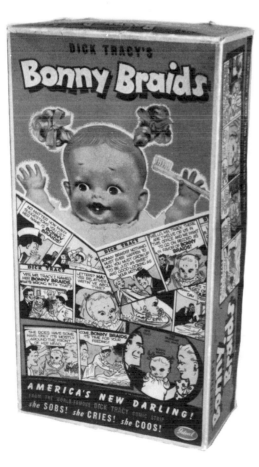

Fig. 3-96

Ideal Toy Company found success again with its 1951 baby doll, "Dick Tracy's Bonny Braids." The doll is 14″ tall and came with a toothbrush. Box reads: "She cries. She sobs. She coos."

Fig. 3-97
Honey Moon, the daughter of Moon Maid and
Junior Tracy, was born in September, 1965, in the
Space Coupe, halfway between Earth and the
moon. Collectors of original art prize strips dealing
with historic events.

Fig. 3-98
Ideal Toy Company made this 14″ doll
in 1965 to coincide with Tracy's gran-
daughter's birth. The doll came wear-
ing a removeable plastic "space"
bubble helmet. The original box also
shows a birth announcement by the
proud parents and reads "Dick Tracy
presents Little Honey Moon."

Fig. 3-99

Little Bonny Braids, born in 1951, is now an adult working as a teacher with Yakima Indians in Washington, with only cameo roles in the strip. Both of Tess Tracy's children were born in the back of a car. Tracy's son Joseph Flintheart Tracy was born in November, 1979. To date in terms of merchandising, Joe has been a total dud. He has also just been a cameo character in the syndicated comic strip.

Toy Guns and Target Games

There have been nearly a dozen different guns and gun sets made over the years. In the mid-1930s Louis Marx made a "Dick Tracy Police Siren Pistol," a "Dick Tracy Sparkling Pop Pistol," and a "Dick Tracy Click Pistol." In the late 1930s Marx made a "Dick Tracy Jr. Click Pistol."

Marx also made two different "Dick Tracy Target" sets in the early 1940s. These included colorful stand-up targets and guns which shot rubber-tipped darts. One set included a 17" circular cardboard bulls-eye type target, and the other set included a 10" × 10" litho tin target. The boxes for the cir-

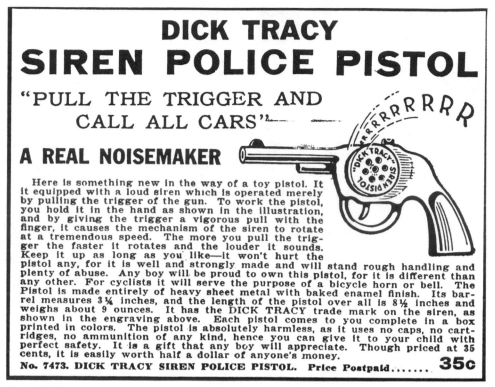

DICK TRACY
SIREN POLICE PISTOL

"PULL THE TRIGGER AND CALL ALL CARS"

A REAL NOISEMAKER

Here is something new in the way of a toy pistol. It it equipped with a loud siren which is operated merely by pulling the trigger of the gun. To work the pistol, you hold it in the hand as shown in the illustration, and by giving the trigger a vigorous pull with the finger, it causes the mechanism of the siren to rotate at a tremendous speed. The more you pull the trigger the faster it rotates and the louder it sounds. Keep it up as long as you like—it won't hurt the pistol any, for it is well and strongly made and will stand rough handling and plenty of abuse. Any boy will be proud to own this pistol, for it is different than any other. For cyclists it will serve the purpose of a bicycle horn or bell. The Pistol is made entirely of heavy sheet metal with baked enamel finish. Its barrel measures 3¼ inches, and the length of the pistol over all is 8½ inches and weighs about 9 ounces. It has the DICK TRACY trade mark on the siren, as shown in the engraving above. Each pistol comes to you complete in a box printed in colors. The pistol is absolutely harmless, as it uses no caps, no cartridges, no ammunition of any kind, hence you can give it to your child with perfect safety. It is a gift that any boy will appreciate. Though priced at 35 cents, it is easily worth half a dollar of anyone's money.

No. 7473. DICK TRACY SIREN POLICE PISTOL. Price Postpaid....... 35c

Fig. 3-100
An original ad for the metal "Dick Tracy Siren Police Pistol" made by Marx Toy Company in the 1930s, 35 cents, postpaid. Working models have a very healthy siren noise.

cular set were very colorful, and are themselves collectible.

In the late 1940s, Parker Johns made an all-metal "Dick Tracy Rapid-Fire Tommy Gun." The only Tracy identification was a sticker on one side of the gun's stock. Purchasers of this gun also received a free brass "Dick Tracy Detective Club" badge.

In the mid-1950s, Tops Plastics made a plastic "Dick Tracy Sub-Machine Water Gun" and a plastic "Dick Tracy 45 Special" water handgun.

Mattel made at least two different Dick Tracy guns in the early 1960s. One was a "Tommy Burst" cap rifle and the other was a "Power-Jet Squad Gun" rifle which was both a cap and water gun.

In the early 1970s, Hubley made a "Crimestopper Play Set" which included a "Dick" cap gun, handcuffs, billfold, magnifying glass, badge and flashlight. The "Dick" cap gun was also sold separately on a bubble-pack card with a Dick Tracy logo and label. This gun has no other "Dick Tracy" identification; thus, many collectors do not consider it a true Tracy collectible without accompanying card.

Louis Marx made a "Dick Tracy Automatic Target Range" in the mid-1960s. It is a BB shooting gun mounted within an enclosed plastic "shooting gallery."

In the late 1960s and early 1970s, Larami Corp. made several different bubble-pack gun and target sets. These included such items as a "Special Ray Gun," a "Camera Dart Gun," a "Repeater Cap Gun," a "Luger Water Gun," rubber-band shooting guns and "Target Sets," and a "Mobile Commander" set with dart guns.

In the 1980s, Ja-Ru made 11 different bubble-pack toy sets, five of which included guns and/or target sets. In 1982, Placo Products made a "Dick Tracy Target Playset." This included a plastic dart gun, a target of

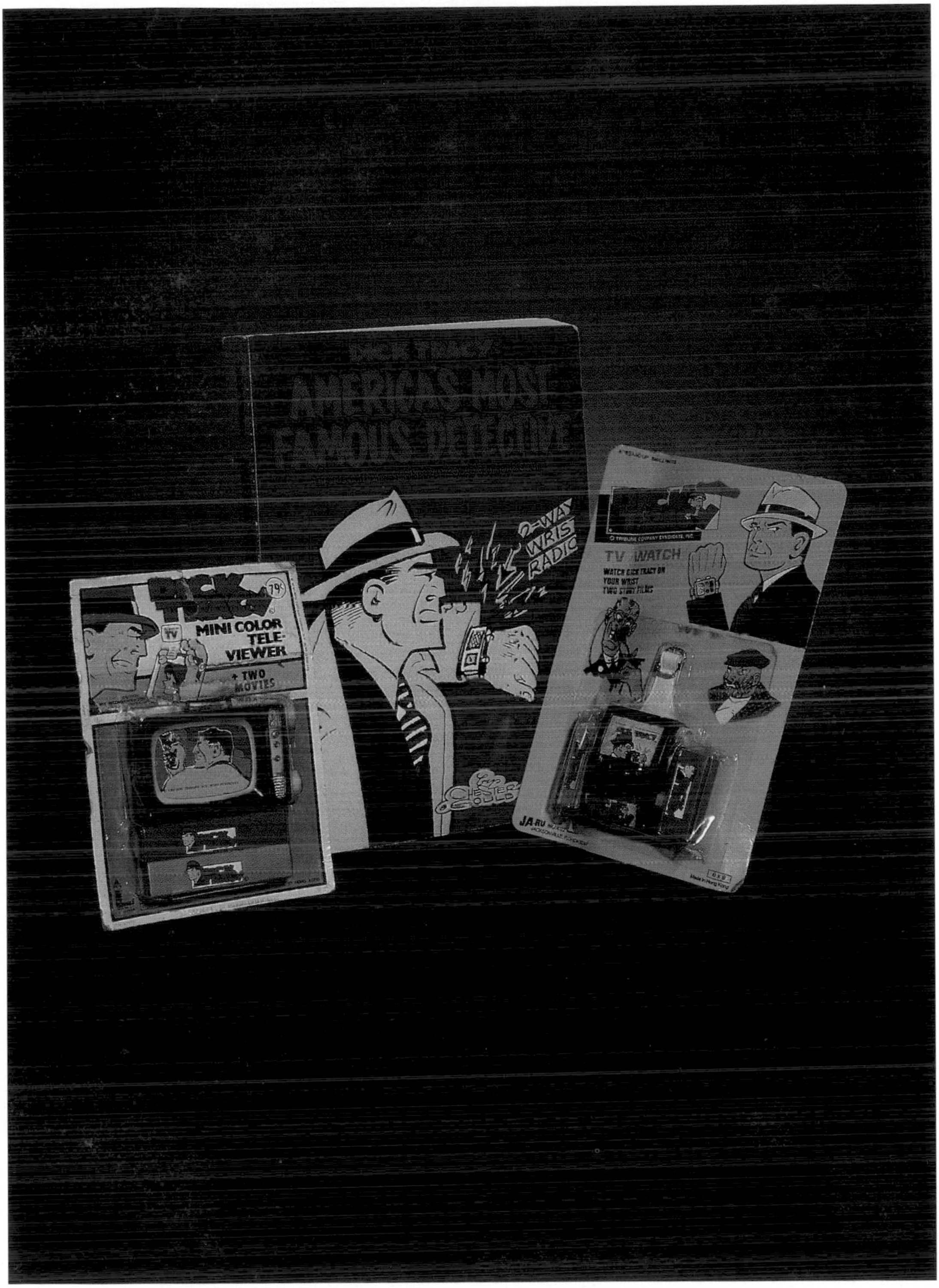
AMERICAS MOST FAMOUS DETECTIVE
2-WAY WRIST RADIO
79¢
MINI COLOR TELE-VIEWER
+ TWO MOVIES
TV WATCH
WATCH DICK TRACY ON YOUR WRIST TWO STORY FILMS

Fig. 14

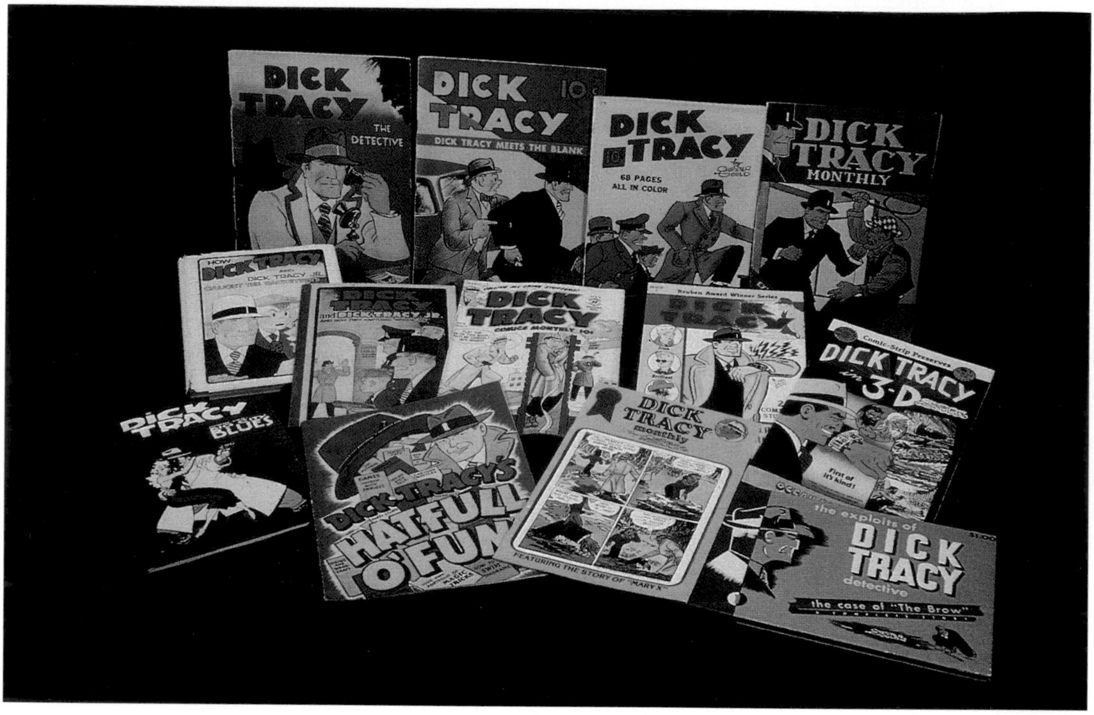
DICK TRACY THE DETECTIVE
DICK TRACY
DICK TRACY MEETS THE BLANK
DICK TRACY
68 PAGES ALL IN COLOR
DICK TRACY MONTHLY
DICK TRACY'S HATFULL O'FUN
DICK TRACY monthly
FEATURING THE STORY OF "MARY X"
DICK TRACY in 3-D
the exploits of DICK TRACY detective
the case of "The Brow"

Fig. 15

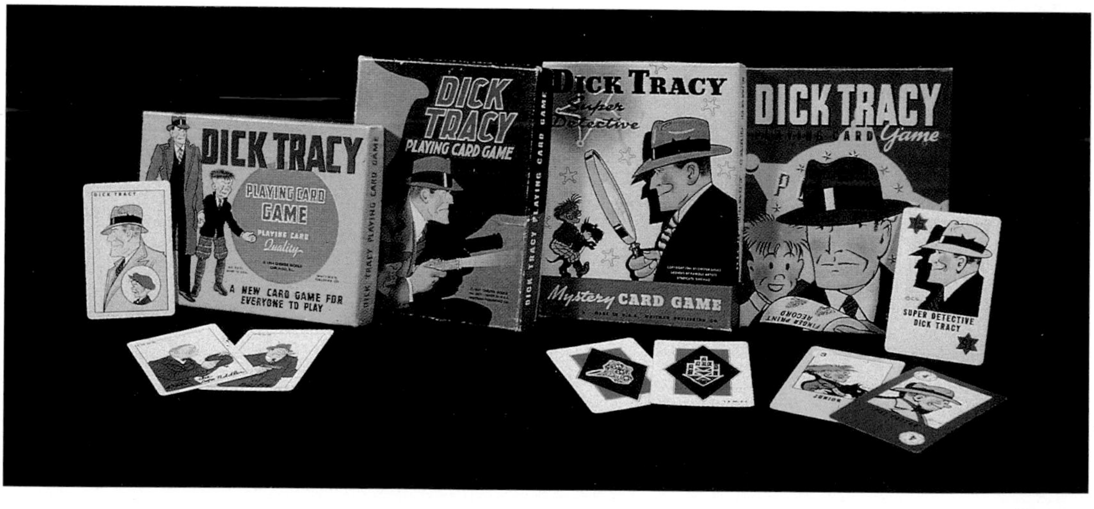
DICK TRACY
PLAYING CARD GAME
A NEW CARD GAME FOR EVERYONE TO PLAY
DICK TRACY PLAYING CARD GAME
DICK TRACY Super Detective
Mystery CARD GAME
DICK TRACY
SUPER DETECTIVE DICK TRACY

Fig. 16

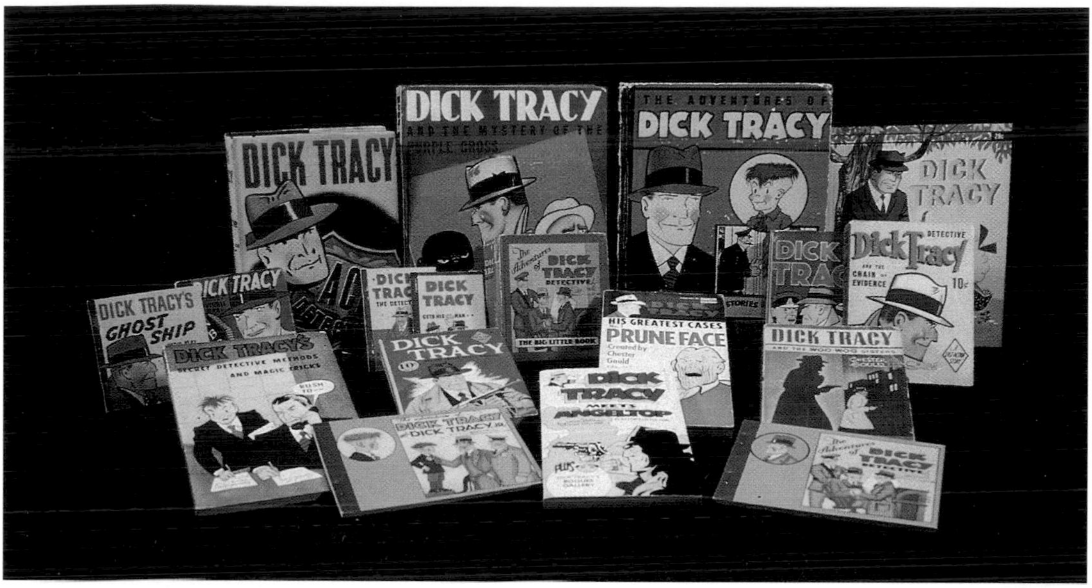
DICK TRACY
AND THE MYSTERY OF THE PURPLE CROSS
THE ADVENTURES OF
DICK TRACY
DICK TRACY'S GHOST SHIP
DICK TRACY'S SECRET DETECTIVE METHODS AND MAGIC TRICKS
THE BIG LITTLE BOOK
HIS GREATEST CASES
PRUNE FACE
Created by Chester Gould
DICK TRACY MEETS ANGELTOP
DICK TRACY AND THE WOO WOO SISTERS
Dick Tracy DETECTIVE AND THE CHAIN OF EVIDENCE
10¢
DICK TRACY AND DICK TRACY, JR.

Fig. 17

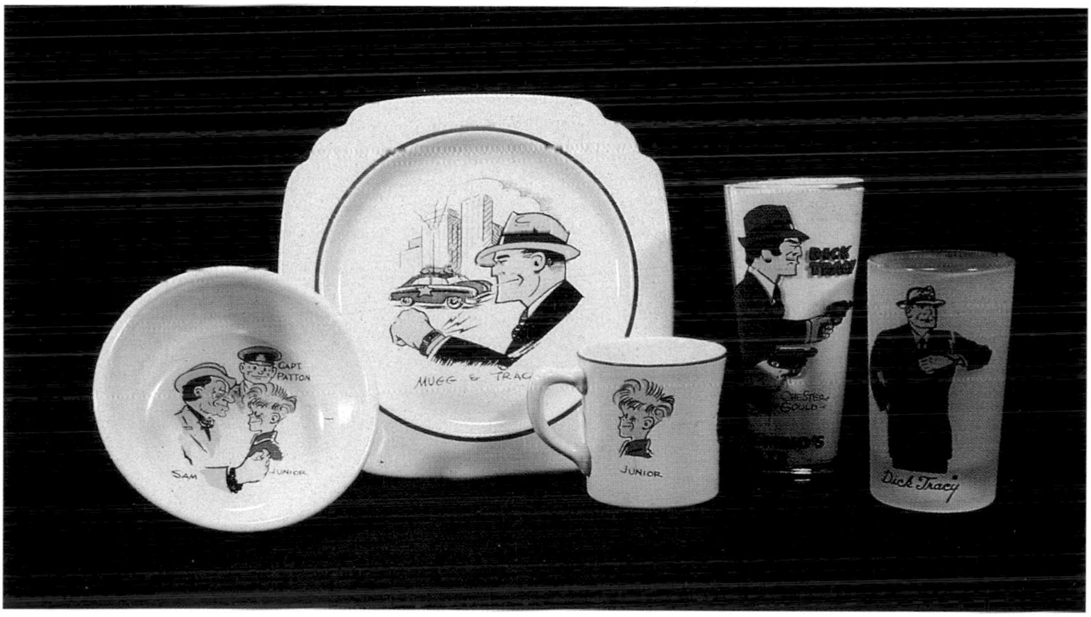
CAPT PATTON
SAM
JUNIOR
JUNIOR
DICK TRACY
CHESTER GOULD
Dick Tracy

Fig. 18

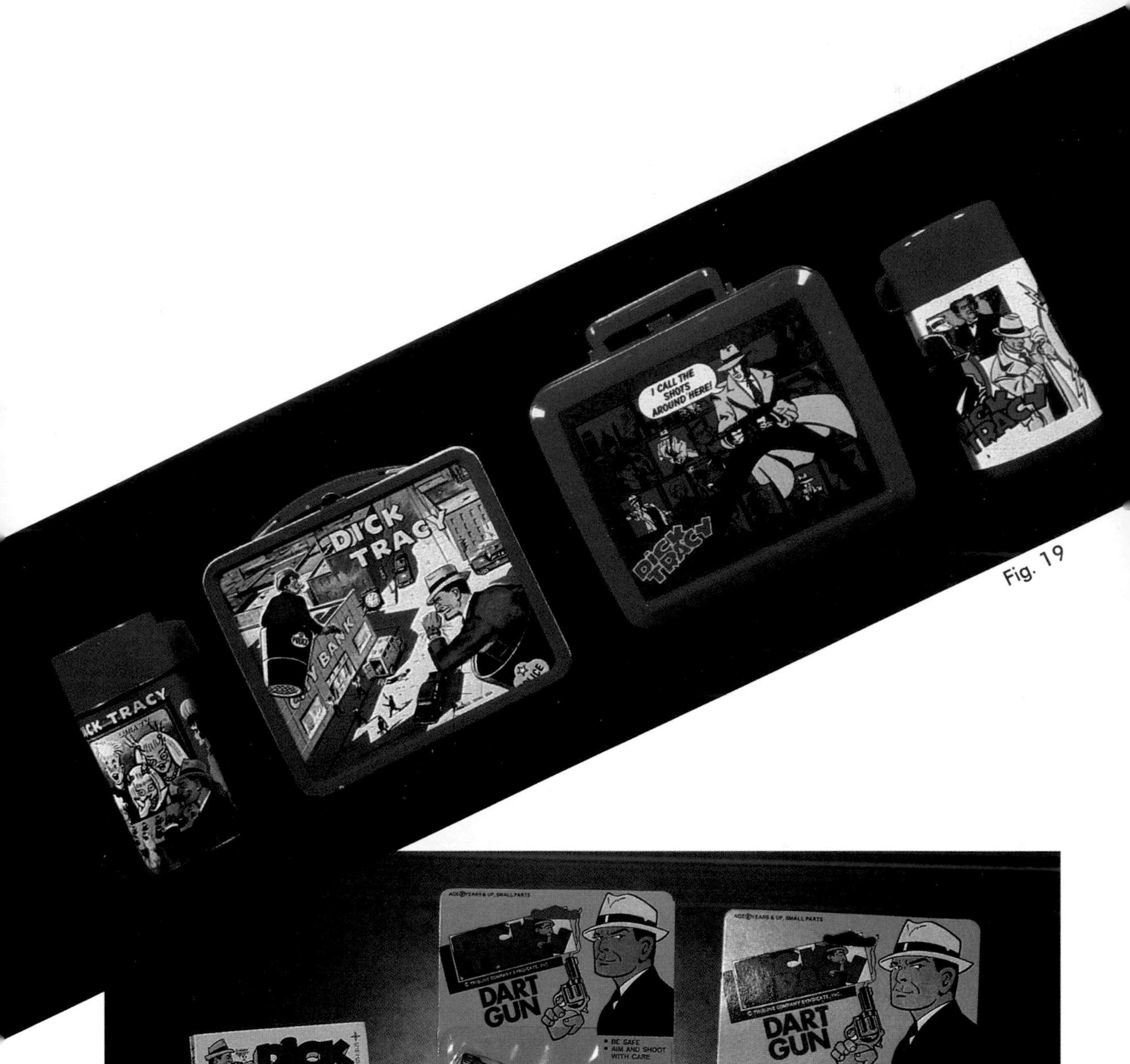
DICK TRACY
CITY BANK
I CALL THE SHOTS AROUND HERE!
DICK TRACY

Fig. 19

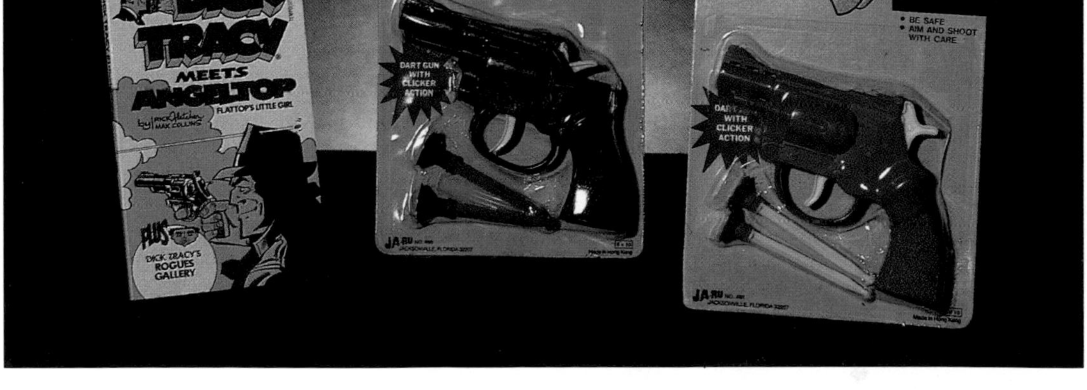
DICK TRACY MEETS ANGELTOP
FLATTOP'S LITTLE GIRL
PLUS DICK TRACY'S ROGUES GALLERY
DART GUN
BE SAFE
AIM AND SHOOT WITH CARE
DART GUN WITH CLICKER ACTION
DART GUN
BE SAFE
AIM AND SHOOT WITH CARE
WITH CLICKER ACTION

Fig. 20

Fig. 3-101
This is the box for an early 1940s Louis Marx target game. Target inside was 17½″ in diameter. Box measures 18″ × 18″ × 1½″. An earlier, rarer box for same game shows a 6-panel cartoon strip.

Fig. 3-102
In the mid-1950s, Tops Plastics made a 12″-long sub-machine-style water gun that held "over 500 shots on one filling." It came in red, green, and light blue models and had a Tracy sticker on the magazine. Julio Santiago identifies it as a toy .45 Caliber Thompson sub-machine gun.

various villains, and a set of handcuffs.

Two different Dick Tracy holster sets were made, but neither came with a gun. An "Official Holster Outfit" was made in the late 1940s by Classy Products. It included a six-shooter type leather holster im-printed with a color Tracy profile. In the early 1950s, J. Hapern Co. made a "Shoulder Holster Set." This included a high-quality leather holster with Tracy's profile embossed into it.

Fig. 3-103
In 1964, Larami Corp. issued this model of a Remington .41 Caliber Derringer as a "Dick Tracy Special Ray Gun." The 5"-long flashlight came with a metal "Dick Tracy N.Y.P.D. Detective" badge.

Fig. 3-104
This 10"-square litho tin "Dick Tracy Target" had a bullseye pattern on the reverse; Marx, 1941.

Fig. 3-105
Larami Corp.'s "Dick Tracy Target Set" from the 1960s shoots rubber bands. The guns came in either red, green or blue. The packaging measures $6\frac{1}{4}$" × 10".

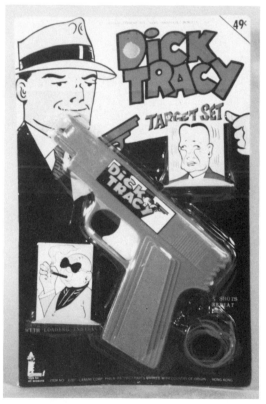

DECEMBER 2 1978

"CHESTER GOULD" CREATOR OF THE "DICK TRACY" COMIC
STRIP AUTOGRAPHS A DICK TRACY CAP PISTOL AND
PRESENTED IT TO THE NAPPERVILLE, ILLINOIS COLLEGE
FUND RAISING AUCTION. AT THE TIME OF PRESENTATION
MR GOULD STATED THAT THIS CAP PISTOL WAS THE
ONLY SUCH ITEM HE HAD EVER AUTOGRAPHED

Fig. 3-106
Chester Gould etched his signature on the barrel and the date on the bottom of
the pistol butt—the only such item he ever etched. The Hubley automatic cap
pistol and the photo of Gould doing the etching are unique to my (Doucet) Tracy
collection.

Fig. 3-107

In 1980, Dick Tracy had a Nite-Site installed on his revolver. The device, developed by former Tracy technical advisers Julio Santiago and Elliel Knutsen, allows accurate direct fire in low level light. Being on the cutting edge of technology is a Dick Tracy tradition.

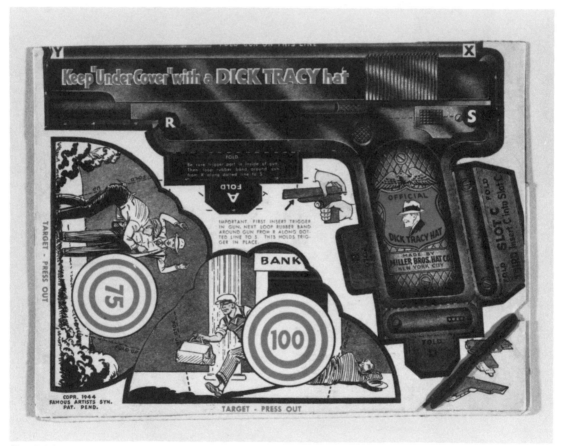

Fig. 3-108

"Dick Tracy's Rubber Band Pistol and Targets" is a premium issued in 1944 by Miller Brothers' Hats. The folded cardboard premium measures $8\frac{1}{4}$" × $6\frac{1}{4}$". Printed on the barrel of this "automatic" is the advertising line, "Keep 'Under Cover' with a Dick Tracy hat."

Fig. 3-109

The "Dick Tracy Shoulder Holster set" of high quality leather was made by J. Hapern Co. in the early 1950s. Tracy's name and image is embossed into the holster. It's shown with its original box, 10″ × 10″ × 2″.

Fig. 3-111

This toy adaptation of a Browning .25 Caliber Automatic by Hubley, made in the 1970s, has no Dick Tracy markings on it except the bubble-pack card it came heat sealed on. Without the card, it isn't a Dick Tracy collectible.

Fig. 3-110

This Dick Tracy holster shown with original box is from the 1940s by Classy Products. Box measures $5\frac{1}{2}″ × 11\frac{1}{2}″ × 1\frac{3}{4}″$.

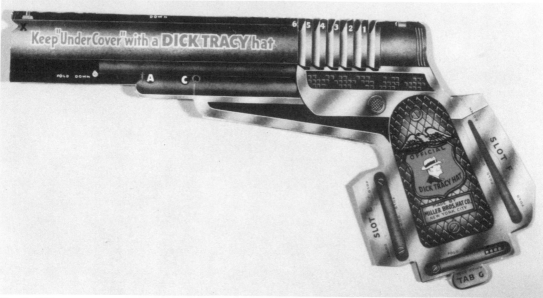

Fig. 3-112
This Miller Brothers' Hats premium rubber-band gun has an 8½" barrel. The Tracy logo on the gun handle says, "Official Dick Tracy Hat."

Games, Cameras, and Viewers

The earliest game was a board game made by Einson-Freeman in 1933, called "Dick Tracy Detective Game." In 1937, Whitman made a totally different board game with the same name. Whitman also made a "Dick Tracy Playing Card Game" which was sold in four different, colorful boxes between 1938 and 1941.

Three different, hand-held games, measuring $3\frac{1}{2}'' \times 5''$, were made in the late 1940s. These were titled "Dick Tracy Bingo Game," "Lock Them Up In Jail," and "Harmonize with Dick Tracy." The object of each was basically to roll BBs into various holes on the face of a glass-framed game card.

One of the most interesting Dick Tracy games was a 1967 bagatelle game by Louis Marx. The characters pictured on the game are all from a 1967 pilot for a Dick Tracy TV show which was never broadcast!

Sel Right made a Dick Tracy board game in 1967 titled the "Master Detective Game." In 1972, Ideal made a Dick Tracy "Sunday Funnies" board game. Ideal also made a battery-operated game titled "Crime Stopper" in 1963.

Acme Toys made at least seven different versions of a Dick Tracy film strip toy. Celluloid strips of cartoon panels were wound through a small, hand-held viewer. Three different Acme sets were made in the mid-1940s, and each included a colorful display box. Acme "Jumbo Movie Style Viewers and Film" sets were sold as late as the mid-1960s.

The most interesting film strip viewer was made by Tru-Vue, Inc., in the late 1940s. The strip was projected in a high-quality 3-D image.

Fig. 3-113
Einson-Freeman made the earliest Tracy board game in 1933. The "Dick Tracy Detective Game" came in two different $10\frac{1}{2}'' \times 14\frac{1}{2}'' \times \frac{3}{4}''$ boxes.

Fig. 3-114

An unusual item because the characters shown are actors from a 1967 Dick Tracy TV pilot that never aired, is Marx Toy Company's bagatelle game. It measures $13 \times 25 \times 1\frac{1}{2}$ inches and is a pinball-style game.

Fig. 3-115
"Dick Tracy in Movie Style" is a film strip viewer toy by Acme in 1948. These toys are quaint and innocent in the age of video cassettes.

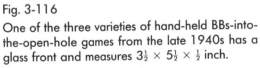

Fig. 3-116
One of the three varieties of hand-held BBs-into-the-open-hole games from the late 1940s has a glass front and measures $3\frac{1}{2} \times 5\frac{1}{2} \times \frac{1}{2}$ inch.

Fig. 3-117
Ja-Ru's "Dick Tracy Pop-Pop Game" has Diet Smith and Flattop as targets. The Ja-Ru line of eleven different toys was available through most of the 1980s.

Fig. 3-118
This tiny 16mm "Dick Tracy Camera" from the 1960s has a box that measures $1\frac{1}{2}'' \times 2\frac{1}{4}'' \times 1\frac{1}{4}''$. It was made in Hong Kong.

Fig. 3-119
Seymour Sales Co. of Chicago made this "Dick Tracy Candid Camera" in the early 1950s. It uses 127 film and has a 50mm lens. It comes with a plastic carrying case. The box is $3'' \times 5\frac{1}{4}'' \times 3''$.

Fig. 3-120
This "Dick Tracy Jumbo Movie Style Viewer" by Acme is from the 1950s. Similar viewers were made by Acme until the mid-1960s.

Fig. 3-121
"Dick Tracy, A Sunday Funnies Game," a 1972 board game by Ideal Toy Company, comes in a 12″ × 16″ × 1½″ box.

Police Sets and Detective Kits

Fig. 3-122
"Dick Tracy Crime Lab" by Ja-Ru, 1980s, has a toy model of a Smith & Wesson .38 Caliber Chief Special. The set includes a magnifying glass and badge. In later years, all Ja-Ru's toy guns were made in bright yellow and orange colors.

J. Pressman & Co. made the first "Police Outfit" in the early 1930s. This included card-mounted handcuffs, a billy club, a whistle, and a silver "Dick Tracy Secret Service Badge." J. Pressman & Co. also made a boxed "Dick Tracy Detective Set including Finger Print Outfit" in the early 1930s.

John Henry Products made several different variations of card-mounted sets with handcuffs, billy clubs, and badges from the mid-1940s to early 1960s.

In the mid-1950s, Deluxe made two different "Dick Tracy Braces Sets." One set included handcuffs and the other a badge, whistle, and magnifying glass. Porter Chemical Co. made a "Dick Tracy Crime Stoppers Laboratory" in 1955. It included a 60-power microscope, glass slides, and fingerprint identification apparatus. This set is among the rarest and most valuable Dick Tracy collectibles.

Laramie Corp. and Ja-Ru made numerous different bubble-packed handcuffs and detective sets in the 1970s and 1980s.

Fig. 3-123

"Dick Tracy Braces for Smart Boys and Girls" consisting of a magnifying glass, a police badge and a whistle, mid-1950s by Deluxe Trademark. The suspenders have a Dick Tracy badge as a holder, sometimes found independently of this outfit. Box is 6" × 12". Another version has only suspenders and no handcuffs.

Fig. 3-124
The "Crimestopper Play Set" by Hubley, early 1970s; 17" × 11" × 2".

Fig. 3-125
This "Dick Tracy Detective Set—including finger print outfit" is by J. Pressman Co. from the 1930s. The box measures $9\frac{1}{2}$" × 15" × $1\frac{1}{2}$". Included in the set are a glass plate, a roller, dusting powder, detective ink, a magnifying glass, and instruction booklet.

Fig. 3-126

This "Dick Tracy Crime Stoppers Laboratory" measures $9\frac{1}{2}'' \times 13'' \times 2\frac{3}{4}''$. Made by Porter Chemical Co. in 1955, it has a 60-power microscope, glass slides, fingerprint apparatus, and a text book.

Fig. 3-127

From the mid-1940s to the mid-1960s, John Henry Products made a number of Dick Tracy sets. "Dick Tracy's Handcuffs for Junior" is from the 1940s. The card measures $5'' \times 10''$.

Fig. 3-128

"Sparkle Plenty Christmas Tree Lights" from the late 1940s came in two sets of 7 or 15 lights. The actual lights were not figurative, just regular tree lights; thus, the decorative box is critical for this collectible.

In the late 1940s, Kalon Radio Corporation made a toy litho tin "Sparkle Plenty Washing Machine." It stood 12″ tall and had all the basic components of a real washing machine. Tracy, B.O. Plenty, and Baby Sparkle were pictured and Gravel Gertie was shown washing and hanging clothes.

In 1950, Styron made a "Sparkle Plenty Islander Ukette." This came with a song booklet and could be played.

Several different sets of "Favorite Funnies Printing Sets" were made between 1935 and the early 1950s. These sets contained rubber stamps, ink pads, and blank strip pads featuring different cartoon characters. A Dick Tracy stamp was included in all sets, and other character stamps may have been included for B.O. Plenty, Chief Brandon, Junior and/or Pat Patton.

A stiff cardboard Sunny Dell Acres dollhouse was made in the late 1940s. A roof-mounted sign read "This is the Home of Sparkle Plenty." It came with stand-up cardboard figures of Tracy, B.O. Plenty, Gravel Gertie and Sparkle in a little crib.

In 1964, Popular Printing made a Dick Tracy Code Printing Set. This included metal, letter type pieces with typesetting and printing apparatus.

In 1967 Louis Marx made a battery-operated "Dick Tracy Talking Telephone." When activated it played 10 different messages such as "Tracy calling—execute Plan B," "Junior, change your disguise," and "Make your arrest now."

In the late 1960s/early 1970s, sets of "Magnetic TV & Cartoon Pals" were made. The Dick Tracy set had 48 colorful, vinyl-covered magnets of different character and villain profiles, including Tracy, Lizz, Sam Catchem, Chief Brandon, The Brow, The Brain, Flattop, Pruneface, Pouch, and Johnny Scorn.

There were three interesting flashlight toys. Bantam-Lite made a 3¼″ pocket flashlight shaped like a disposable cigarette lighter

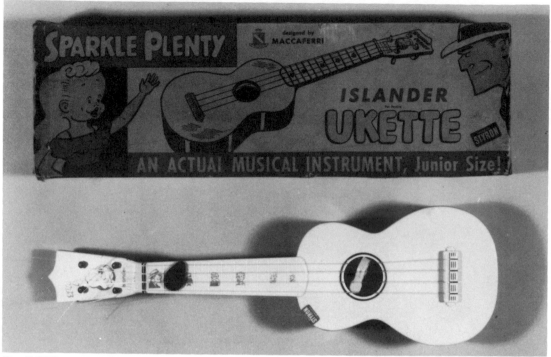

Fig. 3-129

In the comic strip, Sparkle Plenty became a child TV star, singing songs and playing a ukulele. This prompted the "Sparkle Plenty Islander Ukette" made by Styron in 1950. It sold for $5.95, was endorsed by Arthur Godfrey, and came with an instruction and songbook full of Sparkle Plenty drawings. The box is $15\frac{1}{4}'' \times 5'' \times 2''$.

in the 1950s. Plastic, with a blue body and red top, it had Tracy's head and "Dick Tracy Flashlight" etched into the body. Bantam-Lite also made a "Dick Tracy 3-Color Wrist Flashlight" in 1961. The third was a 1975 flashlight by Creative Creations which had a plastic profile of Tracy's head mounted on the light end.

In the 1940s, Miller Brothers Hat Co. sold felt, snap-brim fedora hats with a label on the inside leather band embossed with "Official Dick Tracy Hat." As promotions for their hats, Miller Brothers offered an "enameled hat ring." This was a hefty brass ring showing Tracy's profile with a hat finished in green enamel. Another Miller Brothers Hat premium was a fold-over cardboard "Dick Tracy's Rubber Band Pistol and Targets." Two different sizes and pistol types were made. These, as well as the hat and ring, are scarce and valuable Tracy collectibles.

Two eight-piece sets of frosted tumbler glasses were produced in the late 1940s with decals of different Tracy characters and villains. In the late 1970s, Domino's Pizza gave away glasses featuring a full-length Tracy profile.

In the early 1950s, Homer Laughlib made a ceramic set comprising a Dick Tracy plate, cereal bowl, and mug. (Both 7" and 9"-diameter plates were made.) These pieces were colorfully illustrated with various characters.

Aladdin made a litho tin school lunch box with thermos featuring Dick Tracy in 1967. This was colorful and pictured many of the strip characters. The theme was "space age" as they showed space coupes, air cars, and moon people.

In the mid-1930s, New Haven Clock & Watch Co. made Dick Tracy wristwatches. These pictured Tracy standing with a gun in his hand on both rectangular and circular

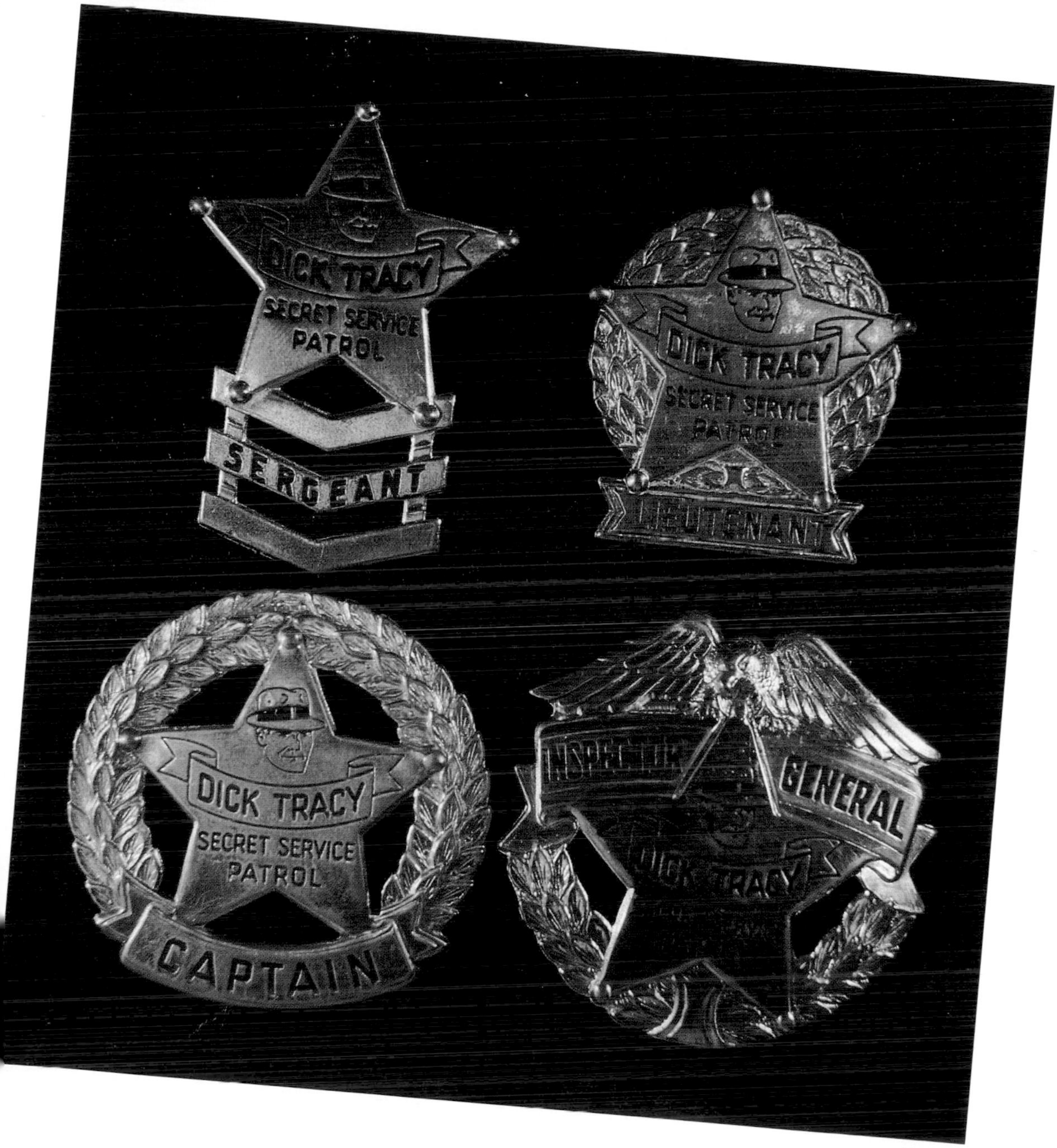
DICK TRACY
SECRET SERVICE
PATROL
SERGEANT
DICK TRACY
SECRET SERVICE
PATROL
LIEUTENANT
DICK TRACY
SECRET SERVICE
PATROL
CAPTAIN
INSPECTOR
GENERAL
DICK TRACY

Fig. 21

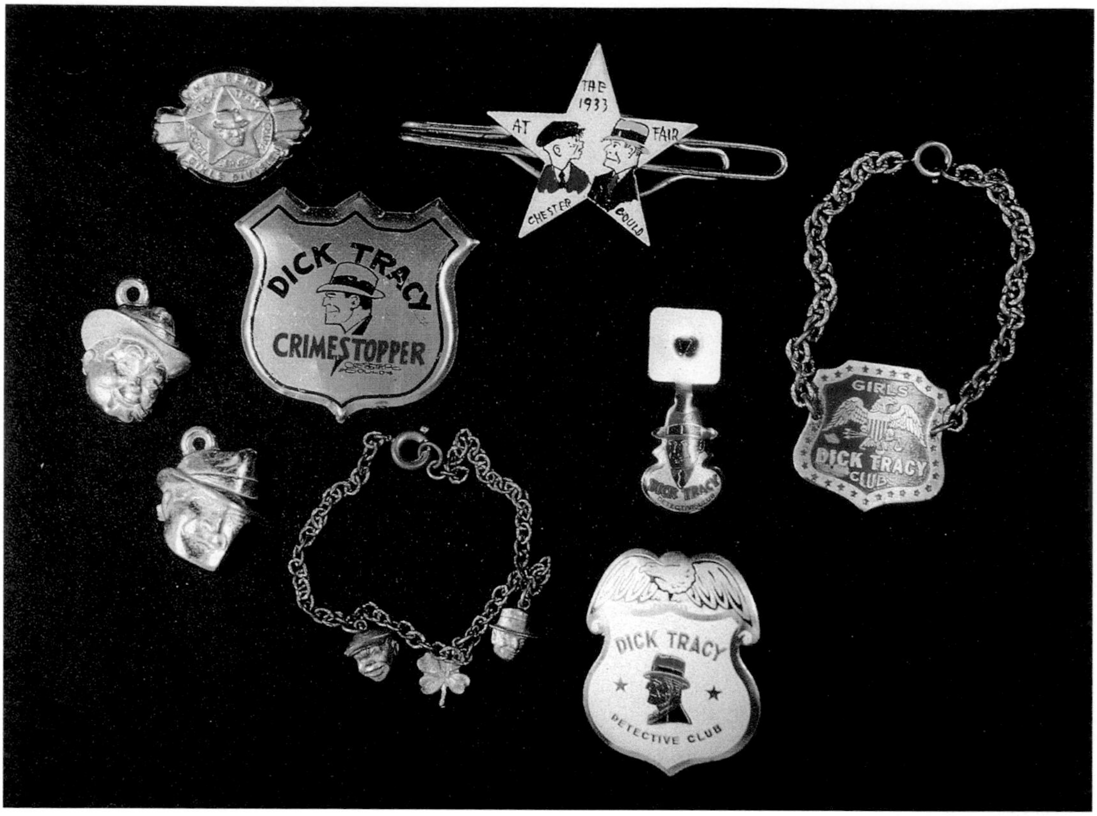
THE 1933
AT
FAIR
CHESTER
GOULD
DICK TRACY
CRIMESTOPPER
GIRLS
DICK TRACY
CLUB
DICK TRACY
DETECTIVE CLUB

Fig. 22

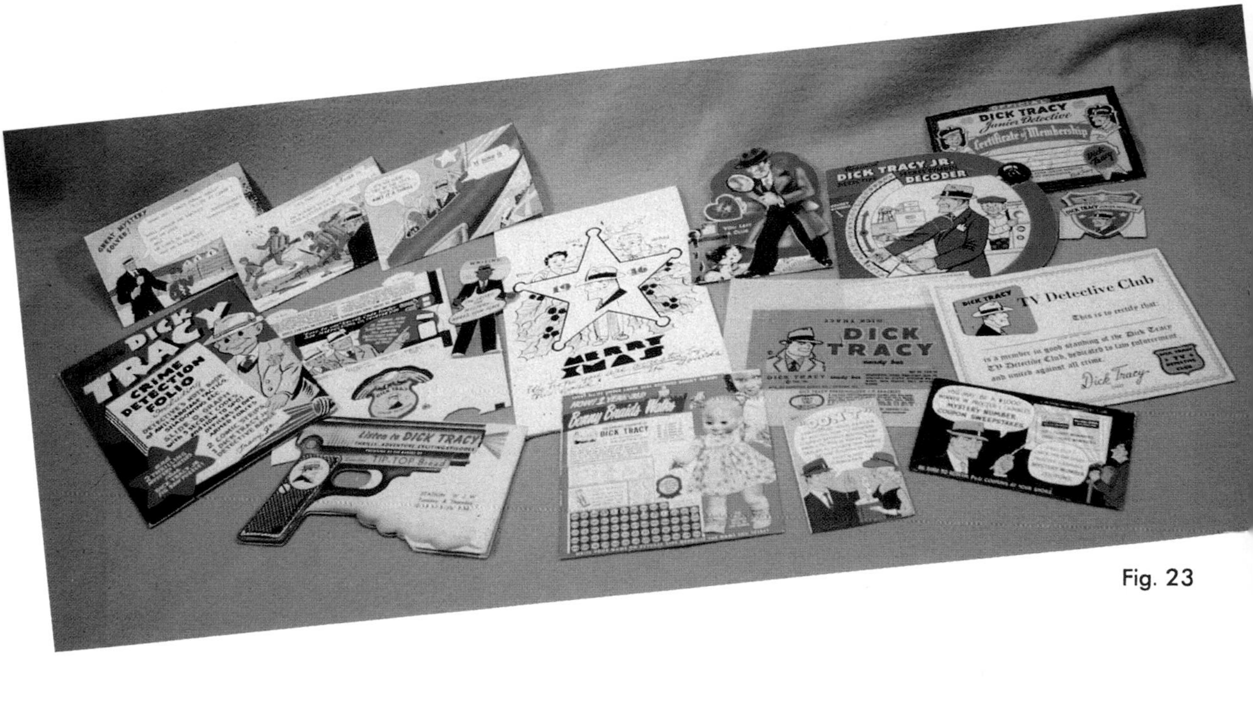
DICK TRACY
Junior Detective
Certificate of Membership
DICK TRACY JR.
DECODER
DICK TRACY
CRIME
DETECTION
FOLIO
MERRY
XMAS
DICK
TRACY
TV Detective Club
This is to certify that:
Dick Tracy
Listen to DICK TRACY
TIP-TOP Bread

Fig. 23

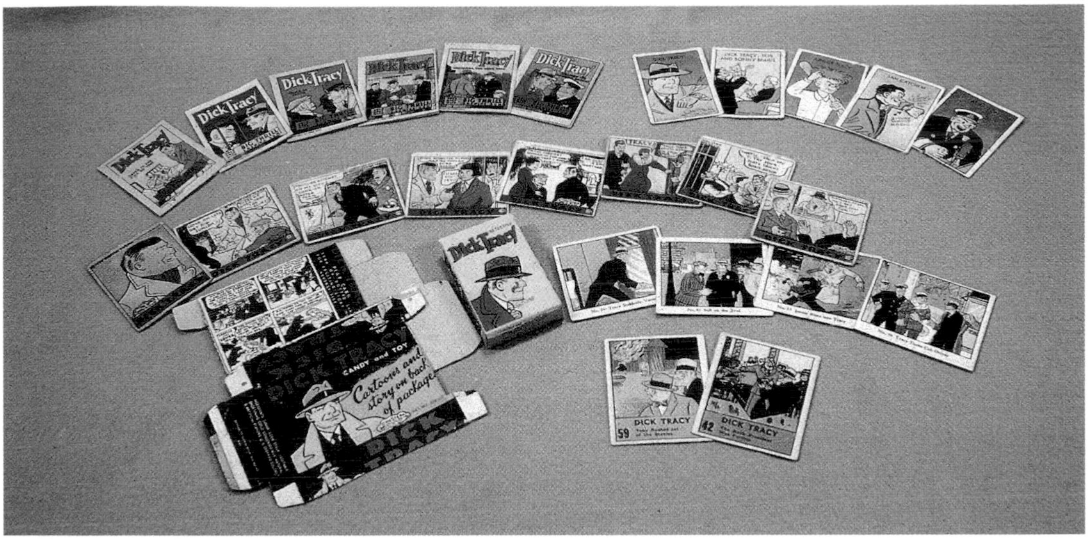
Dick Tracy
DICK TRACY
CANDY and TOY
Cartoons and story on back of package
DICK TRACY
59
42

Fig. 24

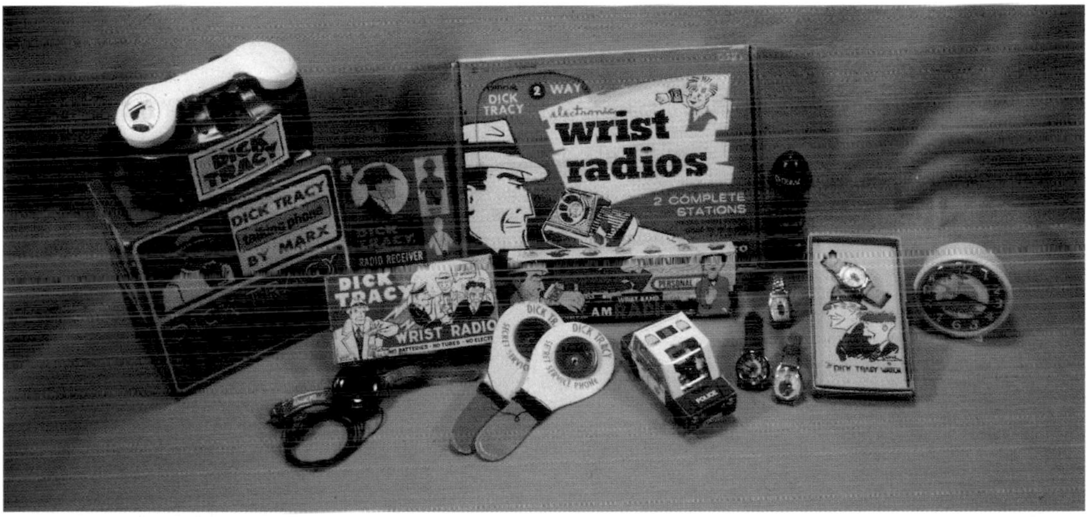
2 WAY
DICK TRACY
electronic
wrist radios
2 COMPLETE STATIONS
DICK TRACY
DICK TRACY
talking phone
BY MARX
RADIO RECEIVER
DICK TRACY
WRIST RADIO
AM

Fig. 25

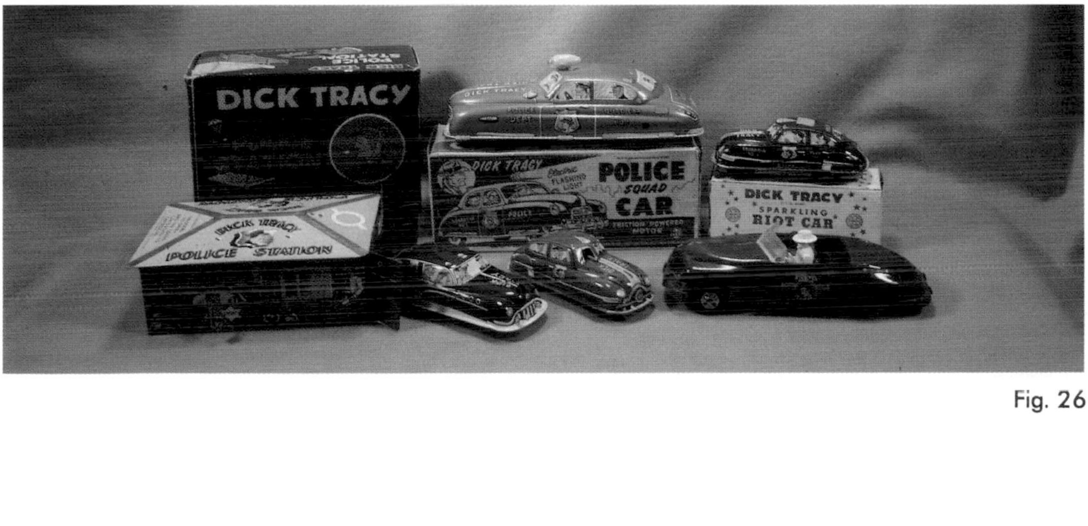
DICK TRACY
DICK TRACY
POLICE SQUAD CAR
DICK TRACY
SPARKLING
RIOT CAR
POLICE STATION

Fig. 26

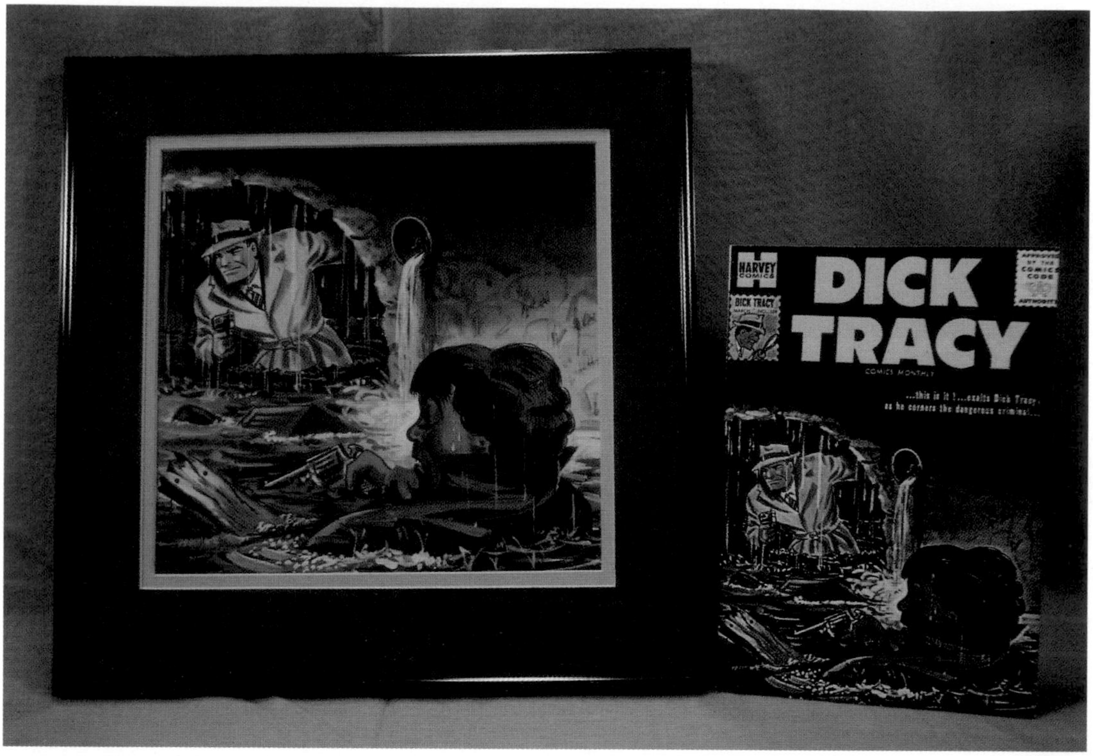
HARVEY COMICS
DICK TRACY
DICK TRACY

Fig. 27

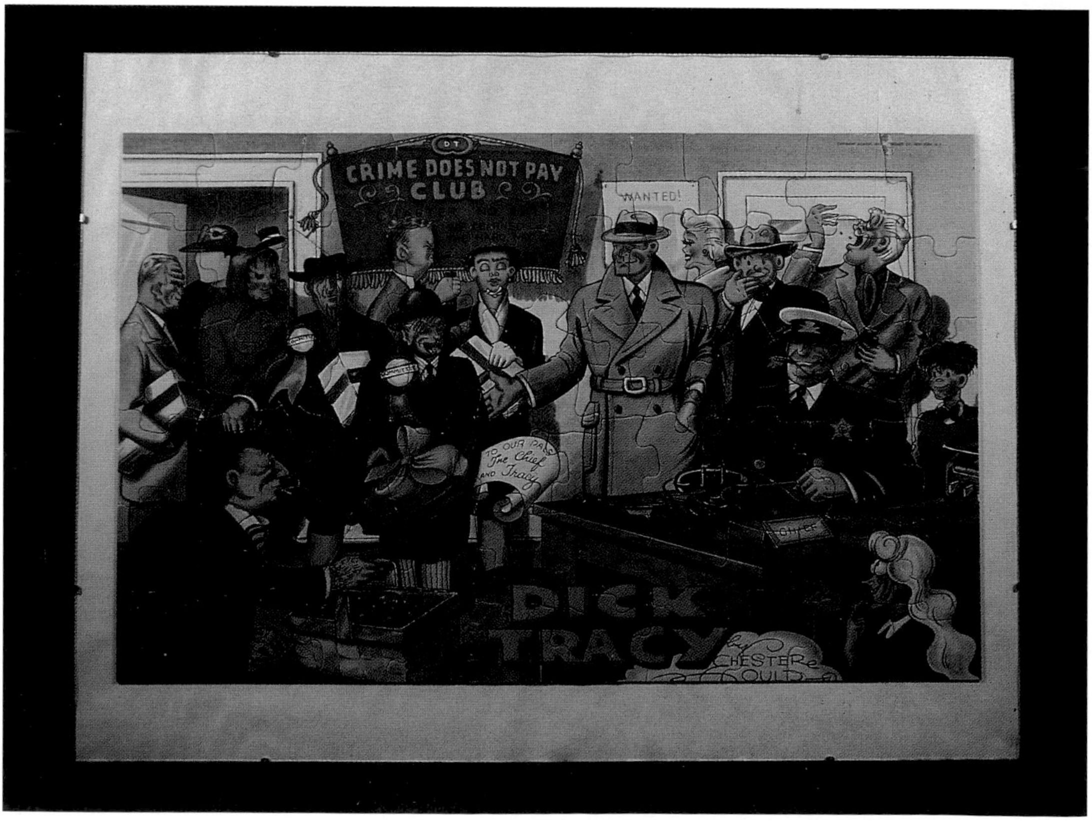
CRIME DOES NOT PAY
CLUB
WANTED!
TO OUR PALS The Chief AND Tracy
DICK TRACY
by CHESTER GOULD

Fig. 28

Fig. 3-130
Mercury Records issued this 10"-diameter "Sparkle Plenty Birthday Party" record in 1947.

dials. In 1951, New Haven issued an animated, or "rocking gun," Dick Tracy watch. This featured a gun in Tracy's hand, at the 6 o'clock position, which moved back and forth as a second hand. These watches, particularly in their original boxes, are prized collectibles.

In the late 1970s and early 1980s, Omni made digital Dick Tracy watches. One came packaged in a box shaped like a police car. The other came in a plastic, space coupe-shaped package. This watch featured an animated display of a space coupe landing on the moon while music played.

In 1947, Mercury made a double record set titled "Dick Tracy in the Case of the Midnight Marauder." The paper record jacket with this set had strips from the Flattop story for kids to color. Mercury also made a "Sparkle Plenty Birthday Party" record in 1947. Coca-Cola issued a "Dick Tracy Original Radio Broadcast" album in 1972 which played a show from the 1930s titled "The Case of the Firebug Murders." In February 1945, the Armed Forces Radio Service Command Performance broadcast a program titled "Dick Tracy in b Flat or For Goodness Sakes, Isn't He Ever Going

To Marry Tess Trueheart?" In this broadcast, Bing Crosby played Tracy, Bob Hope played Flattop, Frank Sinatra played Shaky, Judy Garland played Snowflake, Dinah Shore played Tess Trueheart, and Jimmy Durante played the Mole. Curtain Calls produced this broadcast on a $33\frac{1}{3}$ rpm album in the late 1960s.

In the early 1950s Seymour Sales Co. made a "Dick Tracy Candid Camera." This camera shot 127 film, had a 50mm lens, and came with a plastic case.

In the early 1950s, Camillus Cutlery Co. made "Dick Tracy Glow in the Dark Pocket Knives." Each knife had a $2\frac{1}{2}''$ blade, a crime-stopper whistle, a magnifying lens, and an attached plastic cord. There were four variations of this knife; Tracy and B.O. Plenty and Tracy and Junior. Both came in red or blue.

There have been many different Dick Tracy badges and pin-back buttons produced over the years. Some of these are very scarce and valuable.

At least four different sets of Dick Tracy Halloween costumes with masks and garbs were made. One mask from the late 1940s was made of cheese cloth, and another from

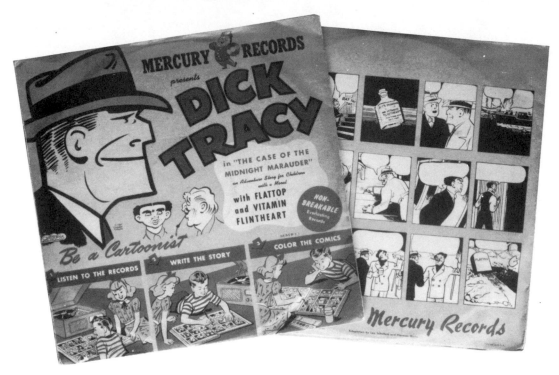

Fig. 3-131
This double record set by Mercury Records in 1947 was of the Flattop story. Children were instructed to listen to the record, write captions in the Tracy strips provided, and then color them.

the early 1950s was made of rubber. The rest were plastic, and one of them had a hinged, moveable lower jaw.

Other varied, interesting, and valuable Tracy collectibles include such items as:

- a "military set" hairbrush
- videocassettes of the Tracy movies, serials and cartoon shows
- audiocassettes of the Tracy radio show broadcasts
- a 1930s tie bar and belt buckle for the "Dick Tracy Jr. Detective Agency"
- plastic and metal charm figures of the heads of Tracy and other characters
- sterling silver rounds (embossed coins) of Dick Tracy
- colorful plastic disks of Tracy characters issued as bread premiums

- a beach towel picturing the Limited Collector Edition Dick Tracy comic book cover
- matchbooks, stickers and napkins from Ernie's Steak House picturing a Gould drawing of Tracy and Junior
- a Dick Tracy paper pop-gun premium from Tip-Top bread advertising the radio show in the 1940s
- a plastic Sparkle Plenty bib

The number and variety of Tracy collectibles are seemingly endless. It would take extraordinary luck, tons of money, and a full-time commitment to acquire a "complete" Tracy collection. However, it is highly unlikely that any Tracy collector will ever be able to amass one of *everything*.

Besides age and rarity, a major reason for the difficulty in finding many collectibles is that the character's popularity transcends many other collectible interests. Tracy purists are continually competing with collectors of cards, radio premiums, toys, cartoon characters, and the like. There are only so many items to go around. Tracy collectors tend to specialize and focus on a specific area of interest, such as original art, premiums or comics. Most are happy with what they have but always eager and thrilled to come upon a new ''find.'' Countless toys, play figures, games, shirts, books, watches, and other items produced in conjunction with the 1990 *Dick Tracy* movie are destined to become Tracy collectibles of the future.

Fig. 3-132
"Dick Tracy in b-Flat," an Armed Forces Radio production, recorded by Curtain Calls. This 1945 performance included Bing Crosby, Frank Sinatra and other outstanding stars.

Fig. 3-133
In 1972, Coca-Cola issued this "Dick Tracy Original Radio Broadcast" record album as a premium. It presents "The Case of the Firebug Murders" from the 1930s radio show.

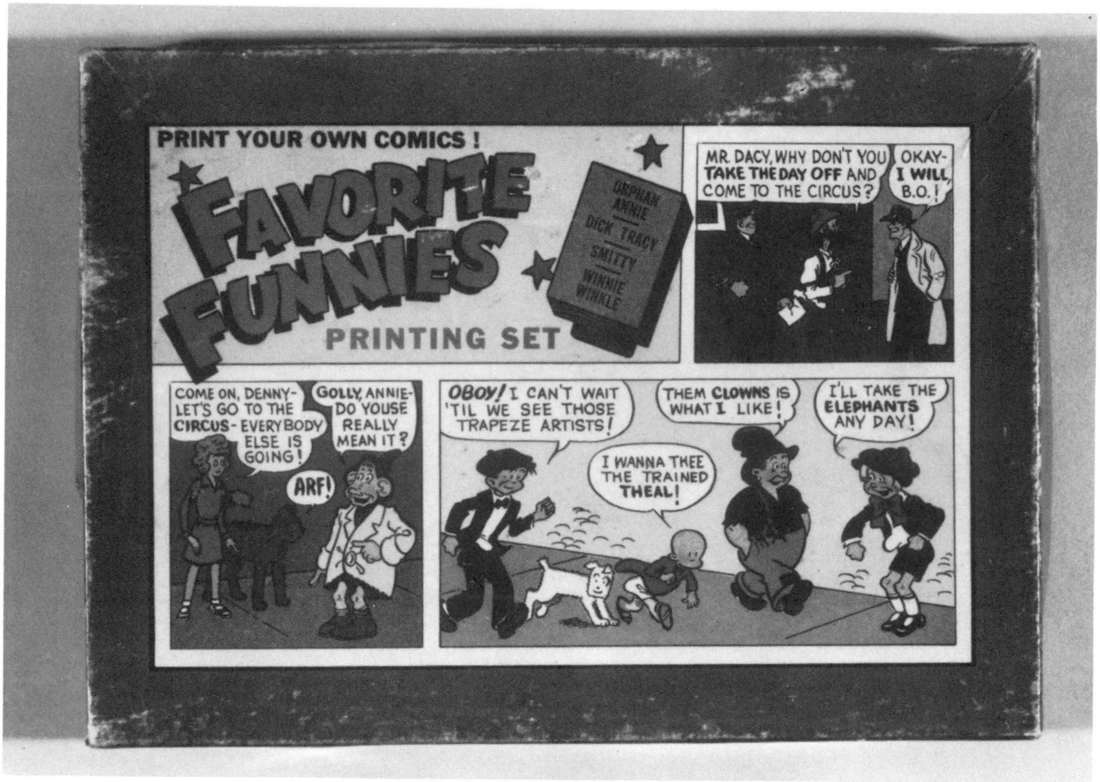
PRINT YOUR OWN COMICS!
FAVORITE FUNNIES
PRINTING SET
ORPHAN ANNIE
DICK TRACY
SMITTY
WINNIE WINKLE
MR. DACY, WHY DON'T YOU TAKE THE DAY OFF AND COME TO THE CIRCUS?
OKAY- I WILL, B.O.!
COME ON, DENNY- LET'S GO TO THE CIRCUS- EVERYBODY ELSE IS GOING!
GOLLY, ANNIE- DO YOUSE REALLY MEAN IT?
ARF!
OBOY! I CAN'T WAIT 'TIL WE SEE THOSE TRAPEZE ARTISTS!
I WANNA THEE THE TRAINED THEAL!
THEM CLOWNS IS WHAT I LIKE!
I'LL TAKE THE ELEPHANTS ANY DAY!

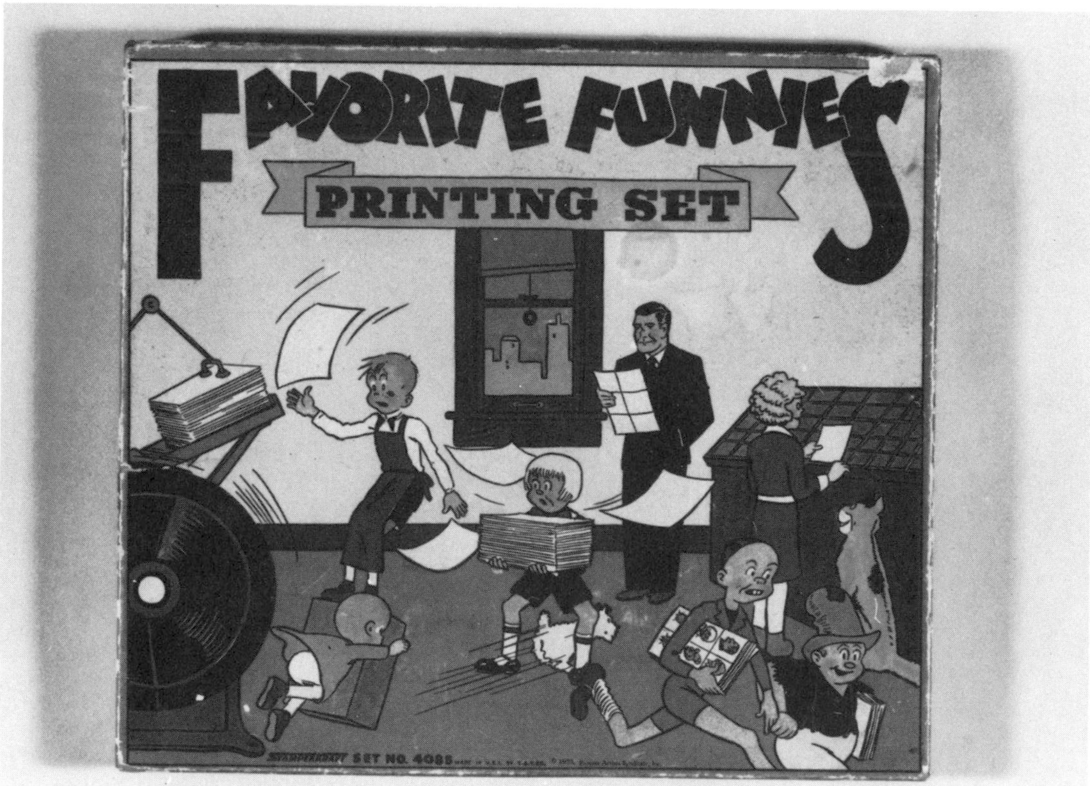
FAVORITE FUNNIES
PRINTING SET
SET NO. 4088

Fig. 3-134
Three different "Favorite Funnies Printing Sets" are shown. Opposite top: late 1940s set includes stamps of Tracy, B.O. Plenty, and Chief Brandon; opposite bottom: 1935 set includes stamps of Tracy, Junior, and Chief Brandon; this page top: 1941 set includes a stamp of Tracy.

Fig. 3-135
Camillus Cutlery Co. made the "Dick Tracy Glow in the Dark Pocket Knife" in the 1950s. This shows a rare, almost complete point-of-sale card. The four different knife variations are still attached. "98¢" price is marked. Any store cards such as this with product attached are rare.

Fig. 3-136

The "Dick Tracy Sparkle Paints" by Kenner came in two different boxed versions in 1963. Shown is the 8″ × 11″ × 1¾″ version with five glitter colors and six pictures to paint. Also available was an 11½″ × 16″ × 1¾″ version that combined the Dick Tracy characters with Mister Magoo.

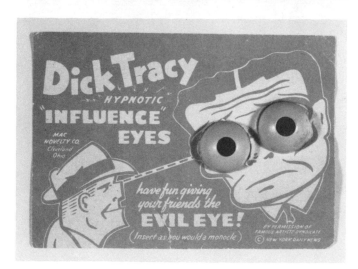

Fig. 3-137

"Dick Tracy Hypnotic 'Influence Eyes'" are from 1947 and mounted on a 7″ × 5″ card. MAC Novelty Co. hyped, "Have fun giving your friends the evil eye."

Fig. 3-138

This "Magnetic TV & Cartoon Pals" store display is vintage late 1960s or early 1970s. The character magnets ranged in size from 2" × 2" to 3" × 2½". 48 magnets were included on the front and back of the mounting board.

Fig. 3-139

This battery-operated "Dick Tracy Talking Phone" by Marx Toy Company is from 1967. The box measures 8½" × 8½" × 4½". The phone is green with an off-white handle. When activated it plays 10 different sayings, such as "Make your arrest now."

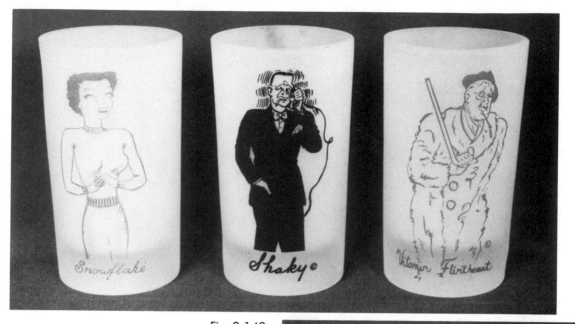

Fig. 3-140
Five characters are shown on these 5"-tall frosted glasses from the late 1940s.

Fig. 3-141
A two-gun Dick Tracy is the theme of this Domino's Pizza glass from the late 1970s. It's 6¼" tall.

Fig. 3-142
This Dick Tracy watch from the early 1930s also comes with a circular dial. It was made by New Haven Clock & Watch Co.

Fig. 3-143
This Dick Tracy watch was made by New Haven Clock & Watch Co. in 1951 and features an animated or "rocking" gun. It sold for $6.95 and the gun "shoots 120 times every minute" according to a magazine ad for the watch.

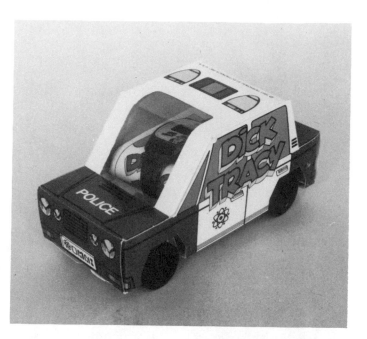

Fig. 3-144
A cardboard police car houses this Omni digital watch from 1981. The package measures 3″ × 5″ × 2¼″.

Fig. 3-145
New Haven Clock and Watch Company's Dick Tracy wrist watch (circa 1930), with its original box.

Fig. 3-146
This Omni watch from the late 1970s is packaged in a plastic Space Coupe with a mini-booklet with Dick Tracy illustrations. In the display, the Space Coupe lands on the moon and a U.S. flag appears while patriotic music plays. The packaging is 6" tall and 2" wide.

Fig. 3-147
A badge and a decal came with this Bonnie-Togs brand Dick Tracy T-shirt from the late 1940s.

Fig. 3-148
Enameled tie-clip, possibly handmade, an example of the type of unique Dick Tracy items that appear. The star design has on it, "at the 1933 fair."

Fig. 3-149
Matchbook from Ernie's Steak House picturing a Gould drawing of Tracy and Junior.

4 COLLECTING ORIGINAL ART

Irony has been an effective literary device in Dick Tracy throughout the years. However, you would not anticipate as much irony as there is in collecting original artwork depicting Dick Tracy.

From Gould to Warhol

The single most expensive Dick Tracy collectible is a piece of art that has little to do with Chester Gould or Tribune Media Services, the owner of Dick Tracy. It is an unlicensed and unauthorized painting of Dick Tracy by the late Pop artist Andy Warhol. Pop artists often felt comic strips were a mass market "lowly" art form and that it was their calling to raise them to fine art.

Warhol's fame as a painter will probably be outlived by his quote: "In the future everybody will be world famous for fifteen minutes." The irony is that while Warhol's Dick Tracy painting, now worth over $100,000, helped make him famous, Dick Tracy has been a super star of American popular culture for almost 60 years.

While fine art elitists wax eloquent on the two Warhol depictions of Dick Tracy, they are a mere novelty to the Dick Tracy collector. If anything, the Warhol artwork has expanded the field of collector interest.

Now, both art and twentieth-century American drawing collectors have a greater interest in Dick Tracy than any other comic strip. (Other strips that have a fine art cult following are Krazy Kat and Nancy.)

In fall 1978, Chester Gould's Dick Tracy artwork was the subject of a one-man show at the Museum of Cartoon Art, Rye Brook, N.Y. A handsome full-color poster is a prized and highly frameable collectible from that show. An oversized catalog printed on newsprint was also published for the show. The newsprint the catalog was printed on has not aged well and mint copies are difficult to find.

Then in 1981, in honor of the 50th Anniversary of Dick Tracy, Chester Gould had his first one-man show in a prestigious New York art gallery. *New York Times* art critic John Russell favorably reviewed the Gould show at Madison Avenue's Graham Gallery. The significance of a good review in

Fig. 4-1

A moon maiden gets a close-up of "earthman at work" as Chester Gould sketches his character Moon Maid at the RCA "Space Age" model TV studio during the annual National Association of Broadcasters convention. Besides his regular work on the strip, Gould did countless special sketches and drawings. This type of publicity photo is itself a collectible.

Fig. 4-2

This special art by Dick Locher with a background by Steve Spencer was published in full color on page one of the Sunday, March 11, 1990, issues of Gannett Westchester Newspapers. (Reprinted with permission of Gannett Westchester Newspapers.)

the *Times* cannot be underestimated. Interest was sparked in some fine art collectors that matched that of syndicated comic strip art collectors. Gould's artwork turned into gold.

Further interest in Chester Gould's originals was created by the extended press coverage of the theft of artwork from the Museum of Cartoon Art. The story began March 24, 1989, on page one of *The Advocate,* a daily newspaper in Stamford, Conn.: "Filched Funnies: Dick Tracy originals are gone!" The most complete account of events is "Chasing Purloined Panels: How the cartoon-theft case was cracked" by Kevin Gray of Gannett Westchester Newspapers published Sunday, March 11, 1990.

In January, 1989, I (Crouch) presented then newly appointed museum director Barbara Hammond with a list of stolen Dick Tracy pieces. Crouch knew which pieces Gould had given to the museum. He also knew that pieces being "shopped" around the country had to be the stolen items. He expressed his opinion that the theft was an inside job.

Although only 28 of some 6,000 pieces of Chester Gould artwork bequeathed to the museum by Gould had been stolen, they included some very important historical pieces from the 1940s with such villains as Flattop, The Brow, and Pruneface. Further investigation by Barbara Hammond revealed Prince Valiant originals by Hal Foster and some Disney animation cels were also missing.

The pressure was on. By March 3, 1989, it became too much for Sherman Krisher, a curator at the museum. He confessed that he had stolen the artwork. He also gave Hammond a written statement that was later used in court against him.

The artwork had been sold and in good faith resold; it had crisscrossed the country. Most of the Dick Tracy originals eventually landed in the hands of a Midwest art dealer. Unfortunately, he and the museum always seemed to be on different wave lengths. Rather than emerging as a hero, he became the target in a sting operation set up by Krisher's defense attorney. Aided by the New York City Police and the Westchester County (N.Y.) District Attorney's office, the operation recovered 44 pieces of art, including the truly important Dick Tracy pieces. The sting took place on October 3, 1989, in the Park Avenue offices of a prominent law firm three days before Krisher was sentenced on the charge of second-degree grand larceny after a guilty plea. The judge sentenced Krisher to 500 hours of community service, five years' probation and directed him to pay the museum $45,000 in restitution.

This case prompted a very interesting and lengthy "At the Bar" column in the October 20, 1989 *New York Times*. The subtitle of the column is "In Dick Tracy's latest caper, 'The Case of the Purloined Panels,' a law firm is embarrassed."

The importance of this theft is that it added to both the mystique and value of Gould's original art. Now the general public, educated by the national wire service stores, is aware of what knowledgeable collectors have been keeping to themselves.

Artist + Content = Value

While completists desire original drawings by Rick Fletcher and Dick Locher as well as Gould, the artwork by Dick Tracy's creator will always remain the most valuable. The next most valuable are pieces drawn by Rick Fletcher but signed "Gould, Fletcher, Collins." This is the creative team of which Gould was only symbolically a member after his December, 1977, retirement.

Rick Fletcher became Gould's assistant in 1961 and was associated with Dick Tracy for 22 years. Handpicked when Gould retired, Fletcher successfully brought verve and excitement to his drawings. While not maintaining Gould's exact style, Fletcher had a homemade notebook of what he called "Gouldisms" that guided him in his artwork.

Fig. 4-3

Angeltop, Flattop's daughter, is shown the actual size of the special drawing by Rick Fletcher for the TMS promotional folder advertising the first story by the creative team of Fletcher and Max Allan Collins. A revenge driven killer, Angeltop had three different stories with Tracy before her demise.

The value of original artwork by Dick Locher is keyed to specific historical events, such as the death of Angeltop or the 1986 origin of the 2-way wrist computer that Tracy now uses. Locher, the Pulitzer Prize-winning editorial cartoonist of *The Chicago Tribune*, worked as Gould's assistant from 1956–1961. He resumed working as the artist on Dick Tracy in March, 1983, after the sudden death of Rick Fletcher.

A beautiful and very exciting piece of Locher artwork is the original cover created

Fig. 4-4

Any original from the 1930s is valuable, but this more so because it is Dec. 4, 1931, the two-month anniversary of the strip. The confrontation between Tracy and sexy gunmoll Texie Garcia enhances the value.

Comic strips were wordier in the early days, when newspapers printed them much larger. Nazi spy The Brow works his evil magic on the doomed Summer sisters. This shows Gould's 1940s style.

The 2-way wrist radio in action, the "high tech" police office, the classic Tracy profile all contribute to the value of this 1950s piece.

for the mystery anthology *Dick Tracy: The Secret Files* published by Tor Books in 1990.

No true artist remains static. Even when drawing the same character, subtle changes in style will occur over time. Gould, for example, made an effort to keep Tracy in tune with the fashion of the day. He's shown

Tracy with everything from a crewcut to longish hair. Some collectors enjoy seeking out these different styles. ''The Aesthetics of Dick Tracy'' by Richard Marschall, a chapter in *Dick Tracy: America's Most Famous Detective*, (the official history of the comic strip) discusses Gould's artistic style

Fig. 4-5
Crop marks and the signature in the middle of the strip were decreed by the Tribune Syndicate's rule that the bottom of the strip be expendable so a newspaper could fit more on a page. Shown both ways to demonstrate the remarkable difference in appearance. This is of special interest to tearsheet collectors.

Fig. 4-6
Gould reduced the size of his original panels to 4" × 5". His art often has a touch of the bizarre. Here, a wife recognizes her kidnapped husband's false leg.

Fig. 4-7

The unknowledgeable dismiss the 1960s as all Gould's "space period." They thereby miss such historical gems as this recap of Junior's origins. Content makes this a valuable strip.

The magnetic Air Car and 2-way wrist TV appear together.

Some collectors seek out villains in original art. Piggy shows his sadistic side as he has his victim's beard shaved—not off, but in half. Gould also knew how to pepper sexiness into his art.

Fig. 4-8

Yes, Chester Gould did show bullets exiting heads. This excellent two-day example of raw, unglamorized violence also shows Mr. Bribery and his sister Ugly Christine. Collectors often try to build a set of originals in an attempt to get six in a row, Monday—Saturday. Finding a full week is rare. Sunday pages are also sought.

A year and a half before retirement at age 77, Gould's writing and art retain a remarkable verve. Art imitates life. Gould's own long and happy marriage is reflected in the playfulness between Tracy and Tess.

Fig. 4-9

This daily has it all: Tracy and Sam with a 2-way wrist TV, the villain Haf-and-Haf, and Lizz in peril. Done by Fletcher in the 1970s. The appearance of a 2-way wrist radio, TV or computer increase the value of an original.

Sam and Tracy tangle with Trendy Lee-Mobile, a murderess who used poison fingernails to scratch her victims to death. Tracy in action, capturing the evildoer, is a theme often sought in the original art. Both this strip and the Fletcher Haf-and-Haf are from stories reprinted in *Dick Tracy: America's Most Famous Detective*, the official history of the strip. Originals from stories reprinted are of special value.

Fig. 4-10

A promotion for Harvey Comics, pen and ink drawing, 10″ × 12″ and *not* by Gould, shows how handsome the Dick Tracy art looks when framed.

Fig. 4-11
A Dick Tracy animation cel from the 1960s pictures Tracy in a tuxedo with his 2-way wrist radio in action.

Fig. 4-12
A collection of Gould correspondence and special drawings show a couple from the early 1930s. Gould was always generous in responding to his fans.

at length. Marschall labels Gould not a realist but an expressionist. He was a master of mood using pen and ink.

In Maurice Horn's essay, "Death in the City," in the same volume, it is noted that hallmarks of Gould's drawing were heavy areas of solid black, a sharp nervous line, and strong contrast and contours.

While the age of a piece is important, nothing is more important in original Dick Tracy art than content. What is in the drawing? Is Tracy duking it out with a villain? Is he in a gun battle? How many main characters are in the drawing? Is there a 2-way wrist radio or TV in use?

Illustrating this chapter are originals in private collections from every decade. They show in orderly progression how Gould's style changed. As Gould was born in 1900, it is easy to note his age when he drew each comic strip. His art remained vibrant right up to his retirement at age 77.

Gould did have other artists assist him on backgrounds and such, a common practice among even fine artists. Gould also wrote Dick Tracy. He never purchased scripts from outside writers, as many cartoonists do. The fact that he worked this way enhances his originals. Dick Tracy was Chester Gould's life and it shows. By contrast, there have been cartoonists who have hired both full-time writers and artists to do *all* their work for them. Gould made occasional use of a photostat on an original. Cartooning is an art with a deadline, but, as a rule, a photostat will decrease the value of an original except if used as the logo on a Sunday page.

Besides the originals for daily and Sunday comic strips, Gould, Fletcher and Locher all have drawn special art. These include drawings for the annual Reuben booklet for the National Cartoonists Society awards banquet, as well as special drawings for fans. Advertising art and packaging design also fall into this category.

Though pieces of Dick Tracy artwork do find their way into formal art galleries, most are available through mail-order dealers or at the summer comicon conventions. The network for original cartoon art is not nearly as organized as that for fine art but it is less expensive when sold this way.

Cels from the animated 1960s version of Dick Tracy do appear occasionally. They are about the furthest thing in the world from a Chester Gould, Rick Fletcher or Dick Locher original, but they *do* have value as a Dick Tracy collectible. In recent years, animation art has been pulling top dollar at the New York City auction houses.

The best way to find out what art is available is to subscribe to the weekly tabloid, *The Comics Buyers Guide*.

5 TODAY'S NEW PRODUCTS— TOMORROW'S COLLECTIBLES?

If it were not for the 1990 Warren Beatty–Madonna *Dick Tracy*, you would not be reading this book—or any of the other new books, comic books, or magazines generated by the renewed interest in Dick Tracy sparked by the film. The June 8, 1983, *Los Angeles Times* headlined "Sparkles Aplenty if Beatty's on to Dick Tracy!" The article noted that Warren Beatty was considering the role of Dick Tracy in a joint venture between Paramount Pictures and Universal Pictures. It added that an October, 1983, production start date might have to be postponed because of negotiations with superstars.

Seven years later, *Dick Tracy,* produced by Warren Beatty and The Walt Disney Company, debuted June 15, 1990. The film and products are licensed by Disney under an agreement with Tribune Media Services which owns Dick Tracy. TMS retained the rights to do non-film-related books and has fully exercised this right.

The amazing diversity of new products in connection with the movie release will become clear, as we consider a few on the market at press time.

The toy line is powered by Playmates Toys with a full line of action figures, vehicles, magnets, a toy wrist radio watch, a Crimestopper kit, and an I.D. composite kit. Tara Toy is manufacturing a vinyl carrying case to hold the 12 action figures.

Another exciting new toy is Tiger Electronics' wrist game. It is the toy equivalent of Tracy's 2-way wrist computer, with the hottest technology of the new products.

The movie features a 2-way wrist radio—a traditional Tracy merchandise item. Ertl Toy Company of Iowa is producing a working "Official Dick Tracy 2-Way Wrist Radio" with three transistors and a 70-foot range. Wendy Gell of New York City is making a costume jewelry non-working wrist radio along with scarves and silk ties. The Tango Division of J. G. Hook is making non-silk neckties, along with a wide range of T-shirts, sportswear, and even Dick Tracy boxer shorts.

Over the years the package design of most Dick Tracy products has been outstanding. By keeping the basic colors of yellow, red, blue, and black, the new merchandise continues this tradition. The colors, the typography, and the emphasis on Tracy's yellow fedora mute the fact that Warren Beatty's nose is featured in the film's logo. The logo does work well: film Tracy and Gould's cartoon Tracy co-exist easily.

Returning to the wrist radio theme and excellent package design, the "Dick Tracy Crime Stoppers Grooming Set" has both.

Fig. 5-1
Ertl Toy Company's working 2-Way Wrist Radio continues the Tracy tradition. © Disney

Fig. 5-2
In the contemporary syndicated comic strip, Dick Tracy uses a 2-Way wrist computer. Mirroring this is the high-tech end of movie merchandise, the Dick Tracy electronic wrist game, complete with voice chip that speaks to the player. From Tiger Electronics. © Disney

Fig. 5-3
The Dick Tracy action figure by Playmates Toys, Inc., is a premier collectible for the future. Tracy stars in an entire line of figures, including vehicles based on cars in the film. © Disney (Photo by Eddie Verlangieri)

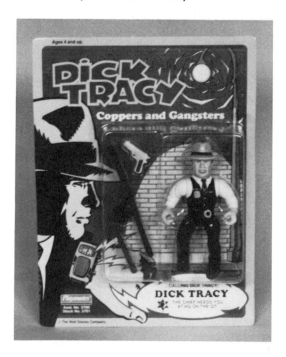

Fig. 5-4

The 2-Way wrist computer was introduced into Dick Tracy's high-tech crime fighting arsenal in June, 1986, by the creative team of writer Max Allan Collins and artist Dick Locher. Collins wrote the novelization of the movie for Bantam Books. It's written in classic hardboiled detective style.

The "Anti-Chap-Lip Radio Watch" has a top that screws off to reveal ointment. The set also contains a comb and a bottle of Dick Tracy after shave. Equally impressive is the "Breathless Cosmetic Glamour Set," also by Cosrich, Inc., of New Jersey. Red kisses against a background of yellow, and a sexy graphic of Madonna as Breathless Mahoney give the set of perfume, lip tints, and folding comb plenty of sizzle.

Lunch box collectors will be pleased with the bright red plastic Dick Tracy lunch box by Aladdin. The firm made a metal Dick Tracy lunch box in the 1960s. Both have fully decorated thermal bottles. The graphics on the new lunch box show Tracy holding a tommy gun and shouting, "I call the shots around here."

ZAK Designs of Los Angeles has been licensed to make pot holders, aprons, oven mitts, and a three-piece set of plastic dinnerware. Gibson Greetings of Cincinnati is producing seven greeting cards printed in five colors, along with foil stickers of the movie logo. Classico of San Francisco is licensed for postcards. They will have 24 images from the film in 4″ × 6″ format and 11 images in a giant 8″ × 10″ format (see color section).

There are too many cloisonné and phototech pins, keychains and magnets, to

mention. Besides posters of Dick Tracy in action poses, One Stop Posters of California is also making 1¾″ buttons in 12 different styles. One features the 2-way Wrist Radio. Others picture villains with their names, including Flattop, Pruneface, Rodent, and Littleface. The Breathless Mahoney button features Madonna in décolleté splendor.

Buttons are one of the oldest forms of Tracy collectibles. The May, 1932, issue of "News Pix" (the *New York Daily News* in-house newsletter), mentioned that a button given to school children with the image of Tracy and the word "Detective" printed on it had been a huge success within the first seven months of the comic strip's debut.

Although the action figures will have some firearms as miniature accessories, it is the policy of The Walt Disney Company not to license toy guns. The graphic image of Dick Tracy blasting away with either tommy gun or handgun is, however, being widely used by T-shirt and packaging designers.

Those collectors who seek toy guns will have to search for the rack toys made by Ja-Ru of Jacksonville, Florida. No longer a Dick Tracy licensee, the Ja-Ru product line was available for most of the 1980s. Don't be surprised if enterprising toy companies market generic toy pistols and tommy guns

Fig. 5-5
ZAK Designs of Los Angeles is making a full line of accessories, including apron and oven mitt. © Disney

Fig. 5-6
Four watches with either the movie logo or other characters on the face are offered by Timex. © Disney

Fig. 5-7
Dick Tracy bicycle from Rand International. © Disney

Fig. 5-8
This lithographed 3-gallon Dick Tracy tin filled with popcorn is made by Holiday Delights of Connecticut and is being marketed nationally in department stores. © Disney

Fig. 5-9
Springfield Instrument Company is making four different Dick Tracy wall clocks, an alarm clock, and a wall thermometer. This is the first Tracy thermometer. © Disney

under such headings as "police detective" gun sets to fill the void.

With so much new Dick Tracy merchandise appearing, a collector would have to mortgage the house to be a completist. Some collectors have chosen to buy the new versions of traditional Dick Tracy products so they can build their collections backward to the older items.

University Games is producing a board game where players join Dick Tracy in helping to capture "scum" such as Big Boy, Pruneface, Flattop, Shoulders, and the mysterious Blank. Its puzzle offering includes a 500-piece puzzle of Madonna as Breathless Mahoney and another of the whole motley crew of villains.

In 1934, the first Dick Tracy wristwatch was made by New Haven Watch Company of Connecticut and sold for $2.65. Now Timex, another Connecticut watch maker, is offering four character watches. Two are variations on the movie logo. A third stars contract killer Flattop brandishing a gun and

threatening, "Eat Lead." The fourth watch design shows Madonna as Breathless Mahoney vowing, "I always get my man."

Also licensed is a neon Dick Tracy wall clock by Worden. Springfield Instrument Co. is licensed for Dick Tracy quartz wall clocks, a table alarm clock and a 12" indoor/outdoor circular thermometer with the movie logo silhouette.

Don Post Studios of California is producing four full-head latex masks of Flattop, the Brow, Influence, and Pruneface. Ben Cooper will be making the children's costume sets for Halloween.

Colorforms, which did a Dick Tracy set in the 1960s, will introduce at least one Dick Tracy set in its 1990 line.

This is the electronic age and Hope Industries of New York City is making a handheld calculator with a bas-relief figural image of Dick Tracy. Hope will also make decorative sneaker snappers, belt biters and Dick Tracy shoe laces. If you don't know what sneaker snappers and belt biters are, you

Fig. 5-10
Dick Tracy T-shirts and nightshirts
abound. Shirt shown by Grandover.
© Disney

are showing your age. Sneaker snappers are three-dimensional plastic decorative accessories for hightop sneakers. A belt biter attaches to your belt and opens to give a small storage compartment.

Disney is an all-American brand name that the public associates with quality products and a fun time. The combination of the Disney organization, Warren Beatty, Madonna and a host of superstar cameo roles in the film is proving very attractive to manufacturers of everything from bubble bath to puffy stickers.

Are these all collectibles? You bet. Even the advertising circulars, company catalogs with Tracy products in them, and actual store displays are collectible.

So build an addition on the house and don't forget the Dick Tracy tricycles and bicycles by Rand International—or the plastic model kit of Tracy's vintage police car by Ertl—or the 3-gallon litho tin with Tracy cartoon strip designs filled with popcorn by Holiday Delights of Connecticut.

The time has never been better for a Dick Tracy fan to indulge in collectibles. New licensees are still being signed and Dick Tracy products should be readily available for quite some time.

Occasionally, a product on the licensed list doesn't make it to market. However, based on information from Disney, you may expect to also find backpacks, sunglasses, jackets, nightshirts, belts, buckles, suspenders, socks and hosiery, canvas shoes, children's underwear, umbrellas, vinyl wallets, beach and bath towels, and dolls, to mention just a few.

Oh yes, don't forget yellow fedoras and trench-coats.

APPENDIX

Books, Articles, and Videos

FEATURE BOOKS
David McKay Publications

Year	Issue No.	Title	Main Characters Featured
1937	nn (No Number)	*Dick Tracy the Detective*	Zora Arson, Boris Arson, Chief Yellowpony
Aug '37	4	*Dick Tracy the Detective*	Zora Arson, Boris Arson, Chief Yellowpony
Oct '37	6	*Dick Tracy the Detective*	Lips Manlis, Athnel Jones, Toyee, Mimi
Jan '38	9	*Dick Tracy & the Famon Boys*	"Cut" Famon, "Bail" Gordon, Maw Famon, Jim Trailer, Bowman Basil

LARGE FEATURE COMIC BOOKS
Dell Publishing Co.

Issue No.	Title	Main Characters Featured
1	*Dick Tracy Meets The Blank*	Johnny Mintworth, Supeena, The Blank
4	*Dick Tracy Gets His Man*	The Blank, Stud Bronzen, Johnny Ramm, Rottur
8	*Dick Tracy Racket Buster*	Johnny Ramm, Naona, Brighton Spotts, Jojo Nidle, Marro, Karpse
11	*Dick Tracy Foils Mad Doc Hump*	Doc Hump, Steve the Tramp, Larceny Lu, Mary Steele, Boris Arson
13	*Dick Tracy & Scottie of Scotland Yard*	Jean Penfield, Spaldoni, Larceny Lu, J. Scotland Bumpstead, Steve the Tramp
15	*Dick Tracy & the Kidnapped Princes*	Pop Gainer, Mitzi, Whip Chute, Nuremoh
3	—	Brighton Spots, Jojo Nidle, Marro, Karpse, Jim Trailer

Note: Issues 1, 4, 8, 11, 13 and 15 were published during 1938–39; issue 3 was published in 1941.

FOUR COLOR COMICS
Dell Publishing Co.

Issue No.	Date	Main Characters Featured
1	1939	Zora Arson, Boris Arson, Chief Yellowpony, Cutie Diamond
		"Cut" Famon, "Bail" Gordon, Maw Famon, Bowman Basil
6	1940	Johnny Mintworth, Supeena, Mrs. Mintworth, The Blank
8	1940	Karpse, Jim Trailer, Pop Gainer, Wolley, Mickey Gainer, Mitzi, Scardol
21	1941	Mayor Chiang, Pete Reppoc, Rottur, Stud Bronzen, Naona, Brighton Spotts
34	1943	John Lavir, Nat Natnus, Stooge Viller, Professor Emirc, Bonnie Viller, Kroywen
56	1944	Mary X, Rudy Seton, Mason, Junky Doolb, Jerome Trohs, Mamma
96	1946	Yogee Yamma, Roloc Bard, Black Pearl, Deafy Sweetfellow
133	1947	Krome, Kitty, Selbert DePool, Mrs. DePool
163	1947	Trigger Doom, Czar, Little Face Finney
215	1948	Sparkle Plenty, Mrs. Volts, Brier Volts

POPULAR COMICS
Dell Publishing Co.
(February 1936 to September 1948)

Issue No.	Main Characters
1–3	Boris Arson
4–7	Toby Townley
8	Toby Townley, "Cut" Famon
9–13	Famon Brothers
14–15	Athnel Jones
16–20	Lips Manlis
21	Lips Manlis, Purple Cross Gang
22–27	Purple Cross Gang

SUPER COMICS
Dell Publishing Co.
(May 1938 to December 1947)

Issue No.	Main Storyline	Issue	Main Storyline
1	Madeline Dell	71	Jerome, Mamma, Yogee Yamma
2	Madeline Dell, Johnny Mintworth	72–74	Yogee Yamma
3–14	Johnny Mintworth	75	Yogee Yamma, Black Pearl
15	Danny Supeena	76	Black Pearl
16–25	The Blank	77	Black Pearl, Deafy
26–32	Stud Bronzen	78,79	Deafy Sweetfellow
33	Stud Bronzen, Naona	80–83	Krome
34	Naona	84–87	Selbert DePool
35	Naona, Ramm	88	Selbert DePool, Ferret
36–40	Ramm	89	Ferret, Trigger Doom
41	Ramm, Jojo Nidle	90,91	Trigger Doom
42,43	Jojo Nidle	92	Little Face
44–47	Marro, Karpse	93	Little Face, Yenom
48–50	Pop Gainer	94	Yenom, Steve the Tramp, Duke
51	Pop Gainer, Scardol	95	Steve the Tramp, Duke
52	Scardol	96	Steve the Tramp, Duke, Mole
53–55	Whip Chute	97	Mole
56	Whip Chute, Nuremoh	98	Mole, Jacques
57	Nuremoh, John Lavir	99	Jacques
58	John Lavir, Natnus	100	Jacques, B-B Eyes
59	Natnus, Stooge Viller	101,102	B.B Eyes
60	Stooge Viller, Prof. Emirc	103	B.B Eyes, Van Dyke
61	Stooge & Bonnie Viller	104	Van Dyke
62	Stooge Viller	105	Van Dyke, Tiger Lilly
63	Stooge Viller, Kroywen	106–108	Tiger Lilly, Frizzletop
64	Kroywen	109	Frizzletop
65,66	Mary X	110,111	Frizzletop, Pruneface
67	Mary X, Jerome, Mamma	112,113	Emil, Mrs. Pruneface
68–70	Jerome, Mamma	114	Mrs. Pruneface, Laffy
		115	Laffy

MONTHLY COMICS
Dell Publishing Co.

Issue No.	Date	Main Characters Featured
1	1/48	Doc Hump, Larceny Lu, Mary Steele, Steve the Tramp in *Dick Tracy and The Mad Doctor*
2	2/48	Boris Arson, Mary Steele
3	3/48	Jimmy White, Spaldoni, Jean Penfield, Big Boy
4	4/48	Jimmy White, Jean Penfield, Alderman Zeld
5	5/48	Jean Penfield, Spaldoni, Mrs. Spaldoni
6	6/48	Mrs. Trueheart, Mrs. Spaldoni, J. Scotland Bumpstead, Steve the Tramp, Larceny Lu, Doc Hump
7	7/48	Boris Arson, Mary Steele
8	8/48	Zora Arson, Boris Arson, Mary Steele
9	9/48	Zora Arson, Boris Arson, Chief Yellowpony
10	10/48	Boris Arson, Zora Arson, Chief Yellowpony, Cutie Diamond, Mary Steele
11	11/48	Toby Townley, Mary Steele, Mark Masters, Bookie Joe, Blake
12	12/48	Bookie Joe, Blake, Toby Townley
13	1/49	Toby Townley, Blake
14	2/49	Mary Steele, Mayor Waite Wright
15	3/49	"Cut" Famon, "Muscle" Famon, "Bail" Gordon, Bowman Basil
16	4/49	Maw Famon, "Muscle" Famon, "Cut" Famon, Jim Trailer
17	5/49	"Cut" Famon, Jim Trailer, Mary Steele, Toby Townley
18	6/49	Mary Steele, Lips Manlis, Jim Trailer, Athnel Jones
19*	7/49	Barker, Muggsie, Mumps in *Golden Heart Mystery*
20*	8/49	Sherry, Snow, Joe, Bertha in *Black Cat Mystery*
21*	9/49	Number One, Scotty in *Dick Tracy Meets Number One*
22*	10/49	Apples Malone, Joe Grenza in *Dick Tracy & the Alibi Maker*
23*	11/49	Loris Low, Jukebox Wilson in *Dick Tracy Meets Jukebox*
24*	12/49	Bubbles, Mrs. Richards in *Dick Tracy and Bubbles*

*Not by Gould

Harvey Publications

Issue No.	Date	Main Characters Featured
25	3/50	Flattop
26	4/50	Flattop, Vitamin Flintheart
27	5/50	Flattop, Vitamin Flintheart, Summer Sisters in *Flattop Escapes Prison*
28	6/50	Vitamin Flintheart, Summer Sisters, Brow in *Case of the Torture Chamber*
29	7/50	Brow, Summer Sisters, Gravel Gertie
30	8/50	Brow, Gravel Gertie, Snowflake Falls, Shaky in *Blackmail Racket*
31	9/50	Shaky, Snowflake Falls, Vitamin Flintheart
32	10/50	Shaky, Snowflake Falls, Vitamin Flintheart, Anna Enog, Gravel Gertie
33	11/50	Anna Enog, Measles, Paprika in *Strange Case of Measles*
34	12/50	Measles, Paprika, Snowflake, Vitamin Flintheart
35	1/51	Measles, Breathless Mahoney, Mrs. Mahoney in *Case of Stolen $50,000*
36	2/51	Breathless Mahoney, Wetwash Wally, B.O. Plenty in *Case of Runaway Blonde*
37	3/51	Breathless Mahoney, Mrs. Mahoney, B.O. Plenty, Itchy in *Case of Stolen Money*
38	4/51	Breathless Mahoney, Mrs. Mahoney, B.O. Plenty, Itchy
39	5/51	Itchy, Kitty (Mrs. B.B. Eyes), B.O. Plenty, Diet Smith
40	6/51	Diet Smith, B.O. Plenty, Irma, Brilliant in *Case of Atomic Killer*
41	7/51	Diet Smith, Brilliant, Rod & Nilon Hoze in *Murder by Mail*
42	8/51	Rod & Nilon Hoze, Themesong, Roach, Shoulders, Honey Doll in *Murder by Mail*
43	9/51	Honey Doll, Shoulders, Themesong, Christmas Early, Gargles in *Case of Underworld Brat, Case of Antiseptic Murderer*
44	10/51	Gargles, Themesong, Christmas Early in *Case of Mouthwash Murderer*
45	11/51	Christmas Early, Influence, Themesong, Vitamin Flintheart, in *Case of Evil Eyes*
46	12/51	Influence, Vitamin Flintheart, Misty Waters, Hypo, Dahlia Dell in *Case of Evil Eyes, Case of the Camera Killers*
47	1/52	Autumn Hews, Coffyhead, Lugi in *Case of Bloodthirsty Blonde*
48	2/52	Autumn Hews, Coffyhead, Lugi, Mumbles, Kiss Andtel in *Case of Bloodthirsty Blonde, Case of Murderous Minstrel*
49	3/52	Mumbles, Kiss Andtel, Shoulders in *Case of Murderous Minstrel, Killer Who Returned From the Dead*
50	4/52	Shoulders, Fence Beardsly, Miss Varnish in *Killer Who Returned From the Dead*
51	5/52	Mrs. Volts in *Case of High Tension Hijackers*
52	6/52	Mrs. Volts, Brier, Diet Smith, Acres O'Riley in *Case of the Pipe-Stem Killer*

Issue No.	Date	Main Characters Featured
53	7/52	Brier, Acres O'Riley, Diet Smith, Heels Beals in *Case of the Pipe-Stem Killer, Dick Tracy Meets the Murderous Midget*
54	8/52	Acres O'Riley, Heels Beals in *Case of the Murderous Midget*
55	9/52	Heels Beals, Acres O'Riley, Brilliant, Big Frost, Flossie in *Case of the Murderous Midget, Case of the Teleguard Terror*
56	10/52	Brilliant, Big Frost, Flossie in *Case of the Teleguard Terror*
57	11/52	Big Frost, Flossie, Auntie, Sam Catchem, Sleet in *Case of the Ice Cold Killer*
58	12/52	Sam Catchem, Sleet, Auntie, Twist in *Case of the Ice Cold Killer*
59	1/53	Sleet, Pear Shape, Mugg in *Case of the Million Dollar Murder*
60	2/53	Pear Shape, Mugg, Pedro in *Case of the Million Dollar Murder*
61	3/53	Talcum Freely, "Sketch" Paree, Spike Dyke in *Case of the Murder's Mask*
62	4/53	"Sketch" Paree, Spike Dyke, Mousey, Papa Rattner in *Case of the Murder's Mask, Case of the White Rat Robbers*
63	5/53	Mousey, Papa Rattner in *Case of the White Rat Robbers*
64	6/53	Wormy in *Case of the Interrupted Honeymoon*
65	7/53	Wormy, Ted Tellum in *Case of the Interrupted Honeymoon*
66	8/53	Blowtop, Toots, Vitamin Flintheart in *Case of the Killer's Revenge*
67	9/53	Blowtop, Vitamin Flintheart in *Case of the Killer's Revenge*
68	10/53	Blowtop, Vitamin Flintheart, Ted Tellum, T.V. Wiggles in *Case of the Killer's Revenge, Case of the TV Terror*
69	11/53	T.V. Wiggles, Vitamin Flintheart, Bubbles Anvil in *Case of the TV Terror*
70	12/53	T.V. Wiggles in *Case of the TV Terror*
71	1/54	Doctor Plain, Mrs. Forchune, Opal
72	2/54	Empty Williams, Bonny
73	3/54	Bonnie, Empty Williams, Bonny Braids
74	4/54	Bonny Braids, Crewy Lou, Sphinx, Mr. & Mrs. Fortson Knox
75	5/54	Carol Knox, King, Crewy Lou, Sphinx
76	6/54	King, Crewy Lou, Brainerd, Bonny Braids, Diet Smith
77	7/54	Crewy Lou, Bonny Braids
78	8/54	Spinner Record
79	9/54	Model Jones, Larry Jones
80	10/54	Model Jones, Larry Jones, Tonsils, Dot View
81	11/54	Tonsils, Dot View, Edward Moppet
82	12/54	Dot View, Mr. Crime, Tonsils
83	1/55	Tonsils, Mr. Crime, Rifle Ruby, Newsuit Nan
84	2/55	Mr. Crime, Newsuit Nan
85	3/55	Newsuit Nan, Mr. Crime (Mr. Alpha), Mrs. Lava

Issue No.	Date	Main Characters Featured
86	4/55	Mr. Crime, Odds Zonn
87	5/55	Odds Zonn, Wingy
88	6/55	Odds Zonn, Wingy
89	7/55	Odds Zonn, Wingy, 3-D Magee, Pony, Uncle "Canhead"
90	8/55	3-D Magee, Pony, Uncle "Canhead"
91	9/55	3-D Magee, Pony, Uncle "Canhead"
92	10/55	3-D Magee, Pony, Uncle "Canhead"
93	11/55	3-D Magee, Pony, Uncle "Canhead"
94	12/55	3-D Magee, Pony, Uncle "Canhead," Mrs Green
95	1/56	Mrs. Green, Dewdrop, Sticks
96	2/56	Mrs. Green, Dewdrop, Sticks
97	3/56	Mrs. Green, Dewdrop, Sticks
98	4/56	Dewdrop, Sticks, Open-Mind Monty
99	5/56	Dewdrop, Sticks, Open-Mind Monty
100	6/56	Dewdrop, Sticks, Open-Mind Monty, Half-Pint
101	7/56	Open-Mind Monty, Dewdrop, Half-Pint
102	8/56	Rainbow Reiley, Wingy, Sparkle
103	9/56	Happy, Rughead, Rainbow Reiley
104	10/56	Rughead, Rainbow Reiley, John Medic, Happy
105	11/56	Happy, Rughead, John Medic, Rainbow Reiley
106	12/56	Happy, Rughead, Fence, Corny
107	1/57	Happy, Rughead, Corny, Fence, Rainbow Reiley
108	2/57	Happy, Rughead, Corny, Fence
109	3/57	Rughead, Mimi, Herky
110	4/57	Flattop, Vitamin Flintheart
111	5/57	Shoulders, Themesong, Roach, Honey Doll
112	6/57	Brilliant, Diet Smith, Miss Irma
113	7/57	Shaky, Snowflake Falls, Vitamin Flintheart
114	8/57	"Sketch" Paree, Spike Dyke
115	9/57	Rod & Nilon Hoze, Uncle Mortimer
116	10/57	Empty Williams, Bonny Braids
117	11/57	Spinner Record
118	12/57	Sleet
119	1/58	Coffyhead, Autumn Hews, Lugi
120	2/58	Mumbles, Kiss Andtel in *Case Against Mumbles Quartette*
121	3/58	Wild Boys, Mumbles, George Ozone in *Case of Wild Boys*
122	4/58	Wild Boys, Mumbles, George Ozone, Cinn in *Case of Poisoned Pellet*
123	5/58	Wild Boys, Mumbles, Cinn in *Case of Deadly Treasure Hunt*

Issue No.	Date	Main Characters Featured
124	6/58	Oodles, Mrs. Vulcan in *Case of Oodles Hears Only Evil*
125	7/58	Oodles, Mrs. Vulcan, "Nothing" Yonson in *Case of Desparate Widow*
126	8/58	Oodles, "Nothing" Yonson, Lizz in *Case of Oodles' Hideout*
127	9/58	Joe Period, Mr. Pocketclip, Julie Marrlin in *Case Against Joe Period*
128	10/58	Joe Period, "Nothing" Yonson, Lizz in *Case Against Juvenile Deliquent*
129	12/58	Joe Period, Flattop Jr. in *Case of Son of Flattop*
130	1/59	Joe period, Flattop Jr., "Nothing" Yonson, Skinny in *Case of Great Gang Roundup*
131	2/59	Flattop Jr., Skinny in *Strange Case of Flattop's Conscience*
132	3/59	Flattop Jr. in *Case of Flattop's Big Show*
133	4/59	Pops, Wooley in *Dick Tracy Follows Trail of Jewel Thief Gang*
134	6/59	Pops, Wooley, Mitzi in *Last Stand of Jewel Thieves*
135	8/59	Pops, Mitzi, "Whip" Chute in *Case of Rooftop Sniper*
136	10/59	Mitzi, "Whip" Chute, Lily in *Mystery of Iron Room*
137	12/59	Mr. Kroywen, Toby Townley in *Law versus Dick Tracy*
138	2/60	Mary X, Mr. Mason, "Junky" Doolb in *Mystery of Mary X*
139	4/60	Yogee Yamma, Roloc Bard in *Yogee the Merciless*
140	6/60	Yogee Yamma, Roloc Bard in *The Tunnel Trap*
141	8/60	Wormy, Tedd Tellum in *Case of Wormy and His Deadly Wagon*
142	10/60	Blowtop, Vitamin Flintheart in *Case of Killer's Revenge*
143	12/60	Measles, Snowflake, Paprika in *Strange Case of Measles*
144	2/61	Shoulders, Brilliant, Big Frost, Flossie in *Strange Case of Shoulders, Stolen Fortune*
145	4/61	Crewy Lou, Sphinx, King, Bonny Braids, Misty Waters, Hypo, Dahlia in *Case of Fiendish Photographers, Case of Camera Killers*

MISCELLANEOUS COMICS

Date	Title	Main Characters
1933	*Dick Tracy & Dick Tracy, Jr. & How They Captured Stooge Viller* (Cupples & Leon, Inc. reprint with hardcover that's not a true comic book)	Stooge Viller, Kenneth Grebb, Broadway Bates
1933	*Dick Tracy & Dick Tracy, Jr. Caught the Racketeers* (Cupples & Leon, Inc. reprint with hardcover in same format as above)	Stooge Viller, Steve the Tramp, Boss Herrod, Big Boy
1946	*The Exploits of Dick Tracy,* "The Case of the Brow" (Rosdon Books, Inc. reprint that's in hardcover)	The Brow
1938	Famous Feature Stories, #1	Toby, Jim Trailer, Ma Moline
1952	Harvey Comics Library, #2 "Blackmail Terror"	T.V. Wiggles, Vitamin Flintheart, Sparkle Plenty
1974	Feature Showcase (published by Alan Light, Funnies Publishing Co.)	Mary Steele, Toby, Bookie Joe, Boris & Zora Arson, Famon Brothers, Lips Manlis
1975	Limited Collectors' Edition, #C-40	Flattop

PAPERBACK REPRINTS

Not true comic book format

Dragon Lady Press

The Best of the Tribune Co., No. 2, October 1985
Dick Tracy Meets Splitscreen by Collins and Fletcher: Splitscreen and Auntie Freedom
Land of Plenty by Collins and Locher: Goodin Plenty, Dye and Oxen Cixot
Quarterly Edition #1, August 1986
50th Anniversary of Dick Tracy by Collins and Fletcher: Angeltop and The Brow's son
Quarterly Edition #2, February 1987
Who Shot Pat Patton? by Collins and Fletcher: Chief Climer and Astral Turf
Quarterly Edition #3, August 1987
The Ghost of Itchy by Collins and Fletcher: Twitchy Oliver
Thrilling Adventure Strips #6, October 1986
Dick Tracy Meets Big Brother by Collins and Locher: Murky, Big Brother, Bugsy
Thrilling Adventure Strips #10, April 1987

The Russian Exchange by Collins and Locher: Frank Diamond

Ken Pierce, Inc

Distributed by Eclipse Comics (U.S. Classics Series)
Tracy's Wartime Memories by Collins and Locher: Flattop, Shaky, Pruneface, and Mrs. Pruneface

Tony Raiola, Pacific Comics Club (1982–1983)

Full-size, virtually identical reprints of Feature Comic Books #4, #6, #9 and Large Feature Comics #1, #3, #4, #8, #11, #13, #15
Dailies and Sundays from March 12–July 13, 1940: Mary X, Jerome Trohs and Mamma
Dailies and Sundays from July 14–October 20, 1940: Yogee Yamma and the Black Pearl

Blackthorne Publishing

Comic Strip Preserves, 1986

Dick Tracy in 3-D—Ocean Deathtrap: The Dropper, Miss Egghead, Chicory, Wunbrow
Dick Tracy Monthly Series (#1–#25, May 1986–December 1987)

1:	Mary X
2:	Jerome Trohs and Mamma
3:	Yogee Yamma
4:	Black Pearl
5:	Deafy Sweetfellow
6:	Krome
7–8:	Selbert Depool
9:	Trigger Doom
10–11:	Pear Shape
12:	Sketch Paree and Spike Dyke
13:	Mousey
14:	Mousey and the Tracy/Tess marriage
15:	Wormy
16–17:	Blowtop
18:	Sparkle Plenty and T.V. Wiggles
19–20:	T.V. Wiggles
21:	Dr. Plain
22:	Empty Williams
23:	Empty Williams and Bonny Braids' birth
24:	Crewy Lou and Sphinx
25:	Crewy Lou

Dick Tracy Weekly Series (#26–#99, January 1988–September 1989)

No. 26	Crewy Lou
27	Spinner Record
28	Junior, Model & Larry Jones
29	Tonsils
30–31	Mr. Crime, Tonsils
32	Newsuit Nan, Mr. Crime
33	Miss Lava, Mr. Crime
34	Odds Zonn
35	Odds Zonn, Wingy
36	Odds Zonn
37–39	Uncle Canhead, 3-D Magee, Pony
40	Dewdrop, Sticks
41	Dewdrop, Open-Mind Monty
42	Open-Mind Monty, Half-Pint
43	Rainbow Reiley
44	Rainbow Reiley, Rughead
45–46	Rughead
47	Wild Boys, Mumbles, George Ozone
48	Mumbles, Cinn
49	Mumbles
50	Oodles
51	Oodles, Lizz
52–53	Kitten Sisters
No. 54	Morin and Blossom Plenty
55	The Clipso Brothers
56–57	Elsa
58–59	Pantsy
60–61	Miss Egghead
62	Miss Egghead, The Dropper
63	Miss Egghead, The Dropper, Chicory
64	Popsie, Mamma
65	Popsie, Headache
66	E. Kent Hardly
67	Rhodent
68	Rhodent, Fatty
69	Willie the Fifth
70–71	Willie the Fifth, Fly Face
72	Haku, Manno, Pala
73	Haku, Fly Face, Willie the Fifth
74	Spots
75	Little Pineapple
76–78	Little Boy Beard
78–79	Little Boy Beard, Aunt SoSo
80–81	Little Boy Beard, Happy Votem
No. 82	Spready, Mona
83	Mary Steele
84	Mr. Pardy
85–86	The Brush
87–88	Auntie
89	Spacecoupe
90	The 52 Gang
91–92	Thistle Dew

93	Thistle Dew, The Raven, Uncle Punky
94–95	Droppy, Pallette Twins
96	Smallmouth Bass
97–99	Moonmaid (#99 last vol. in series)

Blackthorne Publishing
Reuben Award Winner Series, 1984–1989

No. 1	1984	Irma, Brilliant, Diet Smith, B.O. Plenty, Nilon & Rod Hoze
2	1985	Christmas Early, Gargles
3	1985	Coffyhead, Autumn Hews, Lugi
4	1985	Crimestoppers, Bronk, Sparkle Plenty's birth
5	1985	Themesong, Vitamin Flintheart, Influence, Hypo
6	1986	Mumbles, Kiss Andtel
7	1986	Shoulders, Miss Varnish
8	1986	Mrs. Volts, Brier Volts
No. 9	1986	Brier, Acres O'Riley, Heels Beals
10	1986	Brier, Acres O'Riley, Heels Beals, Brilliant, Big Frost
11	1987	Big Frost, Flossie, Sam Catchem, Sleet
12	1987	Sleet
13	1987	Little Face
14	1987	The Mole
15	1987	Jacques, B-B Eyes
16	1987	B-B Eyes, Van Dyke
17–18	1987	Frizzletop, Tiger Lilly
19	1987	Pruneface
20	1988	Pruneface, Nifty
21	1988	Keyes
22	1988	Keyes, Mrs. Pruneface
23	1988	Mrs. Pruneface, Laffy
24	1989	Flattop

PREMIUMS

Comics given away to promote a product

Date	Sponsor	Title	Main Characters
1939	Weather-Bird Shoes	—	Johnney Lavir, Nat Natnus
1939	Buster Brown Shoes	—	Marro, Karpse
1939	Sears	"Merry Christmas from Sears Toyland"	No stories but games and puzzles
1940	Tip-Top Bread	*Family Fun Book*	No stories but games and puzzles
1943	Pan-Am/Gilmore Oil	*Super Book of Comics*	Brighton Spotts, Jojo Nidle
1943	Sears	"Santa's Christmas Comic Variety Show"	No stories but games and puzzles
1944	Omar Bread	*Super Book of Comics, #1*	Brighton Spotts, Junior
1945	Omar Bread	*Super Book of Comics, #13*	Jerome Trohs, Mamma
1946	Omar Bread	*Super Book of Comics, #25*	Jerome Trohs, Mamma, Yogee Yamma
1947	Popped Wheat Cereal	—	Junky Doolb, Jerome Trohs, Mamma
1949	Ray-O-Vac Flashlight	"Dick Tracy Sheds Light on the Mole"	The Mole (not by Gould)
1950–52	Miller Brothers Hats	"Dick Tracy's Hatfull of Fun"	No stories but games and puzzles
1953	Motorola	"Case of the Sparkle Plenty T.V. Mystery"	T.V. Wiggles, Vitamin Flintheart, Sparkle Plenty
1957	Tastee-Freez Ice Cream	No. 6	Pear Shape, Mugg, Pedro Zelene
1958	Esso Service Station	"The Case of the Purloined Sirloin"	Four Square Feeney, Beef (not by Gould)

DICK TRACY FIGHTS
THE MUMBLES QUARTET

Fig. A-1

The cover of Gladstone's Comic Album Series #1 was designed by the series editor Matt Masterson.

COMIC BOOKS LICENSED IN 1990

Gladstone Publishing, Ltd., Box 2079, Prescott, AZ 86302, has been licensed by Tribune Media Services to publish both a bi-monthly comic book and periodic comic graphic albums. A graphic album is a fancy comic book on good stock and is often thick enough to require a binding similar to a trade paperback. This is expected to be a continuing series.

Comic Books	Title
The Original Dick Tracy by Chester Gould, #1	"Dick Tracy versus Mrs. Pruneface"
The Original Dick Tracy by Chester Gould, #2	"Dick Tracy and the Evil Influence"
The Original Dick Tracy by Chester Gould, #3	"Dick Tracy Gets Shaky"
Gladstone Comic Album Series, #1 The Original Dick Tracy by Chester Gould	"Dick Tracy Fights the Mumbles Quartet"

DISNEY GRAPHIC NOVELS

WD Publications, a subsidiary of The Walt Disney Company, has published three graphic novels related to the Warren Beatty/Madonna movie.
Dick Tracy: Big City Blues (#1)
Dick Tracy vs. the Underworld (#2)
Dick Tracy (#3)

BIG LITTLE BOOKS
Whitman Publishing Company, 1932–1967.

Date	Number	Title	Author
1932	GW2	*The Adventures of Dick Tracy, Detective* (First Big Little Book published.)	Chester Gould
1933	GW4	*Dick Tracy and Dick Tracy Junior*	Chester Gould
1933	GW29a	*Dick Tracy from Colorado to Nova Scotia*	Chester Gould
1934	GW59	*Dick Tracy and the Stolen Bonds*	Chester Gould
1934	GW78a	*Dick Tracy Solves the Penfield Mystery*	Chester Gould
1935	GW101	*Dick Tracy and the Boris Arson Gang*	Chester Gould
1935	GW107	*Dick Tracy on the Trail of Larceny Lu*	Chester Gould
1936	GW122	*Dick Tracy in Chains of Crime*	Chester Gould
1936	GW145	*Dick Tracy and the Racketeer Gang*	Chester Gould
1937	GW201	*Dick Tracy and the Hotel Murders*	Chester Gould
1937	GW224	*Dick Tracy and the Spider Gang*	Adaptation of first Dick Tracy movie
1938	GW253a	*Dick Tracy and the Man With No Face*	Chester Gould
1939	SW17	*Dick Tracy on the High Seas*	Chester Gould
1939	SW38	*Dick Tracy Returns*	Adaptation of second Dick Tracy movie
1939	SWp88	*Dick Tracy and the Invisible Man**	Adaptation of radio script
1939	SWp89	*Dick Tracy's Ghost Ship**	Adaptation of radio script
1940	SW70	*Dick Tracy and the Phantom Ship*	Adaptation of radio script
1941	SW74	*Dick Tracy and His G-Men*	Adaptation of third Dick Tracy movie
1941	SW105	*Dick Tracy The Super Detective*	Chester Gould
1942	SW154	*Dick Tracy Special F.B.I. Operative*	Chester Gould
1943	SW171	*Dick Tracy vs. Crooks in Disguise*	Chester Gould
1944	SW216	*Dick Tracy on Voodoo Island*	Chester Gould
1945	SW220	*Dick Tracy and the Wreath Kidnapping Case*	Chester Gould
1946	SW243	*Dick Tracy and Yogee Yamma*	Chester Gould
1947	SW264	*Dick Tracy and the Mad Killer*	Helen Berke
1948	SW273	*Dick Tracy and the Bicycle Gang*	Helen Berke
1949	SW287	*Dick Tracy and the Tiger Lily Gang*	Helen Berke
1967	WW7a	*Dick Tracy Encounters Facey*	Paul S. Newman

*These were 1938–1939 Quaker Premiums.

PENNY BOOKS

32-page softcover books published by Whitman that were either sold for a penny or given away as premiums between 1938 and 1939.

SWp4a	*Dick Tracy Gets His Man*
SWp5	*Dick Tracy Detective*

FAST-ACTION STORY BOOKS
Printed by Whitman for Dell Publishing, 1938–1943.

1938	SD5	*Dick Tracy and the Chain of Evidence*	Chester Gould
1938	SD9	*Dick Tracy and the Maroon Mask Gang*	Chester Gould
1939	SD17	*Dick Tracy and the Blackmailers*	Chester Gould
1941	SD25	*Dick Tracy and the Frozen Bullet Murders*	Chester Gould

MOVIES ON VIDEO

The best source for Dick Tracy videos is Video Communications, Inc., 6535 East Skelly Drive, Tulsa, OK 74145, phone 800-331-4077. Virtually everything ever filmed on Dick Tracy is available including a bootleg tape of a 1967 pilot for a TV series that never aired. It was very much in the tongue-in-cheek style of the 1960's *Batman* TV show.

VCI purchased both the rights and the original master negatives to the four Republic serials and the four RKO feature films a number of years ago. Its videos have the best quality. The Republic Pictures serials are available either in 100 minute feature versions or 300 minute serial versions. Each serial had 15 episodes.

Republic Serials

Dick Tracy (1937) stars Ralph Byrd, Kay Hughes, Smiley Burnette, Lee Van Atta, Francis X. Bushman. The Spider and his clubfooted henchman the Lame One fight Dick Tracy through mind control of Tracy's brother.

Dick Tracy Returns (1938) stars Ralph Byrd, Lynn Roberts, Charles Middleton, and John Merton. Tracy has to overcome Paw Stark and his gangsters sons.

Dick Tracy's G-Men (1939) stars Ralph Byrd, Phyllis Isley (Jennifer Jones), Irving Pichel, and Ted Pearson. Tracy must thwart Zarnoff, an international spy, from stealing America's top secrets.

Dick Tracy Versus Crime, Inc. (1941) stars Ralph Byrd, Jan Wiley, Kenneth Harlan, and Michael Owen. The mysterious Ghost can become invisible at will. Tracy battles this revenge-seeking maniac whose brother Rackets Reagan was sent on a one-way trip to the electric chair.

RKO Feature Films

Dick Tracy Detective (1945) stars Morgan Conway as Dick Tracy, Anne Jeffreys as Tess Trueheart, and Mike Mazurki as the villain Splitface.

Dick Tracy vs. Cueball (1946) stars Morgan Conway, Anne Jeffreys and Dick Wessel as Cueball, the bald-headed hitman for a trio of jewel theives.

Dick Tracy's Dilemma (1947) sees the return of Ralph Byrd in the starring role of Dick Tracy. Kay Christopher plays Tess Trueheart and Jack Lambert is The Claw. A gang of crooks murders a night watchman during a fur heist.

Fig. A-2

Posters such as this for the third Dick Tracy serial, *Dick Tracy's G-Men* (1939) make wonderful collectibles.

Fig. A-3
The villains of the second serial "Dick Tracy Returns" (1938) are cameoed in "Dick Tracy's Rogues' Gallery," a topper for Sunday pages by Max Allan Collins and Rick Fletcher.

Fig. A-4
Ralph Morgan played the villain in the fourth Republic Pictures serial.

Fig. A-5
This advertising cut for the first *Dick Tracy* movie is from the press book published in 1937. All press books are collectible.

Fig. A-6
This framed lobby card from "Dick Tracy's Dilemma" shows what an excellent display piece the 11" × 14" lobby card makes. The Claw was the villain of the film, which also featured Longshot Lillie and Sightless.

Dick Tracy Meets Gruesome (1947) stars Ralph Byrd, Anne Gwynne, and Boris Karloff as the bank robber Gruesome.

See *Dick Tracy: America's Most Famous Detective* (Citadel Press) for more information on Dick Tracy films.

At least two video cassettes documenting Dick Tracy and Chester Gould through the years are available. "*The Documented History of Dick Tracy—Saga of a Crime Fighter*" is a 45 minute film produced by Burbank Video. "*Dick Tracy—The World's Greatest Crimefighter*" is a 50 minute film distributed by Simitar Entertainment, Inc.

Although videos of the animated Dick Tracy TV show are available, the animation is so limited that only diehard Tracy fans will have the fortitude to watch them. Videos of the early 1950's TV show starring Ralph Byrd have now been advertised. Also, as the new film sparks *Tracymania,* audio tapes of the old Dick Tracy radio shows will certainly appear.

Be careful when collecting movie posters and lobby cards. The new interest in Dick Tracy is spawning the reprinting of the old material.

Fig. A-7

This is a special illustration for a National Cartoonists Society Reuben Awards booklet by Gould, Fletcher, and Collins in 1978. It features villains from the RKO feature films of the 1940s.

RECOMMENDED READING

Dick Tracy: America's Most Famous Detective, edited by Bill Crouch, Jr., is the official history of the strip from 1931 to the present. Also two complete stories by Chester Gould, including the first appearance of Sam Catchem, a Fletcher/Collins story and a Locher/Collins story are reprinted. The 256 page trade paperback is published by Citadel Press, Secaucus, NJ.

Dick Tracy: The Official Biography by Jay Maeder is almost a companion volume to the Citadel Press book. These two books are the nucleus of any Dick Tracy library. It is a Plume paperback original, a division of New American Library.

Dick Tracy, the movie novelization by Max Allen Collins is published by Bantam. Collins, who has written the syndicated Tracy comic strip since Chester Gould retired, is an award winning mystery writer. He writes in a fastmoving, hardboiled detective style. This novelization was licensed by Disney. However, Bantam, licensed by Tribune Media Services, has signed Collins to write a series of three more Dick Tracy mystery novels. This first of the series will appear in fall 1990.

Dick Tracy, a Bantam Audio Cassette, is a 180 minute abridgement of the Collins movie novelization performed by actor James Keane who plays Tracy's pal Pat Patton in the film.

Dick Tracy: The Making of the Movie by Mike Bonifer is a 96 page look behind the scenes of the film. Published by Bantam, it has chapters featuring the makeup for Gould's biazarre villains, set design, etc.

The Dick Tracy Casebook: Favorite Adventures, 1931–1990 selected by Max Allan Collins and Dick Locher is published by St. Martin's Press and is basically a reprint book of the syndicated comic strip.

Dick Tracy: The Secret Files, edited by Martin H. Greenberg and Max Allan Collins, is published by TOR Books. This is an anthology of all new Dick Tracy short story mysteries (text only) by leading writers of the genre. Dick Locher did the cover art. Sixteen writers participated.

Dick Tracy, Topps' Offical Movie Souvenier Magazine, edited by Russ Hogan, is a 64 page all-color extravaganza that has enough information in it to almost pass for a book. Topps is also publishing several sets of Dick Tracy collector's cards. The "Dick Tracy Special Edition Collector's Set" includes the 88 cards and 11 stickers from the regular wax wrapper series plus 11 cards only in the collector's set. A normal wax wrapper pack retails for 50 cents and contains 9 cards, 1 sticker, and 1 piece of gum.

Dick Tracy Special, Model & Toy Collector Magazine, summer 1990, published and edited by Bill Bruegman, features numerous photos of new and old Tracy collectibles as well as articles and features. Of particular interest is a Robert Borowski article titled "Dick Tracy—The Series that Never Was" about the 1966 T.V. pilot which never aired.

The Celebrated Cases of Dick Tracy, edited by Herb Galewitz, was originally published as a $10'' \times 13''$ hard cover by Chelsea House in 1970. A trade paperback edition size $8\frac{1}{2}'' \times 11''$ was published by Chelsea House in 1980. Collectors should seek out these editions. The current version pretends to be a new book. The printing and paper qualify isn't nearly as good as the earlier editions. Most misleading is a 1990 copyright by Book Sales, Inc. and absolutely no copyright for Tribune Media Services nor mention that Dick Tracy is a registered trademark of TMS. This is a reprint book using daily strips only.

Dick Tracy: The Thirties, Tommyguns and Hard Times, edited by Herb Galewitz, has a similar publishing history. It was first published in hard cover in 1978. A paperback edition followed. Both were by Chelsea House. The book reprints the first two years of Dick Tracy daily strips. The current Book Sales, Inc. edition lacks the quality of the earlier editions.

CHILDREN'S BOOKS LICENSED BY DISNEY IN 1990

The Dick Tracy Fun Book of Puzzles, Games & Jokes adapted by Nancy E. Krulik, Scholastic, Inc., N.Y., N.Y.

The Official Dick Tracy Giant Sticker Poster Set, Panini U.S.A., Inc. N.Y., N.Y.

Published by Western Publishing Company, Inc.

Item #
_____

4128	Dick Tracy Magic Slate Plus
3312	Dick Tracy Giant Coloring Book
3313	Dick Tracy Giant Coloring Book
2787	Dick Tracy Giant Sticker Fun Book
2847	Dick Tracy Giant Paint with Water Book
15951	Dick Tracy Movie Storybook
12593 12594	Dick Tracy Look Look Books (2 titles)
12400	Dick Tracy, Junior Novelization Book
12401	Dick Tracy, Choose Your Own Adventure Book
2930 2931	Dick Tracy, Digest Activity Books (2 titles)
—	200-piece Dick Tracy puzzle

Collectors are advised that the best time to pick up these items is when *Tracymania* is sweeping the country.

SELECTED BIBLIOGRAPHY OF MAGAZINE ARTICLES

"B.O.'s Wedding Night." *Newsweek,* Aug. 26, 1946.

"Bonny Braids." *The New Yorker,* July 7, 1951.

"Dick Tracy in Orbit." *Newsweek,* Jan. 14, 1963.

MAD Super Special, "The Comics," Fall 1981 (Dick Tracy parodies)

"Miniature Wrist Radio." *Life,* Oct. 3, 1947.

"Sparkle Plenty, The Daughter of B.O. Plenty and Gravel Gertie Becomes a Doll and Starts to Set Sales Records." *Life,* Aug. 25, 1947.

"Too Harsh in Putting Down Evil: Violence in the Dick Tracy Strip." *Time,* June 28, 1968.

"Top Cop." *Newsweek,* Oct. 16, 1961.

Bainbridge, John. "Chester Gould: The Harrowing Adventures of His Cartoon Hero Dick Tracy, Gives Vicarious Thrills to Millions." *Life,* August 14, 1944.

Brandenburg, John. "Gould and Tracy, Partners in Crime for 25 Years." *Editor & Publisher,* Oct. 6, 1956.

Crump, Stuart, Jr. "Chester Gould—the Creator of Dick Tracy." *Personal Communications,* Jan./Feb. 1985.

Culhane, John. "Dick Tracy the First Law & Order Man." *Argosy,* June 1974.

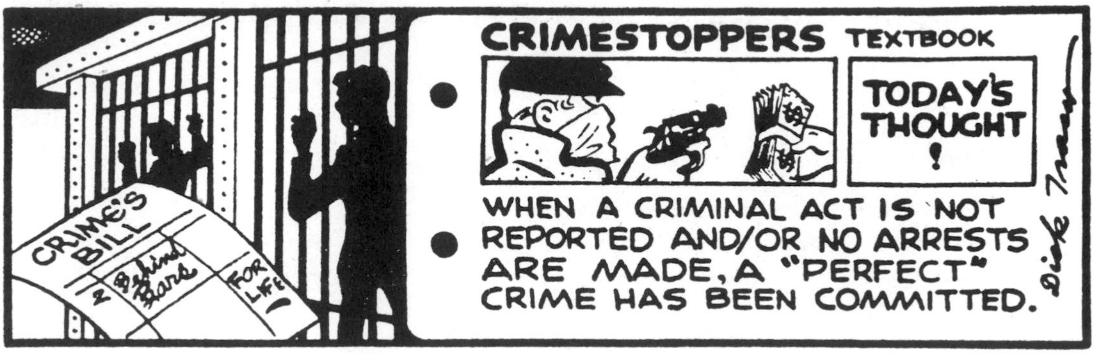
CRIMESTOPPERS TEXTBOOK
TODAY'S THOUGHT !
WHEN A CRIMINAL ACT IS NOT REPORTED AND/OR NO ARRESTS ARE MADE, A "PERFECT" CRIME HAS BEEN COMMITTED.
CRIME'S BILL
FOR LIFE

Fig. A-8

Chester Gould's classic "Crimestoppers Textbook" appeared as a topper with the Sunday comics page logo on September 11, 1949.

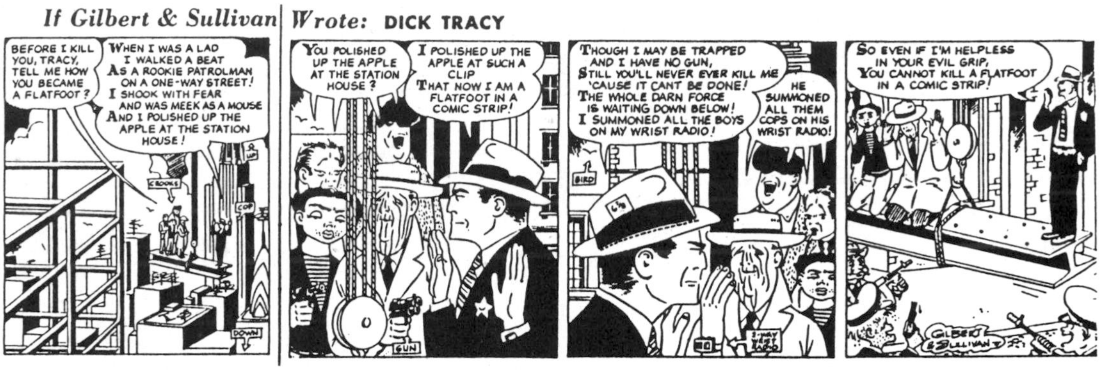
If Gilbert & Sullivan Wrote: DICK TRACY
BEFORE I KILL YOU, TRACY, TELL ME HOW YOU BECAME A FLATFOOT?
WHEN I WAS A LAD I WALKED A BEAT AS A ROOKIE PATROLMAN ON A ONE-WAY STREET! I SHOOK WITH FEAR AND WAS MEEK AS A MOUSE AND I POLISHED UP THE APPLE AT THE STATION HOUSE!
YOU POLISHED UP THE APPLE AT THE STATION HOUSE?
I POLISHED UP THE APPLE AT SUCH A CLIP THAT NOW I AM A FLATFOOT IN A COMIC STRIP!
THOUGH I MAY BE TRAPPED AND I HAVE NO GUN, STILL YOU'LL NEVER EVER KILL ME 'CAUSE IT CANT BE DONE! THE WHOLE DARN FORCE IS WAITING DOWN BELOW! I SUMMONED ALL THE BOYS ON MY WRIST RADIO!
HE SUMMONED ALL THEM COPS ON HIS WRIST RADIO!
SO EVEN IF I'M HELPLESS IN YOUR EVIL GRIP, YOU CANNOT KILL A FLATFOOT IN A COMIC STRIP!

Fig. A-9

Parody is the highest form of flattery and Dick Tracy has been the subject of numerous MAD magazine parodies. This is from "MAD Super Special, The Comics, Fall 1981." Some collectors also seek "Fearless Fosdick" tearsheets from the comic strip Li'l Abner. © E.C. Publications, Inc., 1959.

Doucet, Larry. "Collecting Dick Tracy." *Collectors' Showcase,* Nov./Dec. 1988.

Edwards, William. "How Dick Tracy Gets His Man." *Guns Magazine,* Aug. 1955.

Gould, Chester. "Dick Tracy Looks at Television." *TV Guide,* May 1–7, 1953.

Gould, Chester. "Tracy and Me." *Colliers,* Dec. 11, 1948.

Gould, Chester. "Dick Tracy: The Detective Who Wouldn't Let Me Give Up." *Guideposts,* April 1976.

Hencey, Robert. "Dick Tracy, King of the Detectives." *The Antique Trader Weekly,* May 7, 1986.

Marschall, Richard, ed. "Chester Gould and Dick Tracy, A Comprehensive Look at a Comic Strip Master." *Nemo,* Feb. 1986.

Orphan, Dennis. "Dick Tracy: for 30 Years Flint-Jawed Crime Fighter." *The Quill,* April 1962.

Stuckey, William. "Dick Tracy: The Inner Man." *Northwestern Review,* Winter 1967.

Yoder, Robert M. "Dick Tracy's Boss." *Saturday Evening Post,* Dec. 17, 1949.

RELATED BOOKS, CATALOGS, AND PRICE GUIDES

A Celebration of Comic Art and Memorabilia by Robert Lesser, Hawthorne Books, New York, NY, 1975.

Character Toys and Collectibles (2 volumes) by David Longest, Collector Books, Paducah, KY, 1987.

Collecting Today for Tomorrow by David Alan Herzog, Arco Publishing, New York, NY, 1980.

Collecting Toys—A Collector's Identification & Value Guide, 4th edition, by Richard O'Brien, Books Americana, Florence, AL, 1985.

Comics Buyer's Guide, a weekly tabloid covering the comics industry and a marketplace for comic books, tear sheets of the syndicated comic strip, and original art, 700 E. State St., Iola, WI 54990.

Greenberg's Guide to Marx Toys, Vol. 1, by Maxine A. Pinsky, Greenberg Publishing, Sykesville, MD, 1988.

Illustrated Radio Premium Catalog & Price Guide by Tom Tumbusch, Tomart Publications, Dayton, OH, 1989.

Lowery's—The Collector's Guide to Big Little and Similar Books by Lawrence F. Lowery, Educational Research & Applications Corp., Danville, CA, 1981.

Official Comic Book Price Guide by Robert M. Overstreet is published annually by House of Collectibles, New York, NY. 1990–1991 is the 20th edition.

The Big Little Book Price Guide by James Stuart Thomas, Wallace-Homestead Book Co., Des Moines, IA, 1983.

The Sport Americana Price Guide to Non-Sports Cards by Christopher Benjamin and Dennis W. Eckes, co-published by Den's Collectors Den, Laurel, MD and Edgewood Book Co., Lakewood, OH, 1983.

Toys— Antique & Collectible by David Longest, Collector Books, Paducah, KY, 1990.

COMPLETE DESCRIPTIONS OF ITEMS IN COLOR SECTIONS

See color insert following page 18

Fig. 1. Postcards featuring characters from the 1990 movie. Published by Classico San Francisco, Inc. © Disney.

Fig. 2. Playmates Toys, Inc., special collector's edition poseable dolls of Dick Tracy and Breathless Mahoney from the 1990 movie. Dick Tracy stands 15″ high. Breathless Mahoney stands 14″ high. © Disney. (Photo by Eddie Verlangieri)

Fig. 3. Traditionally, Dick Tracy products have displayed excellent package design. Cosrich's "Dick Tracy Crimestoppers Grooming Set" and "Breathless Glamour Set" continue this tradition. For wrist-radio collectors, the grooming set has an "Anti-Chap-Lip Radio Watch." The top unscrews to reveal the lip balm. Cosrich makes a third set, "Dick Tracy Crimestoppers Bath Set," with two gangster soaps and Dick Tracy bubble bath and Identification Wallet with Badge. © Disney. (Photo by Athena Foto Lab)

Fig. 4. Playmates Toys, Inc., 1990 action figures. Two of the fourteen available figures are shown. Flattop stands 5½″ high and holds a machine gun and noose. Dick Tracy stands 5″ high and holds a standard Colt 45 and billy club. © Disney. (Photo by Eddie Verlangieri)

Fig. 5. "Dick Tracy Crimestopper's Kit" of 1990 is the latest in a long line of Dick Tracy detective kits, this one by Playmates Toys, Inc. Included are handcuffs with secret ring key; "Crimestoppers Textbook" with fingerprinting kit; Dick Tracy official detective I.D. and badge; Junior Detective certificate signed by Dick Tracy; barricade tape and tape measure; magnifying glass and play money; working flashlight; belt with Dick Tracy buckle; colored chalk. © Disney. (Photo by Eddie Verlangieri)

Fig. 6. The Ertl Company produced die-cast Dick Tracy vehicles in both 1/64 scale and a micro scale (not shown in this photo). Ertl also marketed a 1/25-scale model of Tracy's 1936 Ford five-window coupe and a working "Dick Tracy Walkie Talkie Set." All were licensed by Disney for the 1990 movie. © Disney.

Fig. 7. Madonna as Breathless Mahoney, the sultry chanteuse, glitters as a sparkling pin by Wendy Gell Jewelry, Inc. Surrounding it clockwise are a Dick Tracy logo bracelet; earrings to go with the pin; faux Dick Tracy 2-Way Wrist Radios in gold and silver; and a Tracy logo pendant. All were released summer 1990. © Disney.

See color insert following page 50

Fig. 8. Assorted Bonny Braids dolls include 14″ doll (standing) and original box (Ideal, 1951); 6″ hand puppet (rubber head and cloth body, 1951); and 11″-long crawling doll (Ideal, 1952).

Fig. 9. Assorted Dick Tracy figures. Left to right, back row: 13″ composition doll with moveable head, early 1930s; 13″ composition doll with moveable head and mouth (back pull string); 10″ plastic bubble bath bottle ("Soaky") from Colgate-Palmolive, 1965; hand puppet (rubber head and cloth body) from Ideal, 1961. Front row: ceramic pepper shaker, late 1930s; 7½″ doll with bobbing head, early 1960s; 4″ hand-carved bottle stopper with cork base; ceramic salt shaker, late 1930s; 2½″ hand painted Christmas tree light bulb, mid 1940s.

Fig. 10. Sparkle Plenty doll house, 16½″ high, stiff cardboard on wooden base (base measures 23″ × 15½″). Figures on front are 7″ Dick Tracy and 5″ B.O. Plenty. Also includes figures of Gravel Gertie and Sparkle Plenty (not shown).

Fig. 11. Dick Tracy target set, early 1940s, from Louis Marx. Target is cardboard and measures 17½″ across. Box measures 18″ × 18″ × 1½″.

Fig. 12. Assorted Dick Tracy guns. Clockwise from upper right: cap pistol on card (card measures 7″ × 5″), 1973, from Hubley; original box for Louis Marx Sparkling Pop Pistol, 1934; siren pistol, 1934, from Louis Marx; Dick Tracy sub-machine water gun, mid 1950s, from Tops Plastics, Inc.; click pistol, 1934, from Louis Marx; Target Set with rubber-band-shooting gun in original packaging (measures 6¼″ × 10″), 1969, from Larami.

Fig. 13. Dick Tracy Halloween costume with original box, 1962, from Ben Cooper. Mask is plastic, clothing is polyester. Inset: Dick Tracy Halloween masks and original box, early 1960s, plastic, from Ben Cooper. Mask on left has moveable, hinged lower jaw.

See color insert following page 82

Fig. 14. On the cover of "Dick Tracy: America's Most Famous Detective" (Citadel Press), the official history of the Tracy comic strip, Tracy wears a 2-Way Wrist Radio. Flanking the book are toy 2-Way Wrist TVs. Larami's version from the 1970s is on the left and Ja-Ru's from the 1980s on the right. Both toys had paper cartoon strips that could be viewed on the "TV." (Photo by Athena Foto Lab)

Fig. 15. Montage of Dick Tracy comic books. Left to right, upper row: Extremely rare 1937 non-numbered (NN) Feature Book by David McKay Pub.; 1938 Dell Large Feature Book No. 1, 1939 Dell 4-color Comic No. 1, January 1948 Dell Monthly Comic No. 1. Middle row: First two books are scarce 1933 Cupples & Leon Co. hardcover comic reprint books; Monthly No. 25, which is the Harvey Comics first after taking over from Dell in March 1950; Blackthorne Reuben Award Winner Series No. 1; 1986 Blackthorne 3-D comic. Bottom row: 1990 Walt Disney comic, Book One, prequal to the 1990 Dick Tracy movie; mid-1940s Miller Bros. Hat Co. premium comic; Blackthorne Monthly Comic No. 1 from May 1986; 1946 Rosdon Books hardcover book of comic strips.

Fig. 16. Series of Dick Tracy Playing Card Games, all by Whitman Publishing Co. Left to right: 1934 edition; 1937 edition; 1941 edition; 1934 edition. Cards from 1934 sets shown on left, later sets are on right.

Fig. 17. Montage of Dick Tracy books. Left to right, first row from top: Whitman hardcover, *Dick Tracy Ace Detective*, 1943; Whitman Big Big Book, *The Mystery of the Purple Cross*, 1938, scarce; Whitman Big Big Book, *The Adventures of Dick Tracy Detective*, 1934; Little Golden Book, 1962. Second row: two softcover Quaker radio show premium books published by Whitman in 1939, "Radio Play Adventure Scripts"; two Whitman Penny Books, 1938, softcover, of the "Famous Comic Strip Book Series"; the first Big Little Book, "The Adventures of Dick Tracy Detective," 1932, Whitman; Big Little Book, 1941, Whitman, *Dick Tracy and His G-Men*, adapted from movie serial with "flip-it" pages; Dell, Fast Action Book, 1938, softcover, *Dick Tracy and the Chain of Evidence*. Third row: Quaker, 1939, softcover radio show premium book, *Dick Tracy's Secret Detective Methods and Magic Tricks*; Dell, Fast Action Book, 1941, softcover, *Dick Tracy and the Frozen Bullet Murders*; Fawcett paperback book, mid-70s, *Dick Tracy, His Greatest Cases No. 1, Pruneface*; Dell paperback book, 1947, *Dick Tracy and the Woo Woo Sisters*. Fourth row: Karmetz premium book, 1933, softcover, *Dick Tracy and Dick Tracy, Jr.*; Tempo, 1979, paperback book with Fletcher and Collins reprints, *Dick Tracy Meets Angeltop*; Karmetz premium book, 1933, softcover, *The Adventures of Dick Tracy*.

Fig. 18. Dick Tracy place setting and glassware. Left to right: Homer Laughlib, early 1950s, 3-piece ceramic place setting includes cereal bowl ($5\frac{1}{2}$" dia. × $2\frac{1}{4}$" deep), dinner plate (9" dia.), and mug ($3\frac{1}{8}$" tall); $6\frac{1}{4}$" tall glass, late 1970s, Domino's Pizza premium; 5" tall glass, late 1940s, one of a set of 8 frosted tumblers.

Fig. 19. Dick Tracy Lunch Box & Thermos sets by Aladdin Industries, Inc. Set at left is litho tin from 1967 featuring scenes from Tracy's space period. Set at right is 1990 version featuring Disney's Dick Tracy Movie (© Disney).

Fig. 20. Guns and Dick Tracy have traditionally gone together. In later years, toy manufacturers, such as Ja-Ru, changed their toy guns from black barrels to fluorescent colors. However, Disney did not license any toy guns in connection with the 1990 movie. On the left is the 1979 Tempo paperback reprint "Dick Tracy Meets Angeltop, Flattop's Little Girl." The artwork is by Rick Fletcher. (Photo by Athena Foto Lab)

See color insert following page 98

Fig. 21. The top four Quaker radio show premium badges, 1938–1939, for the "Dick Tracy Secret Service Patrol." Clockwise from top left: Sergeant, Lieutenant, Captain, Inspector General. The Inspector General badge ($2\frac{1}{2}$" × $2\frac{1}{2}$") is scarce. Only small quantities of these were produced since not too many youngsters could consume enough Quaker cereal between 1938 and 1939 to qualify for such a high ranking.

Fig. 22. Assortment of Dick Tracy Metal Premiums & Jewelry. Clockwise from top center: Tie bar, rare, painted metal, "At the 1933 Fair", limited edition in connection with the Chicago World's Fair; "Dick Tracy Girls Club" bracelet, silver with red enamel, crest is $1\frac{1}{4}$" × 1", circa 40's; Dick Tracy brass with red enamel Detective Club tab, 1942 radio show premium, $1\frac{3}{8}$" tall × $\frac{3}{4}$" across; "Dick Tracy Detective Club" brass badge with red enamel, 1942 premium, $1\frac{1}{2}$" tall × $1\frac{1}{8}$" across; Lucky Bangle Bracelet, 1938 Quaker premium, brass with four-leaf clover and heads of Junior and Tracy, each $\frac{5}{8}$" tall; metal charms, Sam Catchem and Tracy heads, each 1" tall, circa late 1950s; brass badge, $1\frac{1}{2}$" × $1\frac{1}{2}$", issued in Woodstock, IL, for special event, circa early 1970s; brass badge, 1938–39 Quaker premium, "Member Secret Service Patrol, Girl's Division," $1\frac{1}{8}$" × $\frac{5}{8}$".

Fig. 23. Montage of Dick Tracy paper and ephemera. Upper left: 3 Dick Tracy postcards. First 2 are 1942 WWII Coca Cola premiums issued to GIs. Third is 1943 postcard (scarce). Left center are 3 pieces from the 1942 "Junior Dick Tracy Crime Detection Folio" radio show premium kit. Left lower is a 1944 Tip-Top Bread paper pop gun issued as premium advertisement for Dick Tracy radio show. Center is a mid-40s book marker; original 1946 "Merry Xmas" card by Gould (Jean Gould O'Connell who wrote the foreword is pictured on right of star); "Bonny Braids Walks" punch out card (62 holes) from 1951 (the prize was a Bonny Braids doll). Upper right: 1940's Valentine Day card; 3 items from 1944 "Dick Tracy Junior Detective Kit." Right center: 1950s wax coated wrapper from "Dick Tracy Candy Bar"; 1951–52 "TV Detective Club" membership certificate. Right lower: 2 items from 1960s Proctor & Gamble Sweepstakes.

Fig. 24. A Montage of Dick Tracy Cards. Upper row (left) are the 6 "Big Thrill Chewing Gum" booklets issued in 1934 by The Goudey Gum Co. Upper row (right) are 5 of the cards issued by both Tip-Top Bread and Ammi-dent toothpaste in 1951–52 in connection with the "Dick Tracy TV Show" starring Ralph Byrd. Middle row includes 8 "cartoon comics" cards issued by the Chicago Tribune in 1935. Bottom row (left) is 1950s Novel Corporation candy box front and 4-panel cartoon strip back; a yellow Novel Corporation "Dick Tracy Detective" candy box which has a single colored cartoon panel on back; 4 of the set of 144 caramel cards issued in the early 1930s by the Walter H. Johnson Candy Company. On the extreme lower right are 2 scarce Big Little Book cards issued by Whitman in 1937.

Fig. 25. Dick Tracy watches, radios, and communication devices. From left to right. Back row: Louis Marx Co. "Dick Tracy Talking Telephone" and original box, 1967; American Doll & Toy Corp., "Dick Tracy Transistor Radio" in original box, 1961; late 1950s Remco "Official Dick Tracy 2-Way Electronic Wrist Radio" set in original box; late 1970s Omni digital watch w/LED and musical display, packaged in plastic space coupe (6" tall × 2" dia.). Middle row: Late 1940s Da-Myco Products "Dick Tracy Wrist Radio" (earliest known operable wrist radio), original box with wrist radio in front; Creative Creations "Dick Tracy Personalized AM Wrist Radio," 1975, in original box; mid-1930s New Haven Clock & Watch Co. wrist watch with rectangular dial and original metal band, mid-1930s New Haven Clock & Watch Co. wrist watch with circular dial, leather band and original box, alarm clock, circa early 1980s. Front row: Quaker 1939 radio show premium, "Dick Tracy Secret Service Phones" ($7\frac{1}{2}$" × $3\frac{1}{2}$"); 1981 Omni digital wrist watch in cardboard car-shaped box (5" long × $2\frac{1}{4}$" wide × $2\frac{1}{2}$" high); wrist watch, circa early 1980s; 1951 New Haven Clock & Watch Co. "rocking gun-in-hand" watch.

Fig. 26. Montage of Dick Tracy cars, Louis Marx & Co., early 1950s. Left: "Dick Tracy Police Station with Squad Car," box (9" × $6\frac{1}{2}$" × $4\frac{1}{8}$") in background, litho tin police station in foreground with 7" long litho tin friction car coming out of the station's doors. Next to Police Station box in top row is 11" litho tin, friction drive car on original box. Top row right: $6\frac{1}{2}$" litho tin, friction drive car on original box. Second row middle: $6\frac{1}{2}$" light blue, friction drive car with sparking machine gun protruding through passenger side front window. Lower right: 9" friction drive plastic car with Tracy figure.

Fig. 27. Framed original painting for Dick Tracy comic book cover, Harvey Comics Monthly No. 109, March 1957.

Fig. 28. "Crime Does Not Pay Club, Charter No. 1 'We Learned the Hard Way'" jigsaw puzzle, $21\frac{1}{2}$" × 14", Jaymar, mid-40s.

Price Guide

Introduction

The price guide information presented in this book is based on author Lawrence Doucet's experience. Over the years, he has attended countless auctions, flea markets, antiques and collectibles shows, and public offerings. He has had extensive personal communications and correspondence with many other Dick Tracy fans and collectors across the country.

The prices presented are generally based upon items in average or fine condition; i.e., played with but complete and well taken care of. Prices may vary with location and item condition. An original box with good graphics, particularly for items from the 1930s and 1940s, may increase the price of many items by as much as 50% to 100%. Unless otherwise indicated, the items are priced without their original box.

Several items are either unique or so rare that price guide information is of little value or meaningless. Such items are sold so infrequently, if ever, that their values are herein designated by NRS (No Reported Sales). The new Dick Tracy merchandise in connection with the 1990 movie is designated by a CA (Currently Available).

For all art in chapters 1 and 2, see Tables 1 and 2 in the price guide *except* for the following:

1-7   All items CA.
2-10 and 2-11   NRS.

Fig. #	Price ($)	Fig. #	Price ($)	Fig. #	Price ($)
3-1	1000+	3-7	80–100	3-14	175–200 (complete set)
3-2	250–300	3-8	20–25	3-15	80–100
3-3	100–120 (left)	3-9	30–35	3-16	45–50
	45–50 (right)	3-10	60–70	3-17	20–25 (complete kit)
3-4	350–400	3-11	100–120 (wrapper)	3-18	60–70
3-5	300–350		20–25 (decoder cards)	3-19	80–100
3-6	10–12 (comic alone)	3-12	NRS	3-20	35–40
	80–100 (with mask and	3-13	10–15 (each)	3-21	35–40 (each)
	vest)		100–120 (complete set)	3-22	80–100 (*Adventures*)
					125–150 (*Purple Cross*)

CA (Currently Available), NRS (No Reported Sales)

Fig. #	Price ($)
3-23	80–100 (each)
3-24	150–175
3-25	80–100 (*Frozen Bullet*)
	100–120 (*Chain of Evidence*)
3-26	25–30 (each, with dust jacket)
3-27	10–12
3-28	20–25 (each)
3-29	30–35
3-30	30–35
3-31	175–200
3-32	40–45
3-33	50–60
3-34	40–45
3-35	35–40
3-36	35–40
3-37	8–10 (#1–96, caramels)
	15–20 (#97–120)
	.50–1.00 (each, #121–144)
	250–300 (wrapper)
3-38	15–20 (1942)
	NRS (1943)
3-39	25–30
3-40	80–100 (complete set)
3-41	20–25 (each)
3-42	5–8 (each, Penny Cards)
	100–120 (dispensing machine insert)
3-43	45–50 (each)
3-43a	NRS
3-44	60–70 (each set)
3-45	25–30
3-46	50–60
3-47	60–70
3-48	40–45
3-49	45–50
3-50	100–120
3-50a	30–35
3-51	50–60
3-52	45–50
3-53	60–70
3-54	175–200
3-55	200–250
3-56	175–200
3-57	150–175
3-58	80–100
3-59	150–175
3-60	See Tables 1 & 2
3-61	80–100
3-62	125–150 (left)
	CA (right)
3-63	125–150
3-64	See Tables 1 & 2
3-65	60–70
3-66	80–100
3-67	80–100
3-68	See Tables 1 & 2
3-69	70–80
3-70	25–30
3-71	60–70
3-72	See Tables 1 & 2
3-73	25–30 (left)
	10–15 (right)

Fig. #	Price ($)
3-74	25–30
3-75	NRS
3-76	100–120
3-77	25–30 (each)
3-78	45–50
3-79	15–20 (each)
3-80	50–60 (figure)
	25–30 (mold with box)
	20–25 (powder)
	100–120 (complete set)
3-81	45–50 (puppet only)
	80–120 (puppet and record, orig. box)
3-82	50–60
3-83	NRS
3-84	25–30
3-85	30–35 (unpainted set)
	80–100 (painted set)
3-86	150–175 (each)
3-87	50–60 (complete set)
3-88	See Tables 1 & 2
3-89	250–300
3-90	300–350
3-91	150–175
3-92	125–150
3-93	200–250
3-94	See Tables 1 & 2
3-95	30–35 (walking doll)
	100–120 (crawling doll)
3-96	225–250
3-97	See Tables 1 & 2
3-98	150–175
3-99	See Tables 1 & 2
3-100	See Tables 1 & 2
3-101	50–75 (box only)
	125–150 (game)
3-102	70–80
3-103	30–35
3-104	60–75
3-105	35–40
3-106	NRS
3-107	See Tables 1 & 2
3-108	80–100
3-109	60–70
3-110	60–70
3-111	15–20 (gun without card)
	70-75 (gun on card)
3-112	80–100
3-113	150–175
3-114	70–80
3-115	100–120
3-116	60–70
3-117	10–15
3-118	30–35
3-119	40–50 (without box)
	80–100 (with box)
3-120	50–60
3-121	35–40
3-122	10–15
3-123	50–60
3-124	80–100 (complete set)
3-125	100–120
3-126	175–200
3-127	40–50
3-128	60–70

Fig. #	Price ($)
3-129	100–120
3-130	50–60
3-131	70–80
3-132	35–40
3-133	45–50
3-134	40–45 (top of page 102)
	50–60 (top of page 103)
	70–80 (bottom of page 102)
3-135	NRS (display with knives)
	50–60 (each knife)
3-136	35–40
3-137	50–60
3-138	75–85
3-139	40–45
3-140	100–120 (Dick Tracy glass)
	70–80 (other glasses)
3-141	60–70
3-142	200–225
3-143	175–200
3-144	60–70
3-145	200–225 (not including box)
3-146	80–100
3-147	60–70
3-148	NRS
3-149	15–20
4-1	10–15 (photo)
4-2–	
4-9	See Tables 1 & 2
4-10	NRS
4-11	100–120 (per cel)
4-12	50–60 (each, 1950s and later with preprinted envelopes)
	100–120 (each, 1930s–1940s, autographed sketches)

All items in chapter five are currently available (CA), except for the following:

5-4	See Tables 1 & 2

For all items in appendix see Tables 1 and 2, except for the following:

A-1	CA
A-2	125–150
A-6	25–30

CA (Currently Available), NRS (No Reported Sales)

All items in Figs. 1 thru 7 are currently available (CA).

Fig. #	Price ($)
8	225–250 (doll standing)
	35–40 (hand puppet)
	100–120 (doll crawling)
9	NRS (13" dolls)
	25–30 (10" Soaky)
	45–50 (hand puppet)
	35–40 (salt & pepper shakers)
	NRS (7½" doll)
	NRS (bottle stopper)
	45–50 (light bulb)
10	200–250
11	125–150
12	70–75 (cap pistol/card)
	35–40 (pop pistol, box only)
	80–100 (pop pistol, not shown)
	100–120 (siren pistol)
	70–80 (water gun)
	80–100 (click pistol)
	35–40 (rubber band gun)
13	45–50 (each, mask only)
	85–100 (mask w/costume)
14	CA (book)
	25–30 (Larami, left)
	10–15 (Ja-Ru, right)
15	1000+ (1937 NN McKay)
	250–300 (1938 Dell)
	350–400 (1939 Dell)
	100–120 (1948 Dell)
	100–120 (each, 2 items, 1933 Cupples)
	150–175 (w/dust jacket)
	45–50 (Harvey No. 25)
	6–7 (Blackthorne No. 1)
	3–3.50 (Blackthorne 3-D)
	CA (1990 Disney)
	45–50 (Miller Bros.)
	2–2.50 (1986 Blackthorne)
	60–70 (Rosdon)
16	40–60 (each game)
17	20–25 (1943 Whitman w/dust jacket)
	125–150 (1938 Whitman *Purple Cross*)
	80–100 (1934 Whitman *Adventures*)
	10–12 (1962 Little Golden)
	80–100 (each, 2 Quaker premiums)
	20–25 (each, 2 1938 Whitman Penny)
	80–100 (1932 Whitman Big Little)
	35–40 (1941 Whitman Big Little)
	100–120 (1938 Dell)

Fig. #	Price ($)
	60–70 (1939 Quaker premium)
	80–100 (1941 Dell)
	15–20 (1970s Fawcett *Pruneface*)
	60–70 (1947 Dell)
	80–100 (1933 Karmetz premium)
	20–25 (1979 Tempo *Angeltop*)
	80–100 (1933 Karmetz premium)
18	100–120 (cereal bowl)
	80–100 (dinner plate)
	60–70 (mug)
	60–70 (Domino's glass)
	100–120 (frosted tumbler)
19	70–80 (Aladdin thermos)
	80–100 (Aladdin lunch box)
	CA (1990 Disney lunch box/thermos)
20	10–15 (each, Ja-Ru guns)
	20–25 (1979 Tempo *D.T. Meets Angeltop*)
21	50–60 (Sergeant)
	80–100 (Lieutenant)
	100–120 (Captain)
	175–200 (Inspector General)
22	NRS (tie bar)
	60–70 (1940s bracelet)
	80–100 (red tab)
	60–70 (Detective Club badge)
	125–150 (1938 bracelet)
	15–20 (each, charms)
	20–25 (1970s Crimestopper badge)
	50–60 (1938–39 badge)
23	15–20 (1st 2 cola postcards)
	NRS (3rd postcard)
	125–150 (complete set, Crime Folio)
	80–100 (paper pop gun)
	40–50 (book marker)
	NRS ("Xmas" card)
	40–50 (Bonny Braids Walks)
	25–30 (Valentine card)
	175–200 (complete set, 3 items, Jr. Kit)
	20–25 (candy wrapper)
	40–50 (membership certificate)
	35–40 (sweepstakes items)
24	50–60 (each, "Big Thrill" Nos. 1,2,4,5,6)
	15–20 (No. 3)
	20–30 (each, Tip-Top/ Ammi-dent cards)
	40–60 (*Chicago Tribune* cards)

Fig. #	Price ($)
	20–25 (Novel Corp. candy box)
	40–50 (yellow Novel Corp. candy box)
	8–10 (each, caramel cards, Nos. 1–96)
	15–20 (Nos. 97–120)
	.50–1.00 (Nos. 121–144)
	25–30 (each, Big Little Book cards)
25	40–45 (talking telephone)
	60–70 (transistor radio/ box)
	80–100 (2-way wrist radios)
	60–70 (Omni watch w/space coupe)
	125–150 (wrist radio w/box)
	60–70 (AM wrist radio)
	200–225 (New Haven watch, rect.)
	200–225 (New Haven watch, circular)
	40–50 (alarm clock)
	80–100 (secret service phones)
	60–70 (Omni watch in car box)
	40–50 (1980s wrist watch)
	175–200 (1951 New Haven watch)
26	200–250 (police station/ car)
	175–200 (11" car/box)
	150–175 (6½" car/box)
	150–175 (6½" car, blue)
	150–175 (9" car)
27	NRS
28	40–50

CA (Currently Available), NRS (No Reported Sales)

Table 1. Strip Tear Sheets, Ads and Articles

Era	Daily Newspaper Strip Tear Sheets	Sunday Newspaper Strip Tear Sheets	Magazine & Newspaper Ads & Articles
1930s	$2.00–3.00	$5.00–7.00	$20.00–25.00
1940s	1.00–2.00	3.00–5.00	15.00–20.00
1950s–60s	.50–1.00	1.00–2.00	10.00–15.00
1970s–Early 80s	.25–.50	.50–1.00	5.00–10.00

Table 2. Original Art

Original art for the daily and sunday strips are unique items. Their values are primarily dependent upon age, the presence of Tracy, the villain, the degree of violence and historical significance. Table 2 shows general guidelines as to the values of Dick Tracy original art.

Artist	Era/Strip	Strip Contents		
		No Tracy, No Major Villain & No Historical Event	Tracy & Only Minor Characters	Tracy & Major[1] Villain or Historical Event[2]
Chester Gould	1930s			
	Dailies	$500–800	$800–1000+	$1000+
	Sundays	1000+	$1000+	1000+
	1940s			
	Dailies	150–300	300–600	600–1000+
	Sundays	200–400	400–800	800–1000+
	1950s			
	Dailies	100–150	150–300	300–600
	Sundays	150–300	300–600	600–900
	1960s–70s			
	Dailies	75–100	100–200	200–400
	Sundays	150–200	200–400	400–600
Rick Fletcher	Dailies	50–75	75–150	150–300
	Sundays	100–150	150–300	300–500
Dick Locher		NRS[3]	NRS	NRS

[1] An historical event includes such happenings as the introduction of the 2-way wrist radio, the marriage of B. O. Plenty and Gravel Gertie or Tracy and Tess, and the birth of Sparkle Plenty or Bonny Braids.   [2] Major villains include classics such as The Blank, Pruneface, Mrs. Pruneface, Flattop, The Brow, Shaky, Influence, Mumbles, Sleet, Wormy, Blowtop, Oodles, Flattop Jr., Angeltop, Art Dekko, Torcher, and the like.   [3] No reported sales.